PERSPECTIVES ON CULTURE AND POLITICS
IN THE FRENCH ANTILLES

# LEGENDA

LEGENDA is the Modern Humanities Research Association's book imprint for new research in the Humanities. Founded in 1995 by Malcolm Bowie and others within the University of Oxford, Legenda has always been a collaborative publishing enterprise, directly governed by scholars. The Modern Humanities Research Association (MHRA) joined this collaboration in 1998, became half-owner in 2004, in partnership with Maney Publishing and then Routledge, and has since 2016 been sole owner. Titles range from medieval texts to contemporary cinema and form a widely comparative view of the modern humanities, including works on Arabic, Catalan, English, French, German, Greek, Italian, Portuguese, Russian, Spanish, and Yiddish literature. Editorial boards and committees of more than 60 leading academic specialists work in collaboration with bodies such as the Society for French Studies, the British Comparative Literature Association and the Association of Hispanists of Great Britain & Ireland.

The MHRA encourages and promotes advanced study and research in the field of the modern humanities, especially modern European languages and literature, including English, and also cinema. It aims to break down the barriers between scholars working in different disciplines and to maintain the unity of humanistic scholarship. The Association fulfils this purpose through the publication of journals, bibliographies, monographs, critical editions, and the MHRA Style Guide, and by making grants in support of research. Membership is open to all who work in the Humanities, whether independent or in a University post, and the participation of younger colleagues entering the field is especially welcomed.

### ALSO PUBLISHED BY THE ASSOCIATION

*Critical Texts*
*Tudor and Stuart Translations • New Translations • European Translations*
*MHRA Library of Medieval Welsh Literature*

*MHRA Bibliographies*
*Publications of the Modern Humanities Research Association*

*The Annual Bibliography of English Language & Literature*
*Austrian Studies*
*Modern Language Review*
*Portuguese Studies*
*The Slavonic and East European Review*
*Working Papers in the Humanities*
*The Yearbook of English Studies*

www.mhra.org.uk
www.legendabooks.com

# SELECTED ESSAYS

Each title in *Selected Essays* presents influential, but often scattered, papers by a major scholar in the Humanities. While these essays will, we hope, offer a model of scholarly writing, and chart the development of an important thinker in the field, the aim is not retrospective but to gather a coherent body of work as a tool for future research. Each volume contains a new introduction, framing the debate and reflecting on the methods used.

*Selected Essays* is curated by Professor Susan Harrow (University of Bristol).

*Managing Editor*
Dr Graham Nelson, 41 Wellington Square, Oxford OX1 2JF, UK

www.legendabooks.com

# Perspectives on Culture and Politics in the French Antilles

❖

CELIA BRITTON

*l*

**LEGENDA**

Selected Essays 4
Modern Humanities Research Association
2018

*Published by Legenda*
*an imprint of the Modern Humanities Research Association*
*Salisbury House, Station Road, Cambridge* CB1 2LA

*ISBN 978-1-78188-561-1 (HB)*
*ISBN 978-1-78188-562-8 (PB)*

*First published 2018*

*Copy-Editor: Charlotte Brown*

# CONTENTS

❖

*To my husband Lyle Conquest*

# ACKNOWLEDGEMENTS

❖

Nine of the chapters in this volume have previously been published as articles in journals or chapters in edited books. Chapter 1 appeared in *Small Axe*, 52 (March 2017), 169–79; Chapter 2 in *French Studies*, 66.1 (2012), 41–53; Chapter 3 in *French Cultural Studies*, 22.1 (2011), 61–72; Chapter 4 in *The C. L. R James Journal*, 23 (2017), 43–56; Chapter 5 in *Small Axe*, 30 (November 2009), 1–11; Chapter 7 is my translation into English of my article 'Cacher à l'autre, cacher à soi-même: l'obscurité du langage dans l'œuvre d'Édouard Glissant', *Revue des sciences humaines*, 309 (January-March 2013), 171–87; Chapter 9 first appeared in *Francophone Postcolonial Studies*, 6.1 (2008), 7–23; Chapter 10 in *Ici-Là: Place and Displacement in French Caribbean Literature*, ed. by Mary Gallagher (Amsterdam & New York: Rodopi, 2003), pp. 83–99; and Chapter 11 in *American Creoles: The Francophone Caribbean and the American South*, ed. by Martin Munro and Celia Britton (Liverpool University Press: 2012), pp. 216–29. I am most grateful to all the original publishers for giving me permission to reproduce them here.

C.B., April 2018

# ABBREVIATIONS

❖

AF     Michel Leiris, *Afrique fantôme* [1934] (Paris: Gallimard, 1981)

AP     Peter Hallward, *Absolutely Postcolonial: Writing Between the Singular and the Specific* (Manchester: Manchester University Press, 2001)

AT     René Ménil, *Antilles déjà jadis, précédé de Tracées* (Paris: Jean Michel Place, 1999

BC     Maryse Condé, *La Belle Créole* (Paris: Mercure de France, 2001)

CC     Michel Leiris, *Contacts de civilisations en Martinique et en Guadeloupe* (Paris: Gallimard/UNESCO, 1955)

CD     Jean-Luc Nancy, *La Communauté desœuvrée* [1986], 2nd edn (Paris: Christian Bourgois, 1990)

DA     Édouard Glissant, *Le Discours antillais* (Paris: Seuil, 1981)

ED     Ernest Pépin, *L'Envers du décor* (Paris: Le Serpent à plumes, 2006)

ES     Joseph Zobel, *Et si la mer n'était pas bleue* (Paris: Éditions caribbéennes, 1982)

ESP     Jean-Luc Nancy, *Être singulier pluriel* (Paris: Galilée, 1996)

FM     Édouard Glissant, *Faulkner, Mississippi* (Paris: Stock, 1996)

ME     Édouard Glissant, *Mémoires des esclavages: la fondation d'un centre national pour la mémoire des esclavages et de leurs abolitions* (Paris: Gallimard, 2007)

IE     Chris Bongie, *Islands and Exiles: The Creole Identities of Post/Colonial Literature* (Stanford, CA: Stanford University Press, 1998)

IP     Édouard Glissant, *L'Intention poétique* (Paris: Seuil, 1969)

IPD     Édouard Glissant, *Introduction à une poétique du divers* (Paris: Gallimard, 1996)

LM     Joseph Zobel, *Laghia de la mort* [1946], 2nd edn (Paris & Dakar: Présence africaine, 1978)

NRM     Édouard Glissant, *Une nouvelle région du monde* (Paris: Gallimard, 2006)

PR     Édouard Glissant, *Poétique de la Relation* (Paris: Gallimard, 1990)

QS     Édouard Glissant, *Le Quatrième Siècle* (Paris: Seuil, 1964)

SP     Joseph Zobel, *Le Soleil partagé* (Paris & Dakar: Présence africaine, 1964)

TB     Ernest Pépin, *Tambour-Babel* (Paris: Gallimard, 1996)

TH     Ernest Pépin, *Le Tango de la haine* (Paris: Gallimard, 1999)

TM     Maryse Condé, *Traversée de la mangrove* (Paris: Mercure de France, 1989)

TTM     Édouard Glissant, *Traité du Tout-monde* (Paris: Gallimard, 1997)

# INTRODUCTION

❖

The islands of the French-speaking Antilles — Martinique and Guadeloupe — were among the earliest French colonies, founded in 1635, and have had turbulent histories ever since. The legacy of transportation and slavery is still relevant today; and subsequent political struggles for independence, against France's colonial policy of assimilation,[1] and for or against departmentalization, together with unemployment, strikes and riots, and the always uneasy relations between the majority black population and the *békés* (the plantation owners, descendants of the original white settlers) have resulted in societies that are highly politicized.[2] This in turn is at least partly responsible for the large number, relative to the size of the overall population, of writers and intellectuals. It is therefore not surprising that the literary production of the islands, like that of many postcolonial societies, is centrally concerned with the social and political realities and the distinctive culture of life in Martinique and Guadeloupe.[3]

The present collection of essays therefore discusses both non-fictional, theoretical texts (Chapters 1–7), and novels (Chapters 8–12). All except two of the writers who form the main subjects of the chapters are from Martinique or Guadeloupe, and are recognized there as major, well-known figures (as is Aimé Césaire, who figures prominently in several of the chapters, and Frantz Fanon, Patrick Chamoiseau, and Raphaël Confiant, who are also mentioned in connection with other authors). But they are not all widely studied beyond the Antilles; relatively little international critical work has been done on Ernest Pépin and Joseph Zobel, and René Ménil has also been undeservedly neglected. A large part of this volume is devoted to Édouard Glissant; in the first place this is simply because I have written more on him than

---

1    The policy of assimilation aimed to integrate colonial subjects into French culture and to make them as 'French' as possible through education and other means. It was thus seen as a prime cause of alienation and the difficulty of building an authentically Caribbean collective identity.

2    The 'loi de départementalisation' was passed in France in 1946; it converted the French colonies of Martinique, Guadeloupe, French Guiana, and Réunion into *départements*, i.e. gave them, in theory, the same status as the *départements* within France. They are known as 'Départements d'Outre Mer' or DOMs. Initially welcomed by the left, they soon came to be seen as impediments to independence.

3    Although writers such as Maryse Condé have also protested against this agenda, and claimed the freedom to write about the same range of subjects as metropolitan literature. In her 'Order, Disorder, Freedom and the West Indian Writer' (*Yale French Studies*, 83:2 (1993), 121–35), she argues forcefully that Caribbean literature is in a state of crisis and malaise because of the 'commands enumerated throughout the history of West Indian literature by the various generations of writers' (p. 121): for example, literature should concern itself with collective political struggle (led by a male hero) and should not write about sexuality (and especially homosexuality), the beauties of the landscape, etc.

on other French Caribbean authors, but it is also justified, I would argue, by his exceptional status in the French Caribbean as both novelist and essayist.

However, I have also included two essays on the French ethnographer Michel Leiris, whose perspective on Martinique and Guadeloupe is, obviously, that of a foreigner. Indeed, this is something of which he is keenly aware, and his work explicitly addresses the question of his subjective relationship to the people he is studying. As I shall discuss, he has been praised by both Césaire and Glissant for abandoning the conventional external position of the professional ethnographer in favour of an intersubjective, participatory approach. One could argue, in fact, that Glissant's central concept of 'Relation' may have been partly inspired by Leiris's reformulation of ethnography (Glissant was taught by Leiris at the Musée de l'Homme in Paris from 1953 to 1954). Nevertheless, Leiris does clearly provide a different view of Antillean culture from that of its native writers, as in his delighted reaction, for instance, to the presence in Martinique of traditional forms of French popular culture such as folk songs and roundabouts (Chapter 3).

Equally, the work on community of the French philosopher Jean-Luc Nancy is analyzed in Chapter 6 in relation to Glissant's conception of community, where I argue that despite the differences between them that are mainly attributable to their respective backgrounds, the underlying principles of their theorizations are surprisingly similar.

In addition to Leiris and Nancy, one other non-Antillean writer is discussed in this volume (in Chapters 7 and 11) from the point of view of his relation to Glissant and to Maryse Condé: the American novelist William Faulkner. It is his considerable but ambivalent influence on both Glissant and Condé, the importance of the unconscious in his work, and the way in which their novels rework and at times almost parody his, that forms the basis for the comparison.

It is also noticeable that only one of the authors discussed here is a woman, namely Maryse Condé. Her novels are centrally concerned with issues of gender. It is true that these issues are also prominent in the fiction of Pépin and Zobel, and Glissant's novels contain strong female characters. However, none of the non-fictional texts studied in the first part of this book consider the question of gender at all; there is thus a strange disconnect between the representation of gender in fiction and its non-representation in theoretical essays. There are no doubt female essayists whom I could have considered, most obviously Suzanne Césaire in her articles for the review *Tropiques*, but she does not write about gender either.[4] It does seem that there is a certain masculinist bias in French Antillean theorizations of their culture and politics, as though the urgency of resisting metropolitan French pressures on these overshadows other forms of inequality.

Certain common themes recur in a number of the chapters. The most prominent of these is that of cultural identity. Thus the central focus of Chapter 1 is the way in which Glissant's conception of cultural identity varies from his early to his later works; and in Chapter 6 the relevance of culture is one of the key differences

---

4  *Tropiques* was edited by Aimé Césaire, his wife Suzanne Césaire, and René Ménil in Martinique from 1941 to 1946.

between his and Nancy's definitions of community. Leiris's discussion of departmentalization, in Chapter 3, investigates the extent to which the citizens of Martinique and Guadeloupe identify as French and/or as Caribbean. My analysis of Ménil's work in Chapter 4 shows how in his view cultural identity can be authentic only if it is linked to the struggle for political liberation. And, finally, Chapter 9 discusses how Pépin's novel *Tambour-Babel* represents the determination of the drummers to hold on to their traditional identity as a 'secret aristocracy', while his *L'Envers du décor* presents the cultural identity of Guadeloupeans as the hidden reality of the island, a mystery to tourists.[5]

The relationship between culture and politics is also a theme that is treated in several of the chapters. For Ménil (in Chapter 4), as I have said above, political liberation is the only possible basis for an authentic culture; and for Leiris (in Chapter 3) departmentalization raises the difficult question (although Leiris does not see it as such) of whether cultural autonomy can co-exist with a lack of political independence. The relationship between culture and politics is relevant in a very different way in Peter Hallward's critique of Glissant, which is considered in Chapter 5: Hallward contrasts the commitment to political independence in 'early' Glissant's work with what he sees as the abandonment of any political project in 'late' Glissant, in favour of a depoliticized concern with culture.

Finally, the relationship between the psychological aftermath of slavery and present-day masculinity is treated both by Condé in *La Belle Créole* and by Pépin in *Tango de la haine*.[6] Glissant's analysis of Faulkner's novels is discussed, in very different contexts, in Chapters 7 and 11. The cultural importance of place features in both Glissant's essays (Chapter 1) and his fiction, specifically *Mahagony* (Chapter 10), and also in Pépin's novels, particularly *L'Envers du décor*.[7]

There are inevitably some further minor overlaps between the nine chapters that have previously been published separately, and that are reproduced here with only very small editorial changes. These overlaps involve both their subject matter and their presentation — e.g. re-using the same quotations from the texts. I have added notes to point out the connections between them.

The analysis of theoretical essays obviously requires a different methodology from the analysis of fiction. For the former it is a question of elucidating the author's thought in a discourse that is not essentially different from that of the text studied. I juxtapose those elements of the author's work that are relevant to my topic, point out inconsistencies, ambiguities, significant omissions, changes over time, and discuss the influence on the author in question of other thinkers: for example, Césaire on Leiris; Karl Marx, W. E. B. DuBois, Louis Althusser, and Pierre Macherey on Ménil; Glissant's dialogue with the 'créolité' authors in Chapter 1, and the influence on him of Gilles Deleuze and Félix Guattari in Chapter 6. Less often I bring in other theoretical viewpoints that the author himself does not consider: in

---

5   Ernest Pépin, *Tambour-Babel* (Paris: Gallimard, 1996), hereafter referred to as *TB*; *L'Envers du décor* (Paris: Le Serpent à plumes, 2006), hereafter referred to as *ED*.
6   Maryse Condé, *La Belle Créole* (Paris: Mercure de France, 2001), hereafter referred to as *BC*; Ernest Pépin, *Le Tango de la haine* (Paris: Gallimard, 1999), hereafter referred to as *TH*.
7   Édouard Glissant, *Mahagony* (Paris: Éditions du Seuil, 1987).

the case of Ménil again, Mikhail Bakhtin, comparing his 'double-voiced discourse' with the 'double consciousness' of DuBois and Ménil; or comparing DuBois with more recent work in postcolonial theory. Chapter 6 compares the theorizations of community provided by Glissant and by Nancy, who have apparently not read each other's work. Or it may be a question of evaluating critiques of the author — those of Peter Hallward and Chris Bongie on Glissant, for instance, in Chapter 5. But in all cases, what I am writing is an essay on an essay (or essays), i.e. my discourse belongs to the same general category of what one might loosely call theoretical writing as that of the texts that I am discussing.

Critical analysis of fiction, on the other hand, requires adopting a different discursive position from that of the primary text. It involves, for instance, discussing the effect of a particular narrative point of view (or the interplay of a plurality of narrative points of view, as in Pépin's novels), analyzing characterization, interpreting imagery, identifying intertextual connections, and so on. The critic's use of theory here brings to bear on the fictional text a discourse that is entirely external to it — unlike the theories that influence the writers of essays.[8] Thus when I use Macherey in connection with Faulkner's novels in Chapter 11, for instance, his relationship to Faulkner's text is different from that between Macherey and Ménil in Chapter 4, just as my use of Bakhtin in connection with Ménil is different from my use of the Bakhtinian chronotope in the context of Glissant's fiction. Or again, when I reference psychoanalysis in connection with Condé's treatment of masculine sexuality in *La Belle Créole,* I am 'applying' a theory to a novel in which it has no explicit presence (although I am sure that Condé is perfectly well aware of its relevance). This is a very different process from highlighting Leiris's use of the Freudian uncanny (Chapter 3) or discussing the extent to which Glissant's idea of 'hidden meanings' in his characterization of language use in Martinique relies overtly on the notion of a collective unconscious (Chapter 7).

More generally, fiction does not aim to be *explicit* in the way that an essay does. This is made particularly clear in Glissant's analysis of Faulkner's fiction: he devotes a lot of space to Faulkner's reluctance to identify the nature of the 'original crime', and emphasizes that this lack of explicitness is an essential part of the greatness of his novels. But in a rather different way it is equally true of Zobel's short stories, whose deceptively simple surface covers an intricate representation of social contradictions that are never explicitly discussed.

Also, the identifying of influences on a theoretical text is more straightforward than the study of intertextuality in fiction, which encompasses a range of relationships from *hommage* to parody (for example the treatment of incest in Condé's *Traversée de la mangrove* (1989) as compared with Faulkner's *Absalom, Absalom*

8    Chapter 6 was originally conceived as a kind of postscript to my book *The Sense of Community in French Caribbean Fiction* (Liverpool: Liverpool University Press, 2008), which referred to Nancy in connection with French Caribbean fiction, and so raised the question of the legitimacy of using metropolitan theory to interpret postcolonial literature. This was a much-discussed issue in the early period of postcolonial studies; my own view is that there is nothing wrong with it as long as it is productive. But in any case Chapter 6 has a different focus in that it compares two bodies of theoretical work.

(1936), Chapter 11).[9] In other words, the critical methodology appropriate to fiction is very much one of interpretation.

Nevertheless, it is important not to overstate the differences between analyzing an essay and analyzing a novel. Essays aim to be explicit, but they rarely succeed entirely. Therefore, although the meaning of the imagery relating to the sea in *La Belle Créole*, for instance, is *deliberately* implicit, indeed obscure, while Leiris's reasons for the promotion of departmentalization are not, the latter are in fact just as much open to interpretation and reading between the lines. Glissant is aware of the tension between his anti-essentialism and the political importance of a militant collective identity (Chapter 1), but he does not adequately recognize its full impact on his early theorization of identity. More simply, Ménil's use of Althusser relies on the reader recognizing Althusser's ownership of the idea of 'relative autonomy' — he is not named in the text. My approach to both fiction and essays thus focuses above all on interpretation, on making explicit what in the text is implicit: in other words, on not taking the text at face value.[10]

As all this suggests, the main feature of my methodology — albeit exemplified here to varying degrees — is the practice of close reading. Ever since the early twentieth century, this has been a very mainstream approach to literary texts: attention to the details of wording, repetitions, and variations of phrasing, as a means of teasing out, once again, meanings that are not stated explicitly. It often focuses on figurative language: for instance, the images that Condé employs to describe the sea in *La Belle Créole* that link it to the protagonist's mother and his love for her. My analysis of the novel as a whole is crucially dependent on my interpretation of the details of this imagery. But the most extreme example in the volume of this kind of close reading does not involve figurative language: this is my analysis of Glissant's *Mahagony*, in which the significance of *places*, their identification, and the thematic relationships between them, emerges almost entirely through the textual exploration of repetitions and variations of tiny phrases that are not figurative and that do not draw attention to themselves in any way except through their recurrence in different contexts.

However, the practice of close reading also informs my discussion of the non-fictional texts in this volume. In the case of Leiris, for example, the imbrication of ethnographic fieldwork and personal investment is clearly stated in his writing, but it also means, on a less conscious level, that his subjective relationship to the cultures he studies results in a number of ambiguities and shifts that can only be revealed by close reading, for example his rather tortuous attempt to prove that the 'departmentalized' citizens of the Antilles can be simultaneously both French and not-French (Chapter 3). Or, again, I claim that he was aware that Césaire's attitude to departmentalization, and hence to the Communist Party that supported it, changes radically in the course of the 1950s; but I deduce this solely from the

9     Maryse Condé, *Traversée de la mangrove* (Paris: Mercure de France, 1989), hereafter referred to as *TM*; William Faulkner, *Absalom, Absalom* (New York: Random House, 1936).
10     In a slightly different sense, the connection between the two is particularly close when I bring together Glissant's literary-critical writing on Faulkner with his own fictional practice, in Chapter 11.

fact that a text by Leiris originally published in 1950 omits, when it is republished in 1955, a sentence placing Césaire at the centre of the Party (Chapter 3). Similarly, the recurrence of Glissant's early anxieties about assimilation in his later work (Chapter 1) and the fluctuations in Ménil's attitude to Césaire (Chapter 4) depend on close reading; as does my critique of Hallward's and Bongie's critique of Glissant in Chapter 5, where I analyze the lack of textual evidence for a number of Bongie's claims and the way in which he runs together quotations that in fact refer to completely different situations, and question the contradictions in Hallward's periodization of Glissant's essays and novels.

These examples might suggest that close reading of theoretical texts is inevitably somewhat hostile: a question of pointing out errors and contradictions. But I do not think that this is generally true. In the first place, all discussion of theoretical texts, if it is to go beyond simple exposition, involves critique and argument. But also, my comparison of Glissant and Nancy, for instance, serves not to demonstrate that one of them is somehow 'better' than the other, but to highlight the originality of both thinkers. Equally, my bringing together of essays that Ménil wrote over a long period of time serves to highlight a coherence that is not always obvious in the individual pieces; and close reading of his theorizations of 'double consciousness' shows that, contrary to appearances, it is not in fact an irresolvable contradiction but part of a dialectic of liberation. Close reading, in the case of essays, brings out the strengths of the primary text as much as their weaknesses. Equally, close reading of fictional texts is often the only way to reveal their full richness and complexity.

CHAPTER 1

❖

# Identity and Change in the
# Work of Édouard Glissant

The ambivalence with which Glissant regarded the concept of 'créolité' is well known: on the one hand he considered Patrick Chamoiseau and Raphaël Confiant to be his successors, while on the other he criticized 'créolité' as an essentialist conception of cultural identity: a 'visée à l'être' proposing 'des modèles d'humanité'.[1] The extent to which his own theorizations of identity avoid the charge of essentialism is due, as I shall show here, to the relations he constructs between identity and change.

For much of the period during which Glissant was working, identity has been seen as a problematic, not to say dubious, concept, both politically and intellectually; it has either been associated with a right-wing discourse of ethnic purity or with a sectarian militancy which, while strategically useful to those peoples who are struggling for political independence, elsewhere creates only division and intolerance. Identity was comprehensively dismissed by poststructuralist theory as an essentialist illusion, to be replaced by a more complex concept of the 'subject': for Lacan, for instance, the fundamental dynamic of psychic reality is played out at the level of the subject while identity belongs to the more superficial and in some senses illusory domain of the imaginary.

Glissant, however, continued throughout his career to insist on its necessity and importance. Indeed, perhaps one of the most original aspects of his thought as a whole is his refusal to abandon the concept of identity but instead to rework it with the aim of removing from it all traces of essentialism. That is, he replaced the traditional humanist conception with something relational and dynamic. Identities are always changing, or, more precisely, identity is always constructed in relation to a certain concept of change.

But equally, Glissant's conception of identity also changed radically in the course of his career. There are three main phases. Firstly *Le Discours antillais* in 1981, which analyzes the identity of the Martiniquan people in so far as this is formed and defined against the pressures of the French colonial policy of assimilation; secondly the texts of the mid-1990s, particularly *Introduction à une poétique du divers* and *Traité*

---

1   Édouard Glissant, *Poétique de la Relation* (Paris: Gallimard, 1990), p.103. Hereafter referred to as *PR*.

*du Tout-monde*, dominated by the idea of *créolisation*, in which identity is formed through contacts with others in the 'Tout-monde' — this is perhaps the best-known period of Glissant's thought; and thirdly the much less widely read *Une nouvelle région du monde* of 2006, in which identity is based both on a more general, abstract form of difference and on relationships with place and the natural world.[2]

Therefore, the connection between identity and change implied by the title of this chapter is to be read in two different senses: a conception of identity as changing, but also a changing conception of identity. Moreover, it is not only identity that is re-thought across the three stages: the conception of change changes too, so that from *Le Discours antillais* to *Une nouvelle région du monde*, we are dealing with very different kinds of change.

In *Le Discours antillais* we find ourselves from the outset immersed in the stagnation and inertia that according to Glissant characterized Martiniquan society in the 1970s. A society, in other words, where apparently nothing changes. Thus the first chapter is titled 'A partir d'une situation bloquée', and the first page refers to 'une impuissance à sortir de l'impasse actuelle'. Glissant also emphasizes the paradoxical fact that the present-day societies of the Caribbean were created by the gigantic and brutal *change* that was transportation into slavery, which, he claims, had the advantage of delegitimizing any essentialist notion of a historically continuous collective identity and therefore opening up the possibility of the people's entry into Relation: rather than 'un peuple qui se continue ailleurs, *qui maintient l'Être*', they are 'une population qui se change ailleurs *en un autre peuple* [...] et qui entre ainsi dans la variance toujours recommencée de la Relation (du relais, du relatif)' (*DA*, p. 29). But in the centuries that followed, this possibility of Relation was thwarted by political and, especially, economic realities: the collapse of the world market for cane sugar in the late nineteenth century combined with departmentalization in the 1940s to create a situation in which, according to Glissant, the Martiniquan economy 'produces nothing', and lives on imports and subsidies from France. This was further aggravated by large-scale emigration to France under programmes of the Bureau pour le développement des migrations dans les départements d'outre-mer (BUMIDOM), and by the isolation of Martinique and Guadeloupe, cut off by departmentalization from their neighbouring Caribbean islands.

Glissant makes a direct link between this absence of economic production and the lack of any sense of collective identity, describing it as 'un double carcan: l'impossibilité de produire par et pour lui-même, l'impuissance qui en découla d'affirmer *ensemble* sa nature propre' (*DA*, p. 18); equally, economic inactivity cuts the Martiniquans off from Relation: 'on ne peut entrer en Relation [...] que si on n'est pas perdu dans une pseudo-production' (p. 64). In the Marxist analysis that Glissant adopts for much of *Le Discours antillais*, if there is no 'real' economic production then there are no 'real' social classes either, since these are determined

---

2    *Le Discours antillais* (Paris: Éditions du Seuil, 1981), hereafter *DA*; *Introduction à une poétique du divers* (Paris: Gallimard, 1996), hereafter *IPD*; *Traité du Tout-monde* (Paris: Gallimard, 1997), hereafter *TTM*; *Une nouvelle région du monde* (Paris: Gallimard, 2006), hereafter *NRM*.

by their function in the process of production; and therefore also no possibility of dialectical change that might resolve the social conflicts and create a national identity: 'Artificialiser les "classes sociales". Interdire qu'elles exercent une fonction dans une production [...] Rendre impossible la résolution autonome des conflits de classes, qui aurait fondé la Nation' (DA, p. 57).

In this 'situation bloquée', nothing will change unless people make it change. What is needed is a deliberate concerted effort to change Martiniquan society; and so the people must first become conscious of the need for and possibility of change: they must become 'une communauté s'arrachant de son traumatisme et naissant à sa propre conscience' (DA, p. 93).

This emphasis on consciousness-raising finds a clear echo in Éloge de la créolité, published eight years later, in which Chamoiseau and Confiant, together with Jean Bernabé, claim that 'Notre vision intérieure exercée, notre créolité mise comme centre de créativité, nous permet de réexaminer notre existence, d'y voir les mécanismes de l'aliénation'.[3] In their case, it is not based on the materialist analysis of economic production and social class that we find in Le Discours antillais. In fact, however, Glissant himself arguably departs from orthodox Marxism when he goes on to specify the social sector in which conscious political action will have the best chance of succeeding: given the irrelevance of the economic sector, 'cultural action' assumes a particular and unusual importance, as he explains in the section of Le Discours antillais entitled 'Pour une sociologie culturelle'. Moreover, he attributes to Martinique's traditional popular culture an importance that is also central to the Éloge's formulation of 'créolité', writing: 'La culture populaire vivace est au fondement de nos réflexes [...] C'est à partir d'elle que nous persistons' (DA, pp. 189–90).

Cultural action of course very directly involves collective or cultural identity: the political struggle will be first and foremost a struggle against alienation. In Le Discours antillais Glissant uses the term 'pulsion mimétique' to define the form of alienation specific to the French colonies that had been subjected to the policy of assimilation (especially Martinique and Guadeloupe). This 'mimetic drive' is the obsession with imitating and identifying with French culture, and Glissant (following Frantz Fanon and his Peau noire, masques blancs (1952), of course) sees it as the internalized counterpart of assimilation. It is thus only by overcoming the mimetic drive that Martiniquans will be able to rediscover — or perhaps to create — their own identity.

This opposition between identity and alienation has two consequences. Firstly, it almost inevitably entails a further opposition, between 'true' and 'false' identity: the mimetic drive has resulted in a *false* identity, which must be combatted by restoring the *true* identity of the Martiniquan people. Thus we find Glissant writing, for instance:

> Il semblait que le destin des Antilles de langue française fût de se trouver toujours en porte-à-faux sur *leur* réalité. Comme s'il n'était jamais donné à

3    Jean Bernabé, Patrick Chamoiseau and Raphaël Confiant, *Éloge de la créolité* (Paris: Gallimard, 1989), p. 39.

ces pays de rejoindre leur nature vraie, paralysés qu'ils étaient par [...] une des formes les plus pernicieuses de colonisation: celle par quoi on *assimile* une communauté. (*DA*, p. 15)

But this insistence on 'leur nature vraie' would seem to belong to precisely the essentialist conception of identity that Glissant opposes both elsewhere in *Le Discours antillais* and, with increasing prominence, in his later work. It is also of course what he accuses Bernabé, Chamoiseau, and Confiant of promoting. Secondly, in so far as it is a question of asserting one's identity against assimilation, it leads to a basically defensive attitude towards the French Other: given the inequality of the colonial situation, any attitude other than resistance to the colonial Other risks falling back into the 'mimetic drive'.

But the Other is not in principle limited to the colonial Other; and here another major opposition running through *Le Discours antillais* becomes relevant: 'le Même et le Divers' (title of Chapter 35). For 'le Même', the Other figures as 'Non pas encore l'Autre comme projet d'accord, mais l'autre comme matière à sublimer'; but 'le Divers', in contrast, 'a besoin de la présence des peuples, non plus comme objet à sublimer, mais comme projet à mettre en relation'.[4] Diversity is explicitly the result of anti-colonial struggle: 'Comme le Même a commencé par la rapine expansionniste en Occident, le Divers s'est fait jour à travers la violence politique et armée des peuples' (*DA*, p. 190). Thus we must champion diversity against the pseudo-universalism of the West, because all peoples have the right to affirm their identity, and between all these peoples there can be free and equal relations; that is, diversity makes possible Relation. Thus although Glissant is here talking in fairly abstract terms, 'le Divers' evokes a future in which the Martiniquans too will be able to relate freely, on equal terms, with others.

'Le Divers', the first version of what Glissant will later call 'différence', anticipates his later formulations of identity. But at this stage it lacks any temporal dimension; peoples are diverse in relation to each other, but each one has its 'nature vraie', which would appear to rule out the possibility of radical change. Also, Relation is seen as merely the result, rather than the driving force, of diversity; although later on *Le Discours antillais* does, briefly, move further in this direction, defining cultural identity as 'une identité questionnante, *où la relation à l'autre détermine l'être*' (*DA*, p. 283, my emphasis).

This concept of identity as being formed *through* contacts with the other, rather than *against* the other, becomes the central feature of Glissant's thought in the 1990s — the period dominated by 'créolisation' and the 'Tout-monde'. In the years following the publication of *Le Discours antillais* Glissant seems to have decided that the project of national independence for Martinique was simply not feasible, and to have directed his attention instead to the greatly increased opportunities for

---

4    J. Michael Dash comments: 'Glissant is the first Martiniquan writer to explore the possibility of a Caribbean identity in a thoroughgoing way [...] [He] defines the Caribbean's creole identity in the face of the totalizing sameness of metropolitan assimilation. He sees the all-consuming force of universalizing sameness not only in colonialism but in every manifestation of Western values' (*The Other America* (Charlottesville & London: University Press of Virginia, 1998), p. 11).

contacts between cultures opened up by the early stages of globalization. The world is now envisaged as a multiplicity of communities all communicating and reacting with each other, and characterized by constant, rapid, and unpredictable change on a global level; he sums up the four fundamental characteristics of creolization as follows:

> — la vitesse foudroyante des interactions mises en œuvre;
> — la 'conscience de la conscience' que nous en avons;
> — l'intervalorisation qui en provient et qui rend nécessaire que chacun réévalue pour soi les composantes mises en contact (la créolisation ne suppose pas une hiérarchie des valeurs);
> — l'imprédictibilité des résultantes (la créolisation ne se limite pas à un métissage, dont les synthèses pourraient être prévues). (*TTM*, p. 194)

The struggle for national independence is thus replaced by an awareness of the possibilities offered by a positive version of globalization, in which isolation is transformed into Relation, and stagnation into perpetual movement.

It is, moreover, these relations between cultures that *form* identities. Glissant sets up a major opposition between 'identité-racine' — the traditional essentialist conception, 'unique et exclusive de l'autre' (*IPD*, p. 33) — and 'identité-relation': identity as the product of contacts with the other in the process of creolization: 'l'identité comme facteur et comme résultat d'une créolisation' (*IPD*, p. 23). In so doing, he moves decisively away from the lingering essentialism that characterized his earlier formulation of 'true' identity as the opposite of the alienated identity constructed by the mimetic drive. And this is all the more true in that 'identité-relation' is also always changing, in a network of relations that constantly changes: '*le monde se créolise* [...] les cultures du monde mises en contact [...] les unes avec les autres se changent en s'échangeant' (*IPD*, p. 15). (The formula 'se changer en s'échangeant', to change oneself through exchange with the other, recurs throughout the texts of this period.) Change is part of the very nature of human existence, which therefore can no longer be defined in essentialist terms:

> Je crois que nous sommes arrivés à un moment de la vie des humanités où l'être humain commence d'accepter l'idée que lui-même est en perpétuel processus, qu'il n'est pas de l'être, mais de l'étant, et que comme tout étant, il change. (*IPD*, pp. 26–27)

Chamoiseau and Confiant present 'créolité' in the abstract in very similar terms, as open-ended, constantly and unpredictably changing: the conclusion to their *Lettres créoles* describes it as 'un mélange mouvant, dont le point de départ est un abîme et dont l'évolution demeure imprévisible'.[5] But their more concrete characterization of it in *Éloge de la créolité* does not bear this out; they are describing a particular culture, and one which, moreover, they often see as in danger of disappearing altogether rather than 'evolving'. There is little sense in their work that 'le monde se créolise' — rather, their 'créolité' is almost always restricted to geographically

---

5    Patrick Chamoiseau and Raphaël Confiant, *Lettres créoles: tracées antillaises et continentales de la littérature: Haïti, Guadeloupe, Martinique, Guyane, 1635–1975* (Paris: Hatier, 1991), p. 204.

specific societies defined as Creole in orthodox terms, and is thus substantive,[6] whereas Glissant's 'créolisation' is a process operating on a global level, and the whole point of it is that it is contentless: 'La créolisation [...] n'a d'exemplaire que ses processus et certainement pas les "contenus" à partir desquels ils fonctionneraient. C'est ce qui fait notre départ d'avec le concept de 'créolité' (*PR*, p. 103).[7]

It is noticeable that Glissant now refers to 'cultures', rather than 'peuples' or 'pays': an indication, perhaps, of the extent to which for him identity is no longer *militant*. Now, in the Tout-monde, where relationships are multilateral and less unequal, it is no longer a question of defending one's identity against the colonial Other, but of opening it up *to* the Other: 'des identités maîtresses d'elles-mêmes et qui acceptent de changer en s'échangeant' (*IPD*, p. 42). This stress on the sovereignty of the self contrasts strikingly with the contortions of the mimetic drive. Nevertheless, one can detect a trace of that earlier anxiety about being swallowed up by assimilation, in that the 'grande question' is now: 'comment être soi sans se fermer à l'autre, et comment s'ouvrir à l'autre *sans se perdre soi-même*' (*IPD*, p. 23, my emphasis). Glissant refers insistently to what he calls 'la *difficile* complexion d'une identité *relation*, d'une identité qui comporte une ouverture à l'autre, sans danger de dilution' (*IPD*, p. 24); and again: 'La créolisation ne conclut pas à la perte d'identité, à la dilution de l'étant. Elle n'infère pas le renoncement à soi' (*TTM*, p. 25). Creolization does not mean 'dilution' of the self; it is, rather, a question of 'se changer en échangeant avec l'autre *sans se perdre ou se dénaturer*' (*TTM*, p. 15, my emphasis).

In stark contrast to the situation described in *Le Discours antillais*, everything in the world is now changing of its own accord — unstoppably and uncontrollably. The role of conscious political action in bringing about change has thus become somewhat problematic; Glissant emphasizes not only the sheer speed of change today but also the unpredictability of the results: anything can change into anything. The Tout-monde is also 'le chaos-monde'. Political action has become far more tactical, a question of reacting to local circumstances according to the general principles of Relation.[8]

Equally, while the role of consciousness in relation to change has not been marginalized — it is an integral part of the Tout-monde, which Glissant defines as 'notre univers tel qu'il change et perdure en échangeant et, en même temps, la "vision" que nous en avons' (*TTM*, p. 176, my emphasis), and of creolization, which is defined by 'son caractère de conscience' (*IPD*, p. 27) — it is now significantly different. It is no longer a question of conscious action to bring about defined social change, but in the sense that it is our consciousness of other cultures that allows us to *be changed* by them. Glissant goes so far as to suggest that the project of changing

6    Although they do at one point evoke a future in which 'créolité' will spread throughout the world: 'Le monde va en état de créolité [...] De plus en plus émergera une nouvelle humanité qui aura les caractéristiques de notre humanité créole' (Bernabé, Chamoiseau, and Confiant, *Éloge de la créolité*, pp. 52–53). I am grateful to Richard Price for bringing this to my attention.

7    *Éloge de la créolité* was published in 1989 before Glissant's elaboration of the concept of creolization. In it, therefore, Glissant is associated only with the regional concerns of 'Antillanité' (Bernabé, Chamoiseau, and Confiant, *Éloge de la créolité*, pp. 21–22).

8    See Chapter 5.

the world by revolutionary action is now too deterministic to be viable in the new reality of the 'chaos-monde': 'La belle formule "changer le monde" s'est peu à peu transformée en "mettre le monde en carte, en système"' (*IPD*, p. 102).

Therefore, in preference to orthodox political action based on a rationalist analysis of the situation, one sees in these texts of the 1990s the growing importance of a form of politics based on the collective *imaginaire*: that is, the way in which people conceive of the world, particularly in terms of cultural identity. Although we may be powerless in the face of 'les oppressions concrètes qui stupéfient le monde', we are still 'capables de changer l'imaginaire des humanités' (*TTM*, p. 18). In this far more idealist conception, the object of political action has become to 'changer les imaginaires': that is, to influence people's conception of their own and others' cultures. Thus Glissant comments that:

> Nous commençons de comprendre qu'en marge des guerres économiques et financières, [...] les vrais engagements d'aujourd'hui [...] concernent avant tout les cultures des peuples et des communautés. Le culturel a rencontré le politique et les affrontements majeurs de notre temps en sont empreints. (*TTM*, p. 247)

As with the resurfacing of the old anxiety about assimilation, there is another curious echo here of the earlier *Discours antillais* with its emphasis on 'cultural action'. The objective situation is quite different: previously, the importance of cultural action derived from the particular economic stagnation of Martinique, its lack of any real production, whereas now we are dealing with the social consequences of a rampaging neo-liberal, globalized economy. But, ironically, the overwhelming power of this economy leads Glissant to a similar position: the cultural arena, now more abstractly characterized as 'l'imaginaire des humanités', is still the preferred site for political action. He has been criticized for this, of course.[9] It is tempting to see in Glissant's focus on culture and the *imaginaire* a version of the kind of 'identity politics' that seeks to promote the interests of a particular community, rather than being based on general principles of equality and justice. But this would be to forget that his basic notion of identity formed solely through exchange with others actually *counters* the whole basis of identity politics — and the same cannot so clearly be said for the 'créolité' of Bernabé, Chamoiseau, and Confiant.

In *Une nouvelle région du monde*, identity is subject to a very different kind of change, and is formed in relation to place. Glissant has always attached great significance to 'le lieu' and stressed, both in his novels and his essays, that place is far more than a mere decor; but now its determining influence on the human individual is elaborated far more explicitly. Thus he speaks of a 'géomorphisme' which, as opposed to anthropomorphism, contests the notion of human beings as the centre of the world and resituates them in relation to 'une géographie et une géologie qui les dépassent en les intégrant' (*NRM*, p. 77). Places change us: '*C'est parce que ce sont les pays qui prévalent* [...] Les pays nous changent. Les pays, les

---

9    See Peter Hallward, *Absolutely Postcolonial: Writing between the Singular and the Specific* (Manchester: Manchester University Press, 2001), and Chris Bongie, *Friends and Enemies: The Scribal Politics of Post/Colonial Literature* (Liverpool: Liverpool University Press, 2008). I discuss this in greater detail in Chapter 5.

paysages' (pp. 28–29). As Carine Mardorossian puts it:

> In [Glissant's] later work, and more specifically in *Une nouvelle région du monde*, nonhuman nature adopts a new dimension in its dynamic, reciprocal relationship with humanity [...]. Human and natural history are revealed as reciprocally and deeply transformative, while the representation of the environment questions the humanistic domination and mastery over nonhuman and human life.[10]

Both place and change are invoked by the book's provocatively opaque title, but in ways that turn out to be less than straightforward. It seems to evoke past European enthusiasms for discovery: for geographical and anthropological exploration, and of course for colonization. But in the twenty-first century we know that the world has long been explored: we know that there are no 'new regions'. Nevertheless, the title seems to insist that something has changed and *Une nouvelle région du monde* does contain new formulations of the relationship between identity and change.

In fact the new region turns out to be synonymous with the 'Tout-monde', in so far as this, in its constant reinvention of itself, can never be known: it is always new, always being discovered: 'Bien alors, le monde est tout-à-fait reconnu, et le Tout-monde recouvre le monde entièrement, pourtant et pour nous le Tout-monde est à découvrir et à connaître. C'est une partie du monde, qui ici-là dépasse le monde et le désigne' (*NRM*, p. 97). Is this, then, simply another example of Glissant's fondness for quasi synonyms, concepts that overlap and repeat with subtle differences of emphasis ('créolisation', 'Tout-monde', 'chaos-monde', 'mondialité')? No doubt. But here the point seems to be that introducing the idea of a 'new region' highlights the paradox that this new region is also very old: that is, it signifies a return to an ancient, 'primordial' relation with the natural world — a new and rather different version, perhaps, of the 'vision prophétique du passé'[11] — and a valorization of the distant past which is quite different from the celebration of the present that we find in *Introduction à une poétique du divers* and *Traité du Tout-monde*. Equally, one can detect in *Une nouvelle région du monde* a certain disillusionment with globalization: several passages, for instance, evoke the suffering of the migrants that it has created (*NRM*, pp. 82–86, 122–23, 145–46).

In a long description of the prehistoric cave paintings at Lascaux (*NRM*, pp. 46–52), Glissant interprets them as figurations of the relation between self and other — between the human community that produced them and its surroundings — and notes that they almost never show other human beings (pp. 48–49). In other words, human identity is still relational, as it was in creolization, but now the relationships are not with other humans or cultures but with animals and the natural world. This, he conjectures, is because at the time humans were not yet a dominant species and their communities were not sufficiently numerous to come into contact and/ or conflict with each other very often; therefore their most important relationships

---

10    Carine M. Mardorossian, '"Poetics of Landscape": Édouard Glissant's Creolized Ecologies', *Callaloo*, 36.4 (2013), 983–94 (p. 989).

11    In *Le Discours antillais* Glissant argues that the writer's task is to illuminate the past and project it into the future: 'C'est à démêler un sens douloureux du temps et à le projeter à tout coup dans notre future [... ] C'est ce que j'appelle *une vision prophétique du passé*' (p. 132).

were less with other human communities than with the landscapes and animals with which they lived and on which they depended for survival. It was only later, when competition between different groups of humans became a major factor in their lives, that they began to see the natural world as something to be *owned* and defended from other groups.

Human beings' relation to the natural world — to place, in other words — was therefore one of what he calls 'fusion'; and it is this relationship, as opposed to the later conception of place as a possession to be fought over, that needs to be revived so that it will once again characterize the 'new region of the world'.[12] It connects, in other words, with the ecological strand that became prominent in Glissant's later thought (discussed by Mardorossian in 'Poetics of Landscape').

In so far as this ancient value has been preserved in the modern world, it is by indigenous communities still clinging to their traditions. This is the first time in Glissant's work that we find such emphasis and importance accorded to these communities; there are a few Native American characters in his novels, but overall he has written very little on the indigenous peoples of the Caribbean or elsewhere. Here they are characterized, in rather romantic terms, as people who have not been exposed to outside influences, who continue to exist on the sidelines of the modern world and have very little contact with other cultures: people who 'ne bougèrent pas de leur lieu donné' (*NRM*, p. 98). The effect is to eliminate almost entirely from this text the idea of creolization, which is completely irrelevant to these indigenous communities — indeed, the word 'créolisation' appears only twice in the whole book.

Identity, therefore, in *Une nouvelle région du monde,* is not formed primarily through contacts with other cultures: the indigenous peoples who are presented as a model for the future do not 'changent en s'échangeant'. Indeed, in its implications of 'unmixedness', of a kind of racial purity even, it might be thought to have veered back into a classic form of essentialism. But in fact it is still a relational identity: the result of a relationship (a fusion) with place. 'Les pays nous changent' (*NRM*, p. 29), not once and for all, and not in a deterministic fashion, but in a continuing process of mutual influence between people and places:

> Les lieux [...] tressent un texte baroque [...] dont il nous faut décider s'il soutient ce que nous appellerions notre identité, ou si c'est nous qui lui conférons la densité qui engage chacun des dits lieux plus avant chaque fois dans l'étai de son paysage. (*NRM*, p. 120)

This also implies a different kind of change from that which we saw in the texts of the 1990s: unlike the vertiginous and unpredictable forces that characterize creolization, it is a more gradual, organic form of change, similar to the notion of 'le vivant' that he develops in his late work.[13]

---

12    I have analyzed the notion of 'fusion' in more detail, albeit from a rather different point of view, in ' "La Parole du paysage": Art and the Real in *Une nouvelle région du monde*', in *Language and Literary Form in French Caribbean Writing* (Liverpool: Liverpool University Press, 2014), pp. 154–68.

13    See Alessandro Corio, 'The Living and the Poetic Intention: Glissant's Biopolitics of Literature', *Callaloo*, 36.4 (2013), 916–30, for a discussion of the themes of 'continuity' and 'rupture' in the concept of the 'living'.

*Une nouvelle région du monde*, however, also introduces a second theorization of identity, alongside the idea of fusion: identity as generated by difference, which is more powerful than 'le Divers', because it is generative.[14] Glissant calls it 'la matrice-motrice du chaos-monde' (*NRM*, p. 63), i.e. differences generate more differences in a continuous process: 'Et les différences déroulent à leur tour d'autres différences [...] et ces différences engendrées produisent ensemble, par-delà les diversités, la continuité non prévisible du monde' (p. 97). The conception of identity that results from this is far more abstract and also more general than any of the earlier formulations, in that it applies not only to peoples and cultures but to everything that exists in the world. (A consequence of this is that identity and difference move out of the ethical arena they had previously occupied in Glissant's work; the ethical dimension of *Une nouvelle région du monde* is more prominent in the contrast between 'fusion' and 'possession'.) Identities are created by the generative force of difference; but the very concept of identity (or what he here prefers to call 'variety' because they are always changing or varying: 'Toute identité est aussi une variété qui pour un temps a cessé de bouger', p. 142) has been enlarged beyond the sphere of human identity: places, animals, trees, texts are all identities.

This strange and difficult book, which has received relatively little critical attention, thus arrives at two very different theorizations of identity that, while not actually contradictory, strikingly illustrate Glissant's disdain for what he calls 'systematic thought'. It also testifies to the enduring importance that identity retains throughout his work, from the militant struggle against alienation and the urgency of forcing change on an 'inert' society in *Le Discours antillais*, to the ever-changing contacts between different cultures in the 'créolisation' period, to the ecological perspective of the relations between humans and the non-human world.

The shifts between these three phases are not a simple linear development of Glissant's thought, but rather reflect changes in his perception of the outside world — specifically, two moments of disillusionment: with the project of national independence and then with globalization. It is therefore difficult to assess them outside that historical context or to say that any one of them is more convincing than the others. The militant identity of *Le Discours antillais* is relevant above all to the struggles for national independence that characterized the 1960s and 1970s; but such struggles do still exist in the twenty-first century, and more generally the importance of resisting a dominant political and cultural regime has certainly not gone away; to that extent, Glissant's insistence on consciously building a collective identity, and on respect for other people and other cultures, is still both valid and valuable. Equally, his enthusiasm for globalization now seems rather naive (as he himself later implies); nevertheless, the basic idea that our identities are formed through our relations with others, and change as those relations change, in my view remains powerfully convincing, and a very necessary antidote to essentialist conceptions of identity. Finally, despite the rather romanticized vision of fusion

---

14    See my 'La Parole du paysage' for a more sustained discussion of this theme, including Glissant's reinstatement of a dialectical conception of change that had been more prominent in his much earlier work.

with the natural world that we find in *Une nouvelle région du monde*, its ecological impetus is increasingly relevant to the world we all live in today.

I have argued here, not that Glissant always succeeds in avoiding essentialism, but that his insistence on the necessary relationship between identity and change, in its various forms, is inseparable from his longstanding and consistent anti-essentialist impetus. More generally, I hope to have shown how the notion of identity that runs throughout his writing is a central element in his thought and, in its originality and scope, constitutes one of his major contributions to postcolonial theory.

# CHAPTER 2

❖

# Ethnography as Relation: The Significance of the French Caribbean in the Ethnographic Writing of Michel Leiris

Michel Leiris is known for the close connection between autobiography and ethnography that runs through his work. He developed a practice of ethnographic attention to his own subjectivity, famously becoming an 'ethnographer of himself'; and, conversely, he challenged the idea that the ethnographer must adopt an impersonal, scientific attitude towards the people whose cultures he analyzed. For Édouard Glissant, this position liberated Leiris from the implicitly colonial and racist attitudes of most ethnographers; and in the two articles that Glissant wrote on him, both Glissant's admiration for Leiris and the congruence between Leiris's thought and his own become clear. The first of these articles is an untitled piece in *L'Intention poétique*, the second, 'Repli et dépli', in *Traité du Tout-monde*.[1] In the piece in *L'Intention poétique* Glissant sees Leiris as bringing to bear on his study of others the honesty and rigour of self-analysis that, according to Glissant, characterize the literary writer; thus Leiris is one of those who have 'profité de leur vocation d'écrivain, de l'obligation qui leur est faite d'être sincères et rigides envers eux-mêmes, pour redonner sa vraie signification à l'exercice de cette activité plus que toutes vouée à la "recherche de l'Autre"' (*IP*, p. 121).

The traditional ethnographer, Glissant claims, is hated by his non-European subjects because his 'scientific' stance objectifies and neutralizes them (*IP*, p. 128); but the subjective element in Leiris's ethnographic work makes possible a real engagement with the groups who are being studied. In 'Repli et dépli', equally, Glissant contrasts Leiris with the advent of a new, 'pure' ethnology, by which (judging from an allusion to Lévi-Strauss's *Structures élémentaires de la parenté*) he means structuralism: this approach leads to 'la distanciation, par où on estimait garantir

---

1    The untitled chapter in *L'Intention poétique* (Paris: Éditions du Seuil, 1969, pp. 121–29, hereafter referred to as *IP*, was first published as 'Michel Leiris, ethnographe', *Les Lettres nouvelles*, 14:43 (1956), 609–21; 'Repli et dépli', in *TTM*, pp. 128–38. See Christina Kullberg, *The Poetics of Ethnography in Martinican Narratives* (Charlottesville & London: University of Virginia Press, 2013, pp. 59–65) for a discussion of Leiris's influence on the young Glissant.

l'objectivité [...] Leiris ne souscrit pas à cette tentation de l'universel généralisant' (*TTM*, p. 131).[2] Glissant is also against the type of ethnography, whether traditional or structuralist, that regards its subject matter as ahistorical and unchanging; rather, ethnography must be 'placée dans le rayonnement d'un devenir' (*IP*, p.125), as Leiris's investigations are.[3] Thus the ideal ethnographer is not an observer but a player in a drama unfolding in the present: Glissant concludes the *L'Intention poétique* article with these words: ' "L'observateur attentif" qu'est (ou était) l'ethnographe devra *s'inscrire au drame du monde*: par-delà son analytique — en principe "solitaire" — il devra vivre une poétique (un partage). Ainsi Leiris' (*IP*, p. 129).[4] This kind of ethnography clearly resonates with the concept of 'Relation' that is central to his own work, and in 'Repli et dépli' he makes this explicit, praising Leiris's *Contacts de civilisations en Martinique et en Guadeloupe* as 'une ethnologie de la Relation, une ethnographie du rapport à l'Autre' (*TTM*, p. 131).[5]

The type of engagement demanded by Relation is not merely an emotional attachment; it must also be ethical and political. In *L'Intention poétique* Glissant distinguishes between the early phase of Leiris's ethnographic work, which in 1934 produced *Afrique fantôme* (the diary of his participation in the ethnographic expedition from Dakar to Djibouti between 1931 and 1933, organized by Marcel Griaule), and a later stage, beginning in 1950 with the publication of 'L'Ethnographe devant le colonialisme'.[6] In *Afrique fantôme* Leiris expresses his desire to abolish the barriers between himself and the African people he meets, in order, in effect, to become one of them. He daydreams about never going back to Europe: 'Rester là. Ne plus rien faire. S'installer dans la montagne. Y prendre femme et fonder un foyer. Désir utopique que me donnent ces gens', and is frustrated when the 'écart irréductible de deux civilisations' (*AF*, p. 359) becomes apparent:

> Sensation ardente d'être au bord de quelque chose dont je ne toucherai jamais le fond, faute, entre autres raisons, de pouvoir — ainsi qu'il le faudrait — m'abandonner, à cause de mobiles divers, [...] parmi lesquels figurent en premier lieu les questions de peau, de civilisation, de langue. (*AF*, p. 359)

---

2    *TTM*, p. 130: 'tentative de surprendre, au modèle de sociétés elles aussi supposées pures [...] les structures élémentaires ou les dynamiques de toutes sociétés données'. Claude Lévi-Strauss, *Les Structures élémentaires de la parenté* (Paris: Presses universitaires de France, 1949).

3    Glissant, in making this point, is again going against Lévi-Strauss, who in the final chapter, 'Histoire et dialectique', of his *La Pensée sauvage*, famously attacked Sartre's historical concept of reason (*La Pensée sauvage* (Paris: Plon, 1962), pp. 324–57).

4    Aimé Césaire concurs with this praise for Leiris's engagement and solidarity with the Antillais, but sees it as Leiris going beyond ethnography rather than redefining it: 'Plus qu'un ethnographe, plus qu'un témoin, il était, disons, le complice de l'homme devant son destin', 'Aimé Césaire et Roger Toumson: entretien sur Michel Leiris', in *Michel Leiris: le siècle à l'envers*, ed. by Francis Marmande (Tours: Farrago; [Paris], Léo Scheer, 2004), pp. 71–75 (p. 74).

5    Michel Leiris, *Contacts de civilisations en Martinique et en Guadeloupe* (Paris: Gallimard/Unesco, 1955), hereafter referred to as *CC*.

6    Michel Leiris, *Afrique fantôme* [1934], 3rd edn (Paris: Gallimard, 1981) (all three editions (1934, 1950 and 1981), hereafter referred to as *AF*; 'L'Ethnographe devant le colonialisme' [1950], in *Les Temps modernes*, 58 (1950); *Cinq études d'ethnologie* [1969], 2nd edn (Paris: Gallimard, 1988), pp. 83–112.

In 1950 Leiris wrote a preface to the second edition of *Afrique fantôme* in which he is extremely critical of the attitude he adopted in the text. At the time, he writes, he was disappointed by ethnography because 'une science humaine reste une science et l'observation détachée ne saurait, à elle seule, amener le contact'; and his desire for contact with African culture led him into 'un fallacieux essai de se faire autre en effectuant une plongée — d'ailleurs toute symbolique — dans une "mentalité primitive" dont j'éprouvais la nostalgie' (*AF*, pp. 8, 9). But, he argues, this dichotomy between neutral science and fantasized identification with the other turns out to be false; and he has been able to surmount it through his political commitment to the decolonization movements that had not existed in the 1930s but are now springing up in the aftermath of the Second World War. His friendship with Aimé Césaire, whom he has known since 1946, has also been influential in this regard.[7] As a result, his position is now, he claims, very different; rather than attempting to achieve a 'communion purement formelle', his goal is 'une solidarité effective avec des hommes qui ont une claire conscience de ce qu'il y a d'inacceptable dans leur situation et mettent en œuvre pour y rémédier les moyens les plus positifs' (*AF*, p. 9) — men, in other words, who are actively struggling to change their situation in what Glissant termed 'le drame du monde'.

In fact there is considerably more continuity between the two stages than Glissant, who comments in some detail on the 1950 preface (*IP*, pp. 126–27), and Leiris himself suggest — and, therefore, more overlap between political commitment and psychological fulfilment. The common factor is Leiris's need to participate in the culture he is investigating, which from the start takes precedence over what he calls 'abstract knowledge'. In *Afrique fantôme*, certainly, the participation takes the form of possession in 'Zar' seances in Ethiopia, and an erotic obsession with Emawayish, the woman involved in the seances — as in his oft-quoted remark: 'J'aimerais mieux être possédé qu'étudier les possédés, connaître charnellement une "zarine" que connaître scientifiquement ses tenants et aboutissants, la connaissance abstraite ne sera jamais qu'un pis-aller' (*AF*, p. 324). But some of Leiris's later writings also contain very similar statements of the value of this purely emotional involvement: in his review of *Tristes tropiques*, for instance, published in 1956, he emphasizes approvingly how, even for the theoretically minded Lévi-Strauss, the Nambikwara represent 'le moment *heureux* du livre (son moment idyllique, parce qu'il semble que le contact de cette population [...] lui a fourni une manière d'équivalent de ce *vert paradis des amours enfantines* à quoi Baudelaire rêvait nostalgiquement'.[8] Similarly, in the speech he made on the occasion of Alfred Métraux's death in 1963, he used the same quotation from Baudelaire to preface a clear expression of his continuing fascination with possession:

> Si, en face de ces cultes à base de possession, le rationalisme interdit toute
> autre attitude que celle de l'incrédule, n'est-ce pas dommage et ne vaudrait-il

---

7    Denis Hollier emphasizes the impact that meeting Césaire had on the author's realization of the necessity of a political engagement with colonized societies (Michel Leiris, *La Règle du jeu*, ed. by Denis Hollier and others (Paris: Gallimard, 2003), p. 1402).

8    Michel Leiris, 'A travers *Tristes tropiques*' [1956], in *Cinq études d'ethnologie*, pp. 113–27 (p. 119).

pas mieux, plus naïfs, entrer de plain-pied dans ces merveilles cousues de fil blanc?[9]

Conversely, while the 1950 preface gives the impression that Leiris discovered the iniquities of colonialism only after the war, *Afrique fantôme* actually already contains ample evidence of not only his hostility towards colonialism, but also his awareness of ethnography's implication in it:[10]

> De moins en moins je supporte l'idée de colonisation. Faire rentrer l'impôt, telle est la grande préoccupation [...] Tournées parfois sanglantes dans quel but: faire rentrer l'impôt. Étude ethnographique dans quel but: être à même de mener une politique plus habile qui sera mieux à même de faire rentrer l'impôt.
> (*AF*, p. 169)

There is, therefore, something slightly facile about the very clarity with which the 1950 preface converts identificatory phantasy into political solidarity with the colonized, and about the assumption that the latter automatically absolves Leiris from the charge of narcissism. Now, he modestly claims, his perspective is one of 'très simple camaraderie' (*AF*, p. 9) with the colonized in their struggle for liberation. But decolonization, in fact, offered him a personal emotional liberation: according to Césaire, 'Il a véritablement vibré à la décolonisation'.[11] It is as though the discovery of political solidarity immediately releases him from all his problems of alienation. In other words, the transition from the first to the second phase looks rather less like a substantial change of attitude and more like a kind of sublimation:[12] political commitment is simply the 'sublimated' version of the original desire for identification and participation.[13] A second preface, the 'Préambule' that Leiris

9 Michel Leiris, 'Regard vers Alfred Métraux' [1964], reprinted in *Cinq études d'ethnologie*, pp. 129–37 (p. 134).
10 Seán Hand emphasizes the degree of political commitment already evident in *Afrique fantôme*, referring to its 'moral and political *embarquement* and *témoignage*' and arguing that it 'exposes the imperialist legacy and neo-colonialist maintenance of power-relations deeply ingrained in the assumptions and aims of this African Mission' (*Michel Leiris: Writing the Self* (Cambridge: Cambridge University Press, 2002), p. 55). Sally Price, similarly, defines *Afrique fantôme* as 'even today, the strongest French anthropological critique of colonialism in Africa' ('Michel Leiris, French Anthropology and a Side-Trip to the Antilles', *French Politics, Culture and Society*, 22.1 (2004), 23–35 (p. 28)).
11 Césaire and Toumson, 'Aimé Césaire et Roger Toumson: entretien sur Michel Leiris', p. 74. There is no element of criticism in Césaire's emphasis on the significance of decolonization for Leiris, but he does make its emotional naivety very clear: 'Il a été témoin de la naissance d'un monde nouveau, un monde qui dépasse l'Europe et qu'il veut et qu'il souhaite être le monde de la redécouverte de l'homme par lui-même: le monde de la découverte d'une véritable fraternité, un monde perdu de bonté, de beauté et de tendresse' (p. 74).
12 The definition of Freudian 'sublimation' given by Laplanche and Pontalis is: 'La pulsion est dite sublimée dans la mesure où elle est dérivée vers un nouveau but non sexuel et où elle vise des objets socialement valorisés' (J. Laplanche and J.-B. Pontalis, *Vocabulaire de la psychanalyse* (Paris: Presses universitaires de France, 1968), p. 465). I am not suggesting that Leiris's identification with the colonized is a sexual drive in the Freudian sense, but the process that it undergoes is strikingly similar to the mechanism of sublimation.
13 Evidence for this view is provided by entries in Leiris's diary after his 1945 trip to the Ivory Coast, in which he expresses his affective disillusionment with Africa: 'Mon dernier voyage en Côte d'Ivoire et Gold Coast, qui m'a si fort déplu parce que je refaisais quelque chose à quoi je ne croyais

wrote for the 1981 edition of *Afrique fantôme*, lends support to this interpretation. With a distinctly ironic detachment, he comments not only on the original text of 1934 but also on the 1950 preface, analyzes his motives in 1950, and strongly implies that he was opportunistically taking advantage of the decolonizing movement in order that contact with 'le monde noir' could become a reality for him rather than the 'fantôme' that it had been in 1934:

> Quelque quinze ans plus tard, alors que s'amorçait le processus qui devait aboutir à ce qu'on a nommé présomptueusement la 'décolonisation', il me sembla que le monde noir — africain ou autre — prenait bel et bien corps pour moi, et cela parce que les circonstances me permettaient de penser que, dans la faible mesure de mes moyens de chercheur et d'écrivain, je pourrais apporter un concours indirect mais positif à ceux qui, ressortissants de ce monde noir, luttaient contre l'oppression. (*AF*, p. 3)

And the irony becomes even more evident when he lists the 'buts tonifiants que [...] j'assignais à l'ethnographie quelques années après la dernière guerre' (p. 4).

This does not invalidate either the effectiveness or the sincerity of Leiris's political commitment, which certainly brought about a new emphasis in his view of the discipline of ethnography in which the ethnographer's political responsibility to the colonized was central. But Glissant's comment that in the 1950 autocritique Leiris 'réconcilie recherche de soi et recherche de l'autre, les posant solidairement après avoir cessé de les confondre' (*IP*, p. 127) is an oversimplification. Rather, it is that the political and the personal — the selfless, responsible action in support of the colonized, and the self-serving phantasy of becoming one with them — are for Leiris intertwined in quite complex ways, as I shall attempt to show in the latter part of this chapter.

The ideas on which Leiris's second, more mature, version of subjective ethnography was to be based were elaborated in 'L'Ethnographe devant le colonialisme', which first appeared in *Les Temps modernes* in 1950, and *Race et civilisation*, published in 1951 as part of a UNESCO project on 'La Question raciale devant la science moderne'.[14] The latter work, rather unusually for Leiris but befitting the series in which it appears, places considerable emphasis on anthropology's scientific status as a weapon in the battle against racism: anthropology can prove that there is no such thing as a racially pure society,[15] so that stressing its scientific credentials strengthens the argument.[16] At the same time, however, Leiris quite overtly equates racism with colonialism — a controversial position at the beginning of the 1950s — and often

plus. Me sentir "engagé" vis-à-vis des Nègres, pour qui je n'ai plus cette enfantine sympathie que j'avais quand j'ai fait la mission Dakar-Djibouti' (quoted by Hollier, in Leiris, *La Règle du jeu*, p. 1402). This suggests that the move from emotional to political involvement was itself motivated as much by the loss of a phantasy as by a principled political commitment.

14    Michel Leiris, *Race et civilisation* [1951], in *Cinq études d'ethnologie*, pp. 9–80.
15    Ibid., pp. 12, 17.
16    For example, against the notion that any society can be entirely primitive: 'Les connaissances que la science occidentale possède en matière d'ethnographie, branche du savoir aujourd'hui constituée en discipline méthodique, permettent d'affirmer qu'il n'existe actuellement pas un seul groupe humain qu'on puisse dire "à l'état de nature"' (Leiris, *Race et civilisation*, p. 35).

departs from his neutral, impersonal style to attack it with angry irony.[17] Most importantly, he formulates the idea that anthropology cannot be entirely objective because the anthropologist is inevitably conditioned by his or her own culture: 'Nos idées sur la culture étant elle-mêmes partie intégrante d'une culture (celle de la société à laquelle nous appartenons), il nous est impossible de prendre la position d'observateurs extérieurs'.[18]

It is 'L'Ethnographe devant le colonialisme', however, that constitutes the clearest statement of Leiris's conviction that the ethnographer is directly implicated in colonialism because most of the cultures he studies belong to colonized societies and his missions are made possible by the colonial state; and that he therefore has an ethical and political obligation to place his expertise at the service of the anticolonial struggles of societies in the Third World. Leiris suggests various ways in which he can do so: by speaking up for colonized peoples ('il nous revient d'être comme leurs avocats naturels vis-à-vis de la nation colonisatrice à laquelle nous appartenons');[19] by valorizing their cultures and so helping them to lose their inferiority complex in relation to the West; by studying colonizers as well as the colonized ('une telle étude ne manquerait pas de faire ressortir combien, du point de vue humain, le rapport colonial-colonisé peut être préjudiciable à chacune des deux parties');[20] and, above all perhaps, by facilitating the training of 'native ethnographers' (as Leiris himself would do at the Musée de l'Homme where one of his students, in 1953–54, was Glissant) who would be able to provide a different point of view, not only on their own societies but also on European ones, so that ethnography could become a real intersubjective partnership between the West and the Third World.[21]

It is with this idea of reciprocity that Leiris comes closest to Glissant's concept of Relation.[22] Glissant's hostility to traditional ethnography stems precisely from its refusal to enter into relation with its subjects: 'Nous haïssons l'ethnographie: chaque

17    For instance: 'Ironie non moins étrange, c'est dans la mesure où les races réputées inférieures prouvent qu'elles sont à même de s'émanciper que, les antagonismes devenant plus aigus dès l'instant que les hommes de couleur font pour les blancs figure de concurrents ou se voient reconnaître un minimum de droits politiques, le dogme racial est affirmé avec une énergie plus manifeste' (Leiris, *Race et civilisation*, p. 12).

18    Ibid., p. 70.

19    Ibid., p. 88.

20    Ibid., p. 106.

21    This is one of the themes of James Clifford's *The Predicament of Culture: Twentieth-Century Ethnography, Literature, and Art* (Cambridge, MA: Harvard University Press, 1988); in the chapter entitled 'On Ethnographic Authority' (pp. 21–54) he writes, for instance, 'now that the West can no longer present itself as the unique purveyor of anthropological knowledge about others, it has become necessary to imagine a world of generalized ethnography' (p. 22). Later in the book he accords Leiris an important role in this process, and also credits him with being, in 1950, 'perhaps the first ethnographer to confront squarely the political and epistemological constraints of colonialism on fieldwork' (p. 89).

22    Interestingly, however, Irene Albers argues that a kind of reciprocity is already evident in *Afrique fantôme*, in that the theatricality of the Zar ceremonies provided a basis for a reciprocal staging of roles: 'Fieldwork [...] turns out to be a situation in which the ethnographer and the possessed, the European and the African culture, stage themselves for each other' ('Mimesis and Alterity: Michel Leiris's Ethnography and Poetics of Spirit Possession', *French Studies*, 62 (2008), pp. 271–89 (p. 286)).

fois que, s'achevant ailleurs, elle ne fertilise pas le vœu dramatique de la relation'; its refusal, in other words, to grant its subjects the possibility of 'looking back' at the ethnographers' own culture: 'La méfiance que nous lui vouons ne provient pas du déplaisir d'être regardés, mais de l'obscur ressentiment de ne pas voir à notre tour' (IP, p. 128). Leiris makes exactly the same point when he notes that up until now no non-Western society has been able to produce researchers who could carry out ethnographic studies of our Western civilization; and that this results in 'une sorte de déséquilibre qui fausse la perspective et contribue à nous assurer dans notre orgueil, notre civilisation se trouvant ainsi hors de portée de l'examen des sociétés qu'elle a, elle, à sa portée pour les examiner'.[23] The other's view of our society reveals to us its limitations, and this is the counterpart to the 'ethnography of oneself' that Leiris also promotes. The ultimate goal is to have four perspectives, all interacting with each other: the self's and the other's view of the self's culture and of the other's culture.

The ability to be critical of one's own culture is enhanced both by the other's view of it and by one's ethnographic knowledge of other cultures; but, equally, it is a precondition of being able to study other cultures without bias: 'recherche de soi' and 'recherche de l'autre' again necessarily implicate each other.[24] As Glissant also makes clear in L'Intention poétique, the importance of the reciprocity, of being able to 'voir à notre tour', is not that it would demonstrate the equality of the two sides but that it would transform the ethnographic activity into a 'relation': his objection to 'one-sided' ethnography is 'non point pour ce qu'elle nous sèvre du contentement d'équivaloir, mais pour ce qu'elle offusque et saccage (du moins telle qu'ainsi pratiquée) la richesse de tous rapports' (IP, p. 128).

It is in this sense that ethnographic study has to be 'relational', in Glissant's terms, or, as Leiris puts it, based on the conviction that 'il n'est aucune observation qui ne soit un rapport entre quelqu'un qui regarde et quelque chose de regardé'.[25] But one can perhaps make a more general connection between Leiris and Glissant on the level of personal identity. Leiris's initial desire for authentic contact with primitive societies had more to do with his own psychological needs — the need to escape the confines of his own identity, to lose himself in possession, and so on — than with furthering his ethnographic research.[26] This, indeed, was one of the reasons for abandoning it in favour of political solidarity with the colonized and the construction of a politically responsible ethnography. I have interpreted this shift as a kind of sublimation of the original desire; and the sublimated version, the 'relational' ethnography inaugurated in 1950, still entails a certain conception of subjectivity. It is not merely a set of professional techniques but an attitude of

23    Leiris, 'L'Ethnographe devant le colonialisme', p. 107.
24    In the 'Introduction' to Cinq études d'ethnologie Leiris spells this out very clearly: ethnology is 'une science, certes, mais une science dans laquelle le chercheur se trouve engagé personnellement peut-être plus que dans toute autre. Son effort pour pénétrer une culture différente de la sienne [...] l'amène, en effet, à se détourner [...] de cette dernière et, par contraste, lui en montre les limites' (pp. 5–6).
25    Leiris, 'Regard vers Alfred Métraux', p. 135.
26    As he himself put it in Afrique fantôme, 'J'ai besoin de tremper dans leur drame [...] Au diable l'ethnographie!' (p. 352).

respect, openness, and solidarity towards people whose cultures are different from our own, and hence also a certain conception of personal identity: the earlier simple identification with the other gives way to a more subtle, balanced conception in which self and other, autobiography and ethnography, are held in an interdependence that is equally necessary to both.[27] And this conception of self and other as 'solidaires' (*IP*, p. 127), as Glissant expresses it, is very close to what he himself would later, in *Poétique de la Relation*, call 'identité-relation', an identity that does not define itself by its differences from others but is constituted through its relations with others: '[l]'identité comme système de relation, comme aptitude à "donner avec"' (*PR*, p. 156), which he defines further as 'liée [...] au vécu conscient et contradictoire des contacts de cultures [...] donnée dans la trame chaotique de la Relation' (*PR*, p. 158).[28]

Glissant sees *Contacts de civilisations en Martinique et en Guadeloupe* as the culmination of all Leiris's ethnographic work. His admiration for this particular text is motivated partly by its fulfilment of his criterion of contemporaneity: it focuses on the Antilles as an evolving society and speculates on its future development. But his approval stems above all from the book's central theme: as a study of the contacts, precisely, between the different ethnic groups in the French Caribbean, the work 'engage dans le présent un avenir [...] et confirme (malgré le racisme qui sévit dans ces pays) qu'il n'est pas utopique de concevoir l'avènement un jour d'une véritable civilisation composite' (*IP*, p. 127). The enormous importance of this idea of contacts for Glissant is that it echoes another of his own major concerns, namely the value he attaches to cultural mixing or creolization.[29] But it is, in fact, equally important to Leiris, on two different levels, and to understand this we need to return to *Afrique fantôme* and the transition from its attempt at phantasmatic identification with the other to the later politicized solidarity.

If the move in which identification becomes solidarity does indeed, as I have argued, follow the logic of sublimation, then that would also provide a framework within which to explain why the theme of contacts between cultures becomes so dominant in Leiris's work from the 1950s. The concept of contact starts off on the personal level: Leiris's own desire for 'un contact vrai' (*AF*, p. 3) with the African cultures he encounters, and in principle with any other, in the strong sense, culture. Such contact proves elusive, not to say illusory, and so Leiris sublimates it into political solidarity; but it also — in another act of sublimation — migrates to

27    Although Hand argues convincingly that *Afrique fantôme*, through realizing the failure of its initial desire for identification, builds on this a self-analysis that already results in exactly this kind of ideal of relational identity: 'a phenomenological reflexivity that raises ethnography to the stage of existential reciprocity' (*Michel Leiris: Writing the Self*, p. 59).

28    Christina Kullberg touches on the connection between this text and Leiris's conception of ethnography: 'The knowledge that Leiris extracts from other cultures is not just relative. Glissant's ethnography of Relation places the process of understanding in the zones between the observer and the observed [...] In *Poétique de la Relation* from 1990, the notion of Relation is immediately presented as a concept of identity. Glissant explains that this theory asserts the idea that "each and every identity is extended through a relationship with the Other"' (*Poetics of Ethnography*, p. 63).

29    Glissant develops this theme throughout his later work but particularly in *Introduction à une poétique du divers* and *Traité du Tout-monde*. See also Chapters 1 and 6 of this volume.

the professional ethnographic level. If Leiris cannot himself achieve 'real contact' with the groups that he observes, then he will observe the contacts that do really exist between different groups: according to Glissant, '[l]'effort de Leiris consistera désormais à incliner la pratique de l'ethnographie dans le sens de cette étude des contacts réels' (*IP*, pp. 126–27).

The political need for ethnography to confront colonialism will also, of course, result in the study of the contacts or clashes between European and non-European cultures, and so would provide an alternative explanation for this shift in Leiris's interests. But the exaggeratedly severe condemnation in 'L'Ethnographe devant le colonialisme' of those who persist in analyzing 'pure' primitive societies reads very much like a rationalization of Leiris's frustration at his inability to enter into contact with such primitive societies.[30] Equally, his argument that the individuals who are most worth studying are not those least touched by European civilization but, on the contrary, the educated *évolués* whose understanding of colonialism makes them, rather than the 'brave type de la brousse' beloved of colonial administrators, the most 'authentic' of all Africans is not entirely convincing.[31] They are, certainly, the leaders of the anticolonial movements, but it does not necessarily follow that they are the only ones affected by colonialism and therefore the only ones worth studying.

The importance of contacts between civilizations is also an important theme in *Race et civilisation*, although here it is not so centrally linked to colonialism, and the contacts are seen as entirely benign and 'fruitful' (one section is titled 'Fécondité des contacts'). Leiris quotes Franz Boas to the effect that the more racially mixed a society is — the greater the number of contacts it has with other cultures — the more it can flourish.[32] At this point he brings Africa into the discussion as an example of a civilization that has not, according to him, benefited from as many contacts as most other parts of the world.[33] From this point of view, Africa is the exact opposite of the Caribbean, which, as Glissant frequently points out, is the geographical region that has benefited from the most intense process of creolization, or cultural and ethnic mixing. Hence, of course, the title of Leiris's study of Martinique and Guadeloupe: *Contacts de civilisations en Martinique et en Guadeloupe*. There is, therefore, a very close connection between Leiris's investment in the theme of contacts between cultures and his discovery of the French Caribbean.[34] It is only after his first visit

30   'Mais il faut réagir — et mettre les étudiants en garde — contre une tendance trop fréquente chez les ethnographes, [...] celle qui consiste à s'attacher de préférence aux peuples qu'on peut qualifier, relativement, d'intacts, par goût d'un certain "primitivisme" ou parce que de tels peuples présentent par rapport aux autres l'attrait d'un plus grand exotisme' (Leiris, 'L'Ethnographe devant le colonialisme', p. 102).
31   Ibid., pp. 102, 103.
32   Leiris, *Race et civilisation*, p. 64.
33   Ibid., p. 65.
34   J. Michael Dash emphasizes the significance of the Caribbean as an area of cultural contact for Leiris, citing the title of the lecture Leiris gave in Haiti at the end of his first trip, 'Antilles, poésie des carrefours', and commenting, '[t]he title of Leiris's presentation in 1948 points to the new poetics of cultural clash, which he sees as the main preoccupation of modern ethnography', 'Le Je de l'autre: Surrealist Ethnographers and the Francophone Caribbean', *L'Esprit créateur*, 47 (2007), pp. 84–95 (p. 92).

in 1948 that the promotion of intercultural contact becomes a regular theme in his writing, not only in texts concerned with the Antilles but also in the more general works. His experience of the Antilles was quite different from that which he had had in Africa and seems to have played an important role in re-orientating his ethnographic work.[35]

Having been to Martinique and Guadeloupe, Leiris was no longer interested in the 'intact' primitive, which he did not find there.[36] Even his commitment to anticolonial struggle was temporarily suspended, since Martinique and Guadeloupe had recently become *départements d'outre mer* — a status of which he approves in *Contacts*, despite referring to them more disparagingly as 'pays semi-coloniaux' in the 1950 preface to *Afrique fantôme* (p. 8) — and Haiti had been independent since 1804.[37] His interest was wholly focused on the contacts between the different groups, mainly, in practice, the mulatto and black communities, the *békés*, and more recently arrived French people from the metropolis, with some discussion also of the Indian community and the Native Americans. His discovery of the Antilles, therefore, made it possible for Leiris to move from his desire for personal contact with the primitive to a sublimated desire for a culture that was itself predicated on contact with otherness, as Glissant implies: 'il accomplira dans le réel cette dialectique jadis déformée (dans l'imaginaire) par ses premiers livres. Deux séjours aux Antilles le confirment dans son intention d'ausculter là des contacts de civilisations. Ces pays offrent un exemple privilégié de symbiose culturelle' (*IP*, p. 127).

But the Antilles did not offer only this sublimated version of contact. It is very clear from *Contacts* that Leiris also found it much easier than he had done in Africa to form genuinely close relationships with the people he met in Guadeloupe and, particularly, in Martinique. Césaire emphasizes the importance of the friendships Leiris formed there in helping him to understand the Antilles;[38] he in fact arranged for Leiris to meet and interview all his own friends in Martinique, including people such as René Ménil, Aristide Maugée, Georges Desportes, and Georges Gratiant — intellectuals and communists like Césaire himself, but mainly from the mulatto community, whom Leiris found very congenial company and with whom he kept in touch on his return to Paris.[39] Even beyond this circle, the informants whom he interviewed were largely middle-class, and although he claims that his work brought him into contact with very varied milieux, 'visitant Noirs aussi bien que mulâtres, gens du peuple aussi bien que bourgeois' (*CC*, p. 176), there is no textual

35    Later, in *Frêle bruit*, Leiris writes that 'à l'époque où je voyageais encore professionnellement, les Antilles, confluent de l'Afrique et de l'Europe et lieu où culturellement il s'est produit bien des hybridations curieuses, étaient devenues mon terrain d'élection' (in *La Règle du jeu*, p. 962).

36    Sally Price perhaps overgeneralizes when she states that '[w]hat interested [Leiris], anthropologically, were not pristine worlds on the wane, but rather a phenomenon he called clash, the dynamic of potentially messy contact zones' ('Michel Leiris, French Anthropology and a Side-Trip to the Antilles', p. 28), but this is certainly a good characterization of his response to the Caribbean.

37    See Chapter 3 for a fuller discussion of Leiris's attitude to departmentalization.

38    Césaire and Toumson, 'Aimé Césaire et Roger Toumson: entretien sur Michel Leiris', p. 72.

39    In the introduction to *Contacts de civilisations en Martinique et en Guadeloupe*, Leiris refers to them as 'amis aujourd'hui des plus chers que j'ai rencontrés lors de mon séjour de 1948' (*CC*, p. 12).

evidence that he actually interviewed any of the agricultural workers who made up the bulk of the population (there would, of course, have been language problems, but far less difficult than those he had overcome in Africa). The overwhelming majority of his contacts, as listed in the Introduction and referenced in footnotes, are with teachers, university professors, mayors, a bishop, several military officers, social workers, businessmen, bankers, and lawyers; the closest he comes to working-class life is four trade union officials.

The book as a whole is very different from *Afrique fantôme* because of the complete absence of any sense of the exotic. In fact it hardly reads like a piece of orthodox ethnographic research at all, because of the cultural similarity between Leiris and his informants and, indeed, the impression one has that much of his fieldwork consisted of being invited to dinner. His insistence in 'L'Ethnographe devant le colonialisme' on the importance of studying *évolués* is put into practice here; and the political reason for it — that these are the people whose education and social position have brought them into closest contact with Europeans, so that they are in the best position to criticize colonialism and European society generally — is fully justified, at least by the circle of Martiniquan Communists, and, of course, by Césaire himself, whose *Discours sur le colonialisme*, first published in 1950, was a devastating critique of European civilization.[40] Césaire praises Leiris by saying that 'ce qu'il a su faire, dans les Antilles, c'est fraterniser véritablement avec les Antillais, les comprendre, les aimer, comprendre leurs luttes',[41] suggesting that *Contacts* was a true product of the politically engaged conception of ethnography outlined in 'L'Ethnographe devant le colonialisme'. But another, rather different reason for the concentration on *évolués* also becomes apparent: the Antillean communist intellectuals were simply much easier to work with and to relate to than the African informants whom Leiris had described, often with some bitterness, in *Afrique fantôme*.

However, in another twist typical of the relation between the political and the personal, this also means that the aspiration expressed in 'L'Ethnographe devant le colonialisme' of making ethnography into a genuinely intersubjective partnership (a 'relation', in other words) between Western and non-Western researchers can perhaps be realized. In a lecture he gave in Paris in 1949 Leiris stated that one of the aims of his 1948 visit to Martinique and Guadeloupe was to 'prendre contact avec les intellectuels antillais en vue du développement de la recherche ethnologique dans les Antilles françaises';[42] and he went on to recount how he had discussed with the

---

40   Aimé Césaire first published his *Discours sur le colonialisme* in 1950, but in a later version of the text *Discours sur le colonialisme* (Paris & Dakar: Présence africaine, 1955) he also supported his friend's vision of ethnography, defending Leiris against Roger Caillois's attack on *Race et civilisation* for its opposition to the idea of a hierarchy of cultures (p. 48) and parodying Caillois's dismissal of the idea of native ethnographers: 'C'est l'Occident qui fait l'ethnographie des autres, non les autres qui font l'ethnographie de l'Occident' (p. 52). Roger Caillois's article, 'Illusion à rebours', was published in two parts: *Nouvelle revue française*, 24 (December 1954), 1014, 1017–18, & 25 (January 1955), 58, 67–68.

41   Césaire and Toumson, 'Aimé Césaire et Roger Toumson: entretien sur Michel Leiris', p. 74.

42   Michel Leiris, 'Perspectives culturelles aux Antilles françaises et en Haïti', lecture given on 4 March 1949 to the Centre d'études de politiques étrangères; published in *Le Siècle à l'envers*, ed. by F.

'Groupe d'études martiniquais' (an association 'dont font partie plusieurs membres du corps enseignant et des professions libérales') the possibility of the Musée de l'Homme helping them to carry out research in ethnography and folklore.[43] Indeed, one of the main recommendations to come out of this first contact with the Antilles was, according to this lecture, to set up 'directives et facilités données aux groupes d'études et aux associations culturelles pour les engager dans la voie de la recherche ethnologique ou au moins folklorique'; and Leiris adds: 'De tels efforts pourraient être menés en liaison avec l'activité du musée de l'Homme et avec celle du musée des Arts et Traditions populaires'.[44] No such initiatives are mentioned six years later in *Contacts*, however, and it is not clear that they were ever put into practice. But Leiris's meeting with Antillean intellectuals did result in one publication that realizes something like the kind of collaboration he foresees in 'L'Ethnographe devant le colonialisme'. This is the issue of *Les Temps modernes* (no. 52) that he edits in 1950, and it consists of a mixture of poems, elements of popular culture such as songs and the names given to road vehicles, and a dream narrative.[45] Leiris writes the introduction, and the presentation of the songs from Martinique and Guadeloupe, and of the names of the trucks and buses; Métraux contributes a piece on Haitian religious songs; the authors of the poems are from all three islands and the dream narrative is from a Haitian architect. The volume as a whole is therefore a real collaboration between French ethnographers and Caribbean writers; its preparation involved lively discussion between Leiris and the Martiniquan Communists, who were not entirely happy at being published in *Les Temps modernes* because of what they viewed as Sartre's dubious political position.[46] It is still, of course, a long way from the collaboration with native ethnographers that Leiris envisaged in 'L'Ethnographe devant le colonialisme', but it exemplifies the alternative possibility he recommended in this text (p. 109) that ethnographers should seek out and learn from intellectuals — politicians, writers, or artists — from colonized or 'semi-colonized' countries, and organize their work in accordance with the latter's perception of priorities. Compared with Africa, in any case, the Antilles certainly offered far greater potential for the development of ethnographic or quasi-ethnographic 'relations' with European intellectuals.

From the late 1940s onwards, then, Leiris's work was significantly influenced by his friendship with Antillean intellectuals, above all with Césaire, and by the new intellectual and emotional satisfactions that his contact with the Antilles had given him. Glissant belongs to a later generation, and in his case the influence goes in the opposite direction; but, as one of the most perceptive readers of Leiris, he also forms part of the nexus of 'contacts' linking Leiris with the French Caribbean. In this chapter I have tried to show how the (inter)subjective element in Leiris's ethnography both evolved in parallel with his relation to the Antilles and enabled

Marmande (Paris: Farrago, 2004) pp. 45–67 (p. 45).
43   Ibid., p. 49.
44   Ibid., p. 57.
45   Leiris was clearly charmed by the Antillean practice of giving to road vehicles the same kind of poetic names as to fishing boats.
46   See A. Armel, *Michel Leiris* (Paris: Fayard, 1997), p. 495.

him to become a partner in Antilleans' efforts to understand and change their situation in 'le drame du monde'.

CHAPTER 3

❖

# Dual Identities:
# The Question of 'Départementalisation' in
# Michel Leiris's *Contacts de civilisations*
# *en Martinique et en Guadeloupe*

*Contacts de civilisations en Martinique et en Guadeloupe* (1955) is a study of relations between the different ethnic groups in the two islands, based on material that Leiris acquired during two periods that he spent in the French Caribbean in 1948 and 1952. The first trip was suggested and organized by Aimé Césaire, who had been a *député* for Martinique since 1945 and whom Leiris had met in Paris. Césaire asked him, as a specialist on African culture, to investigate the continuing African influence in the culture of Martinique and Guadeloupe; his report was widely circulated but never appeared in officially published form. Between 1948 and 1952, however, Leiris published a number of other texts, some directly concerned with the Antilles (such as the issue of *Les Temps modernes* (no. 52, 1950) on the culture of the French Caribbean which he edited) and some more general, notably 'L'Ethnographe devant le colonialisme', in which he formulated the principles on which a politically responsible ethnography should be based. The second trip to the Antilles in 1952 was organized on behalf of UNESCO by Leiris's fellow ethnographer Alfred Métraux, who commissioned *Contacts* on the basis of a 1952 UNESCO resolution concerning the social integration of ethnically diverse groups in societies, as he explains in the preface (*CC*, p. 5). Métraux was the director of the large-scale anti-racism project, entitled 'Race et société: la question raciale devant la science moderne', that UNESCO had initiated in the wake of the Second World War, and he had already published Leiris's essay *Race et civilisation* in the same series.[1] *Contacts* was thus conceived from the start within the context of combating racism, and Métraux's preface stresses this.

This emphasis on integration goes some way towards explaining Leiris's strangely positive presentation of the 'départementalisation' of the Antilles which, voted

---

1 See M. Brattain, 'Race, Racism, and Antiracism: UNESCO and the Politics of Presenting Science to the Postwar Public', *American Historical Review*, 112:5 (2007), 1386–1413, for an interesting analysis of the shortcomings of this project.

through as 'la loi d'assimilation' in March 1946, had been implemented in January 1948, that is, just before his first visit. Throughout *Contacts* he is wholly and warmly in favour of departmentalization. While he does not pretend that it has cured all the considerable social problems of the Antilles, he believes that it will do so in time (p. 44), and, although he warns that the people's patience will not last forever (p. 187), that it is the only possible solution. From raising salaries (p. 33) to encouraging the population to use Western medicine and put their children in crèches where they will be exposed to the French language from a very young age (pp. 100–01), departmentalization is bringing practical improvements and cultural enrichment to the Antilles, and Leiris's only criticisms of it relate to the delays in its implementation (p. 183).

His position here at first seems very much at odds with his longstanding commitment to independence for the colonies, reiterated in 'L'Ethnographe devant le colonialisme'. But the Antilles are an exception to the rule; in *Contacts* he notes the lack of any significant independence movement in the islands (*CC*, p. 116), and observes that what their black population wants is to have equal status with metropolitan French citizens: departmentalization 'répondait à une aspiration ancienne des Antillais français revendiquant dès longtemps le droit à être entièrement "assimilés" à des Français métropolitains' (p. 183). At the time departmentalization was supported by the Communist Party and most of the rest of the left in France (and opposed by the right, especially the *békés*). It was seen as the way to ensure racial and social equality between the citizens of the islands and those of metropolitan France; an enactment of republican universalism, it would counter the power of the *békés* and ensure equality through assimilation. Métraux's preface to *Contacts* explains that the reason for including the French Antilles in the UNESCO project was that studying the anti-racist effects of assimilation there would provide insights that could be put to practical use elsewhere (p. 6). In this context it would clearly have been difficult for Leiris to criticize departmentalization. More mundanely, he was also very conscious of the need not to offend the French authorities in Martinique, since his first visit in 1948 had resulted in the Prefect making an official complaint to his employers at the Musée de l'homme about his 'attitude de partisan politique, lancé dans une amitié ostentatoire envers les calomniateurs attitrés du Gouvernement et de l'administration Préfectorale' — which in turn had caused great difficulties in organizing and funding the second trip in 1952.[2]

It is nevertheless strange to read Leiris, who in the past had always been so fervently committed to preserving and celebrating cultural otherness, praising the inculcation of French cultural and social norms into the Antillean population, particularly since his ethnographic work is always also the site of considerable personal investment on an emotional level — ethnology is 'une science dans laquelle le chercheur se trouve engagé personnellement peut-être plus que dans toute autre'[3] — and this imbrication of ethnography and autobiography, first manifested in

2    See Armel, *Michel Leiris*, pp. 492, 520, for an account of this.
3    Leiris, 'L'Ethnographe devant le colonialisme', p. 5.

*Afrique fantôme* in 1934, always required a strong coefficient of otherness.[4] But the man who wrote of his African informants 'J'ai besoin de tremper dans leur drame, de toucher leurs façons d'être, de baigner dans la chair vive' (*AF*, p. 352) is now writing of the need to 'intégrer à la vie de la communauté française des groupes que leur origine différencie sensiblement des autres constituantes de cette communauté, cela veut dire amener les groupes en question à prendre leur part entière de la culture française' (*CC*, pp. 9–10). Moreover, although his first trip to the Antilles was explicitly dedicated to researching the African roots of the culture, he now argues that the French influence is so omnipresent in Antillean culture that African traces are negligible, and 'le problème de diffusion culturelle posé ici s'avère être, essentiellement, un cas particulier du problème général de l'éducation populaire' (p. 10). Education is seen as synonymous with the diffusion of French culture. Indeed, the provision of education, which in 1950 he had severely criticized because of the inadequate number of schools and lack of reading materials,[5] is now the object of sustained, albeit measured, praise: there are still practical and financial problems, but 'l'application aux Antilles des lois scolaires métropolitaines est aujourd'hui chose acquise et — après une période qu'il n'est pas excessif d'appeler héroïque — l'instruction publique dans les deux nouveaux départements ne se heurte plus guère qu'à des difficultés d'ordre publique' (*CC*, p. 72). He emphasizes the population's eagerness to acquire education (p. 73), and even adduces the literary genius of Césaire and Joseph Zobel as evidence of the effectiveness of the French education system in Martinique (p. 81).

This does not, however, mean that Leiris no longer attaches any value to the cultural specificity of the Antilles. The educational curriculum is identical to that of metropolitan France, and while he justifies this 'd'un point de vue démocratique' as 'une absence de discrimination', he admits that it causes 'certains inconvénients' (*CC*, p. 89); and goes on to quote Fanon's *Peau noire, masques blancs*, published just three years earlier, on the alienating effect of such an education (p. 90). Despite its universalist principles, then, the education system results, not in a 'liquidation (ainsi qu'on l'attendrait d'un enseignement que l'on sait dispensé dans un esprit démocratique), mais un affermissement du sentiment d'infériorité hérité de l'époque esclavagiste' (p. 91). This, however, turns out to mean that the Antillais have not truly understood what European culture consists of: they are alienated because their inferiority complex leads them to 'adopter la culture européenne dans ses formes extérieures (celles qui expriment de façon manifeste qu'on est en possession de cette culture: langage, vêtement, etc.) plutôt que dans son esprit' (p. 91) (as though Fanon's problem was that he was too fond of expensive French suits). But Leiris does also devote considerable space to the discussion of how the Antilles can preserve their own culture, especially in the section of *Contacts* entitled 'Le problème d'une

4    Seán Hand writes: 'L'ethnographie de Leiris, de même que son autobiographie, s'occupe de la possibilité d'une proximité absolue au sein de la différence', in his article 'Hors de soi: politique, possession et présence dans l'ethnographie surréaliste de Michel Leiris', in *L'Autre et le sacré: surréalisme, cinéma, ethnologie*, ed. by C. W. Thompson (Paris: L'Harmattan, 1995), pp. 185–95 (p. 189).
5    In *Les Temps modernes* 52, p. 1347. Much of this introduction reappears in *Contacts*, but, significantly, not this passage.

culture spécifiquement antillaise' (pp. 106–16). The ideal form of assimilation is not passive, as he explains in his introduction: it implies that the people concerned 'ne se borneront pas à recevoir passivement [la culture française] mais participeront à son élaboration' (p. 10), and that this 'élaboration' will include the 'apport original' of their own 'particularismes régionaux' (p. 10). Antillean culture can thus make a specific contribution to the overall national French culture within which it is integrated. But this is a two-stage process, as Leiris emphasizes: the Antilleans have first to become integrated into French culture before they can start to add on elements of Caribbean culture: they 'contribuent dans la mesure exacte où ils y sont intégrés et se trouvent, par conséquent, à même d'exercer leur influence' (p. 10). In practice, then, this means that only the intellectual elite already saturated with French education are in a position to develop their Antillean cultural specificity[6] — and indeed, the section devoted to this question consists of a survey of Antillean literary reviews and movements.

This rather narrowly based attempt to promote Antillean culture also suffers from another problem. Departmentalization is reconciled with cultural specificity through a combination of *political* union and *cultural* autonomy, which, although he never quite formulates it explicitly, Leiris is in effect recommending; and this implies that Antillean culture is autonomous with regard not only to metropolitan France but also to politics. This separation, however, is often seen as highly problematic; ever since departmentalization the whole question of how far cultural autonomy can meaningfully co-exist with a lack of political autonomy has been much debated within the French Antilles.[7] For Édouard Glissant, who in the 1960s and 70s would become one of the most vehement opponents of departmentalization, culture depended crucially on political freedoms, and the political status of Martinique was directly responsible for its lack of a vigorous collective culture; as he writes in *Le Discours antillais:* 'Jusqu'à la loi de départementalisation de 1946 qui constitue en la matière une apothéose, les Antillais sont ainsi conduits à se nier en tant que collectivité, afin de conquérir une illusoire égalité individuelle' (*DA*, p. 17). Departmentalization, he insists, has been a sham ('la fausse semblance des Départements d'Outre Mer') and a pernicious distortion: 'Comme s'il n'était jamais donné à ces pays de rejoindre leur nature vraie, paralysés qu'ils étaient par [...] une des formes les plus pernicieuses de colonisation: celle par quoi on *assimile* une communauté' (*DA*, p. 15). Surprisingly perhaps, in view of these later pronouncements, Glissant, who studied at the Musée de l'Homme from 1953 to 1954 when Leiris was preparing the manuscript of *Contacts*, wrote a very favourable review of the latter in 1956, praising its vision of culture as an evolving rather than an immutable phenomenon and its emphasis on the theme of contacts between

6    Despite the fact that elsewhere Leiris remarks that it is the popular culture of the Antilles that retains most of the non-European forms (*CC*, p. 45).

7    See, for instance, Guadeloupean Jacky Dahomay's 'Cultural Identity versus Political Identity in the French West Indies', whose conclusion is: 'let me simply say that reflecting on the articulation between cultural identity and political identity in the French West Indies as well as the latter's political future is a mind-boggling task' (in *Modern Political Culture in the Caribbean*, ed. by H. Henke and F. Reno (Kingston, Jamaica: University of the West Indies Press, 2003), pp. 90–108 (p. 106).

cultures.[8] Nevertheless, he did express courteous reservations regarding its support for departmentalization and the alienation that, in his view, resulted from this:

> Un Antillais engagé dans la problématique nationale qui tôt ou tard surgira dans ces pays reprocherait peut-être à ce livre de ne pas assez y définir des constantes. Mais ce n'est pas à Michel Leiris de faire le travail des Antillais, ou de les dégager des profondeurs de l'aliénation. (*IP*, pp. 127–28)

In any case, Leiris does not seem to have been at all influenced by Glissant's views on the Antilles, mentioning him only once in *Contacts* (p. 104). Césaire, in contrast, is repeatedly referenced throughout the text and was clearly Leiris's most important mentor in the Antilles; during his second trip, when Césaire was himself in Fort-de-France, they saw each other 'presque quotidiennement', and it would not be an exaggeration to say that for the most part Leiris saw Martinique through Césaire's eyes.[9] They also continued to be close friends after Leiris returned to Paris at the end of 1952. One would therefore expect Leiris's view of departmentalization to be in accord with that of Césaire. But — and this is perhaps the most puzzling aspect of Leiris's enthusiasm for departmentalization — it is not.

More precisely, Leiris's position differs from that held by Césaire in the early 1950s when Leiris was writing *Contacts*. Together with Léopold Bissol and Raymond Vergès, *députés* for French Guiana and Réunion respectively, Césaire had led the campaign for departmentalization after the Second World War; he had done so because of his belief that the republican universalism of the French state would protect the inhabitants of the Antilles from the exploitation of the *békés* (he also demanded that the sugar plantations should be nationalized), and in order to get for his people the metropolitan levels of social welfare that were particularly badly needed in Martinique and Guadeloupe after the deprivations that had been inflicted by the war.[10] But all the evidence suggests that by 1955 Césaire had already become disillusioned with departmentalization. As early as 1948, as part of the celebrations of the centenary of the abolition of slavery, he gave a speech in Paris furiously denouncing its failure.[11] *Soleil cou coupé*, the collection of poems he published the same year, has been read as expressing his disillusionment with it.[12] His *Discours sur le colonialisme*, first published in 1950, does not specifically mention departmentalization, but is such a devastating attack on France as a colonial nation that it is hard to believe he was happy with the current situation. Georges Ngal

8    Glissant, 'Michel Leiris ethnographe'. It is probably true to say that in 1956 Glissant was not yet seriously involved in anti-colonial politics; he would found (together with Albert Béville) the 'Front Antillais-Guyanais' only in 1959, as a reaction to riots in Fort-de-France against not the *békés* but the metropolitan French who were on the island as a direct result of departmentalization. Nevertheless, the fact that he chose to reprint the piece in 1969 in *L'Intention poétique* indicates the depth of his respect for Leiris despite their political differences.

9    Armel, *Michel Leiris*, p. 512.

10   See H. Hintjens, 'Constitutional and Political Change in the French Caribbean', in *French and West Indian: Martinique, Guadeloupe and French Guiana Today*, ed. by R. D. E. Burton and F. Reno (Basingstoke: Macmillan, 1995), pp. 20–33 (p. 23).

11   See Armel, *Michel Leiris*, p. 490.

12   Aimé Césaire, *Soleil cou coupé* (Paris: Éditions K, 1948). See also Georges Ngal's commentary in his *Lire le Discours sur le colonialisme* (Paris & Dakar: Présence africaine, 1994), p.23.

quotes Césaire as saying of the *Discours sur le colonialisme* that 'C'était un peu pour moi l'occasion de dire ce que je ne pouvais pas dire à la tribune de l'Assemblée nationale';[13] he claims that Césaire was already feeling that he had been 'duped' by the French government; observes that his level of activity as a *député*, measured by the number of interventions he makes in debates at the Assemblée nationale, falls drastically after 1950; and concludes that '*Discours sur le colonialisme* ne se comprend pleinement que replacé dans le contexte des déceptions liées à la faillite des espoirs nés de la libération'.[14] The culmination of this process was Césaire's break with the French Communist Party (PCF) in 1956 and the formation two years later of his Parti Progressiste Martiniquais based on a demand for greater autonomy from France.

It is therefore almost inconceivable that Leiris would not have been aware of the strain that his friend's adherence to the PCF, and hence to departmentalization, was under just one year prior to this. Indeed, one of the revisions he makes to his introduction to the 1950 issue of *Les Temps modernes* when he reproduces it in *Contacts* in 1955, suggests that he knew Césaire was already distancing himself from the party. A paragraph explaining why many Antillean intellectuals joined the Communist Party after the war is recycled in a slightly expanded form from the *Les Temps modernes* issue (pp. 1346–47) to *Contacts* (p. 110), but the earlier version goes on to place Césaire at the head of this movement:

> Prise de conscience décisive, dont l'artisan le plus notoire aura été le grand poète Aimé Césaire, que son désir passionné de voir s'organiser un monde plus vivable, non seulement pour les habitants des taudis de Martinique mais pour les hommes de tous pays, voue depuis plusieurs années aux tâches les plus arides.[15]

This sentence is missing from the later version in *Contacts*. Since Leiris's admiration for Césaire had in no way diminished (and the latter's political tasks were by then even more 'arides'), the only possible reason for this omission must be his awareness that Césaire was already reconsidering his commitment to the PCF; and, since the reason for that (as an open letter Césaire wrote to Maurice Thorez (the PCF's general secretary) in October 1956 made quite clear) was that the party did not see any need for greater autonomy for the DOMs, Leiris must have known that Césaire was by now thoroughly disillusioned with departmentalization.

There was also independent evidence that departmentalization was not in reality achieving the racial equality that Métraux's preface to *Contacts* saw as its *raison d'être*. The late 1940s and early 1950s saw a series of strikes by civil servants protesting that they were not treated equally with their metropolitan counterparts working in the islands; in 1949 Léopold Bissol, who had earlier argued for departmentalization alongside Césaire, complained that 'Things are getting worse and worse in the new departments. They are left with the impression that the metropole has taken them

---

13    Ngal, *Lire le Discours sur le colonialisme*, p. 27.
14    Ibid., p. 29.
15    *Les Temps modernes*, 52 (1950), 1347.

to her bosom in order to suffocate them'.[16] Universal suffrage in the DOMs would not be introduced until 1956. As Jacky Dahomay comments, 'Departmentalization never really ended practices inherited from the colonial past'.[17]

Given that departmentalization was not realizing the ideals that had underpinned its creation, and that Césaire had turned against it, not to mention the fact that it conflicted with his own belief in the absolute value of cultural difference, one has to wonder why Leiris supported it so uncritically throughout *Contacts*. Was he simply trying to keep out of trouble with the authorities?[18] But if this had been his only motive, it would have been sufficient to abstain from criticizing departmentalization, and so preserve the apolitical stance that the authorities required of him. The fact that he seems to go out of his way to praise both the principles underlying it and its present and projected future effects suggests that other less circumstantial motives may also be involved. I want to argue that this is in fact the case, and that these other motives are far more deep-seated. One of Leiris's most prominent characteristics, as I have mentioned, is the constant interaction of his own subjective impulses with his objective observation of other cultures. Previously his most evident desire had always been to escape the limits of his own selfhood through contact with radically different cultures.[19] This leads one to assume that departmentalization constituted the exact opposite of an object of desire for him: that on an emotional level he could relate only to scenarios of otherness in which he could experience an ecstatic loss of self — as Glissant puts it, 'Il est conquis par ce contraire de lui-même' (*IP*, p. 123) — and that the assimilated Antillean DOMs therefore failed to supply him with any emotional sustenance. In fact, however, there is evidence that they were for Leiris the source of a different and very particular kind of psychological investment.

This has to do with the ambiguous collective identity of the citizens of the DOMs. Although the notion of political unity with France plus cultural autonomy is perfectly coherent in the abstract, it occasionally leads Leiris into rather awkward formulations of the relationship that Martiniquans and Guadeloupeans have with France. How is it possible to describe the extent to which they do not conform to the 'French' way of life since, as French citizens, they are supposedly just as French as metropolitan French citizens? For instance, within the 'population des Antilles françaises [...] la partie la plus pauvre de cette population demeure plus éloignée de *ce qu'on peut regarder comme les normes de la vie française* que sa partie la plus fortunée' (*CC*, p. 70, my emphasis). Leiris's solution is to substitute 'européen' for 'français' when referring to ethnic Frenchness: he goes on to recommend 'une intégration

16   Quoted in Hintjes, 'Constitutional and Political Change in the French Caribbean', p. 27.
17   Dahomay, 'Cultural Identity versus Political Identity in the French West Indies', p. 106.
18   The rather cryptic last sentence of *Contacts*, which so blatantly contradicts the emphasis on political engagement expressed in 'L'Ethnographe devant le colonialisme' that it is difficult to read it as anything other than ironic, suggests that this might be the case: 'Mais on touche, ici, aux grands dilemmes sociaux en face desquels se trouve l'ensemble du monde contemporain et il ne convient pas à l'observateur sans passion qu'on s'attend à ce que soit l'ethnographe de s'engager sur ce terrain' (*CC*, p. 192).
19   See Chapter 2 for more discussion of this. Hand (in *Michel Leiris*) gives a full analysis of the process.

complète de ces couches originairement non européenne ou partiellement non européenne de la population martiniquaise et guadeloupéenne' (p. 70) but is nevertheless forced to finish the sentence by referring to a 'French' culture that is essentially metropolitan:

> dont la récente promotion sur le plan des droits politiques est fort loin de signifier que, sur le plan de la culture (dans l'acceptation la plus large du terme) elles ne demeurent pas en position quelque peu marginale par rapport aux Français nés à la métropole ou issus d'immigrants venus de la métropole. (*CC*, p. 70)[20]

But what on the intellectual level was a tricky problem of definition for Leiris corresponded on an emotional level to something far more powerful and valuable. The anomalous position of the DOMs, simultaneously 'inside' and 'outside' France, has been the subject of much commentary and analysis. It is usually seen as an identitarian problem: in his introduction to one of the most influential studies of the topic, Richard D. E. Burton speaks of the 'double-bind' in which 'in a peculiar way, coloured French West Indians have asserted their identity by denying it or, more precisely, they have asserted one identity (as French) by denying another (as West Indians)'.[21] Similarly, Jacky Dahomay comments: 'The malaise continues. How can one be at the same time West Indian and French?'.[22] But for Leiris it seems to have been the opposite of a problem: rather, a positive advantage, not to say a unique opportunity, on the level of his own psychology.

There is little evidence of this deeply personal significance attributed to departmentalization in the generally rather arid prose of *Contacts*. But at the end of his first trip to the Caribbean in 1948, Leiris gave a lecture in Haiti entitled 'Antilles et poésie des carrefours' (not published in France until 1992) in which he expressed in a far more lyrical and openly emotional way the 'choc émotif' that the Caribbean had on him; as the title suggests, it is the combination of the cultures of Africa and Europe that not only fascinates Leiris but profoundly moves him: 'J'ai été si fort ému par quelques-uns de ces "carrefours" où viennent se fondre ou se couper des trajectoires distinctes'.[23] One on level he seems to be aware that this is something of a cliché; in *Contacts* he describes in rather dismissive tones the typical delight of the European at the cultural mixing of the Caribbean in general.[24] But what

---

20 Sometimes he defines traditional French culture (as taught in schools, for instance) as the culture of the dominant ethnic group within France: the education system accords too much importance to 'la culture du groupe ethnique qui, aujourd'hui encore, occupe la position prééminente et se regarde par rapport aux autres groupes comme le plus civilisé' (*CC*, p. 91); elsewhere, however, it is simply 'French culture' *tout court* (while the Antillais are still 'French'): 'l'actuelle société antillaise offre donc cette particularité d'être un agrégat humain dont les membres, pour la plupart, diffèrent notablement *des autres Français* par leurs origines alors que la culture française s'y avère fortement prépondérante' (*CC*, p. 113, my emphasis).

21 R. D. E. Burton, 'The French West Indies *à l'heure de l'Europe*', in *French and West Indian*, ed. by Burton and Reno, pp. 1–19 (p. 3).

22 Dahomay, 'Cultural Identity versus Political Identity in the French West Indies', p. 105.

23 Michel Leiris, 'Antilles et poésie des carrefours', in *Zébrage* (Paris: Gallimard, 1992), pp. 67–87 (pp. 69, 75).

24 'Est-il besoin d'indiquer que ce fameux charme des Antilles dont tant de voyageurs ont parlé (en

'Antilles et poésie des carrefours' allows us to see is that Leiris has nevertheless discovered a new kind of positive psychological investment in the specific situation of the citizens of the DOMs, i.e. in the *ambiguity* of their identity, as evidenced above by the difficulty he has in *Contacts* in defining them as simultaneously French and not-French. 'Antilles et poésie des carrefours' gradually puts in place an implicit distinction between his usual desire to lose himself in radical otherness, and a new delight in contact with something which is *both* other *and* part of himself. Leiris describes coming across a black girl in Martinique herding goats while singing an old French folk song, and conveys emphatically the very particular kind of emotion that it arouses in him: 'un état d'incertitude délicieuse qui tient à ce qu'on est en face de quelque chose qui semble être à la fois le comble de l'insolite et le comble du familier'.[25]

In the light of this formula which, consciously or unconsciously, echoes Freud's definition of the uncanny, Leiris begins to feel that his journey to the Antilles has in fact been 'un retour', a kind of homecoming to something that is 'secretly familiar'.[26] He is in fact enacting the exact reverse of the trajectory which Glissant would describe the following year in his *Soleil de la conscience*: the no longer colonized but 'departmentalized' subject from Martinique encountering France and finding in it the same combination — although for Glissant it is markedly less euphoric — of familiarity and strangeness.[27] He himself describes it as the double 'regard du fils et la vision de l'étranger'.[28] He makes no explicit references in this text to Leiris, but does describe himself in eminently Leirisian terms as 'ethnographe de moi-même';[29] the common features of their experiences perhaps explain why Glissant's opposition to departmentalization does not prevent him from praising *Contacts* as highly as he does.

omettant trop souvent d'insister sur les ombres du tableau) tient, autant qu'à leurs beautés naturelles, à la combinaison syncrétique qui s'y est opérée entre cultures africaines et culture européenne pendant les quelques trois siècles que compte aujourd'hui leur histoire?' (*CC*, p. 63.).

25   Leiris, 'Antilles et poésie des carrefours', pp. 75–76.

26   Ibid., p. 76. See Sigmund Freud, 'The Uncanny', in *The Standard Edition of the Complete Works of Sigmund Freud*, ed. by J. Strachey and others, 24 vols (London: Hogarth Press, 1957–74), XVII, 217–52 (p. 245).

27   Édouard Glissant, *Soleil de la conscience* (Paris: Éditions du Seuil, 1956). The chapter entitled 'L'Expérience vécue du noir' in Fanon's *Peau noire, masques blancs* constitutes another version of the first journey from Martinique to France, and for Fanon it is of course violently negative.

28   Ibid., p. 11. J. Michael Dash comments: 'The fragmented texts that make up *Soleil de la conscience* can be read as a series of entries in the author's journal of his first journey to Europe. This cannot be a voyage of discovery in the conventional sense because his colonial education has already made it familiar. So the travel narrative becomes a voyage of self-discovery, for a visitor is both the same and other, as he says at the beginning and end of this work, and has "the look of the son and the vision of the outsider"' ('*Caraïbe fantôme*: The Play of Difference in the Francophone Caribbean', *Yale French Studies*, 103 (2003), 92–105 (p. 96). See also Kullberg, *Poetics of Ethnography*, pp. 64–77.

29   Glissant, *Soleil de la conscience*, p. 15. Kullberg's *Poetics of Ethnography* discusses in detail the influence of Leiris on *Soleil de la conscience*, commenting for instance that 'As a colonial subject, Glissant's narrator is both inside and outside the city where he now lives, caught up in a strange feeling of being part of Parisian life — knowing its culture, its literature, having seen pictures of monuments and learned their symbolic importance — and, at the same time, being completely foreign' (p. 57).

Unlike Glissant, Leiris does not define himself as the son of the country he has arrived in; however, the familiar side of the double response has the intimate flavour of memories of his childhood.[30] Hearing the girl sing, he is 'face à face avec mon enfance elle-même';[31] and the next example he cites, of wooden horses on merry-go-rounds, also reminds him specifically of his childhood:

> Pour qui connaît la France et sait ce qu'un manège de chevaux de bois peut receler comme potentiel de féerie pour un enfant de la ville aussi bien que pour un enfant de la campagne, ma réaction n'a rien de surprenant.[32]

Thus, he concludes, Martinique has brought about 'une redécouverte de mon enfance [...] dans une région fort éloignée, au moins kilométriquement, du Paris où je suis né'.[33] Rather than a loss of self, it is an uncanny rediscovery of his past self accomplished through this precise combination of strangeness and intimate familiarity.

Leiris's lecture goes on to describe some of the discoveries he has made in Haiti, especially that of *vodou*; but, although the syncretic character of *vodou* makes of it another 'carrefour', it is noticeable that the emotions it arouses in Leiris are entirely those of fascination with its unambiguous otherness; there is no sense of the double reaction that we find in all his Martiniquan examples. Possession, the central feature of *vodou* and one of Leiris's long-standing obsessions, involves a radical escape from the confines of the self into total strangeness, not the mixture of strangeness and familiarity that he experiences in Martinique. It is a case of abandoning one's own self completely, as he puts it in his preface to Métraux's *Le Vaudou haïtien*: 'Être un autre que soi, se dépasser dans l'enthousiasme ou dans la transe, n'est-ce pas l'un des besoins fondamentaux des hommes?'[34] He also claims that Métraux's fascination with possession was motivated by 'un violent désir d'évasion hors des murs de la banalité quotidien';[35] whereas, significantly, his own attitude towards the Antilles as he describes it in 'Antilles et poésie des carrefours' does not reject the French culture which remains his basic 'daily bread', but just wants to add something more exciting

---

30    As a phenomenon that appears strange only because it has been repressed for a long time, the Freudian uncanny is closely linked to childhood. Equally, one of the most typical manifestations of the uncanny that Freud discusses is the *double*; and although it is not quite the same thing, it is tempting to make a connection between the double and the split identity of the French Caribbean 'departmentalized' subject.

31    Leiris, 'Antilles et poésie des carrefours', p. 76.

32    Ibid., p. 77. *Contacts* also includes a description of these wooden horses, which constitutes one of its rare departures from the dry, official tone that Leiris generally adopts in this text, evidence no doubt of the deep impression they made on him: 'ces sculptures très rudimentaires [...] atteignaient grâce à leur dépouillement une sorte de classicisme et sont parfois bouleversantes par leur simplicité' (*CC*, pp. 57–58).

33    Leiris, 'Antilles et poésie des carrefours', p. 76.

34    Leiris, 'Préface', in Alfred Métraux, *Le Vaudou haïtien* (Paris: Gallimard, 1958), pp. 7–10 (pp. 9–10). Cf. Séan Hand's comment that 'Dans son ensemble, l'œuvre de Leiris repose ainsi sur le désir d'être hors de soi, et son analyse ethnographique de la possession trahit ce rêve plus profond de devenir un(e) possédé(e) et d'atteindre par là une présence pure sans conscience de soi' ('Hors de soi', pp. 189–90).

35    Leiris, 'Préface', p. 10.

to it: 'un Européen comme moi qui, certes, est bien loin de n'avoir que mépris pour la forme de culture qui est son pain quotidien, mais est avide, intensément, d'une nourriture plus savoureuse et plus stimulante'.[36]

Only Martinique offers the magical, uncanny yet 'delicious' possibility of becoming other while remaining the same — being both inside and outside a culture, that is, inside and outside oneself. Moreover, Leiris constructs a direct parallel between the political status of the islands and the type of escape from selfhood they can offer him. In the course of the lecture he differentiates between independent Haiti on the one hand and on the other Martinique and Guadeloupe which are 'la banlieue de mon propre pays'; and, finally, makes it quite clear that the 'inside/outside' ambiguity of these latter, which is so precious to him, derives precisely from their status as DOMs: 'Ce mélange d'exotisme et de familiarité [...] s'explique le plus simplement du monde par l'histoire de ces deux îles, devenues maintenant des départements français dont la singularité est d'être situés sous les tropiques'.[37] Leiris's attitude towards departmentalization in *Contacts* thus turns out, despite the latter's very impersonal discourse, to be motivated on a level that is at least as irrational and emotional as the overt excitement and frustration of *Afrique fantôme*. There is of course nothing dishonourable about being in favour of departmentalization. But in so far as Leiris's motives had more to do with his individual psychology than with the social situation in Martinique and Guadeloupe, his position does call to mind the warning in 'L'Ethnographe devant le colonialisme' when he wrote, perhaps thinking of his own attachment to the Antilles, that 'l'on n'est que trop porté à regarder comme heureux un peuple qui nous rend, nous, heureux quand nous le regardons, en raison de l'émotion poétique ou esthétique que son spectacle nous donne'.[38]

36    Leiris, 'Antilles et poésie des carrefours', p. 70.
37    Ibid., pp. 68, 76.
38    Leiris, 'L'Ethnographe devant le colonialisme', p. 95.

# CHAPTER 4

# 'Double consciousness':
# Cultural Identity and Literary Style
# in the Work of René Ménil

The concept of 'double consciousness', as a characterization of black subjectivity, originates with W. E. B. Du Bois, who in a famous passage in the first chapter of his *The Souls of Black Folk* (1903) wrote that the American Negro lives in a world:

> which yields him no true self-consciousness, but only lets him see himself through the revelation of the other world. It is a peculiar sensation, this double-consciousness, this sense of always looking at one's self through the eyes of others, of measuring one by the tape of a world that looks on in amused contempt and pity. One ever feels his two-ness, — an American, a Negro ... two thoughts, two unreconciled strivings; two warring ideals in one dark body, whose dogged strength alone keeps it from being torn asunder. The history of the American Negro is the history of this strife, — this longing to attain self-conscious manhood, to merge his double self into a better and truer self.[1]

Du Bois was describing the position of black people in the United States at the very beginning of the twentieth century; and yet we find something strikingly similar in the work of René Ménil, another Marxist, but living half a century later in the very different world of a French Caribbean colony and, from 1946, a French Overseas Department.[2] Double consciousness is not as explicit in his writing as in that of Dubois, but it is extremely pervasive. In *Tracées* he writes:

> On peut dire que notre conscience antillaise est nécessairement parodique parce qu'elle est prise dans un jeu de dédoublement, de redoublement, de miroitement, de séparation face à la conscience coloniale française matérialisée par les institutions du régime et des mass media.[3]

In an earlier article in *Tracées*, originally published in 1964, he links it to Fanon's analysis in *Peau noire, masques blancs* (*AT*, p. 37) and comments: 'L'homme colonisé,

---

1    W .E. B. Dubois, *The Souls of Black Folk* [1903], 2nd edn, ed. by Brent Hayes Edwards, Oxford World Classics (Oxford: Oxford University Press, 2008), pp. 8–9.
2    Ménil, however, consistently refers to Martinique as a 'colonial' regime, even after 1946.
3    René Ménil, *Antilles déjà jadis, précédé de Tracées* (Paris: Jean Michel Place, 1999), pp. 225–26, hereafter referred to as *AT*. *Tracées* was originally published as *Tracées, identité, négritude, esthétique aux Antilles* in 1981.

sous la pression de l'appareil colonial, devient un étranger pour lui-même' (p. 38); and describes how black Martiniquans who identify with the colonizers 'porteront à l'intérieur même de leur conscience une fissure' (p. 39). The actual term 'double conscience' appears in a later article in *Tracées*, 'Psychanalyse de l'histoire': 'La société martiniquaise tout entière, dans le régime colonial actuel, est fourvoyé dans l'impasse d'une double conscience' (*AT*, p. 48). And right at the end of *Antilles déjà jadis*, he comments: 'La séparation. Une tension en moi [...] une barrière et une dualité que je dois franchir pour rejoindre quelque chose de moi-même [...]. Telle serait ma destinée: une tension pour rejoindre l'autre de ma dualité, ce qui apaiserait un manque' (*AT*, p. 317). Not only does the idea of double consciousness thus feature in his writing from 1964 through to 1999; it also recurs in some far more specific contexts. Even looking at the sea results in a 'Double regard, l'un impregné de l'imagerie occidentale [...] l'autre appliqué [...] au concret des circonstances et de l'histoire' (*AT*, p. 268). Or, he is surprised to discover how accurate are the portraits of black subjects painted by European artists such as Rubens and Rembrandt, compared with those done by French Caribbean painters, who 'pensent le nègre au-dedans d'eux-mêmes subjectivement. Il résulte de là qu'ils le modèlent imaginairement avec les traits et la couleur de la réussite coloniale qui est blanche' (*AT*, p. 271). This example from the visual arts is similar to a more extensive *literary* phenomenon: the internal split revealed in the 'self-exoticizing' tendency of French Caribbean literature. Ménil critiques this kind of literature in 'L'Exotisme colonial', originally published in 1959, arguing that here the writer portrays *himself* as exotic, because he sees himself through the eyes of the metropolitan French: 'Je suis "exotique-pour-moi", parce que mon regard sur moi c'est le regard du blanc devenu mien après trois siècles de conditionnement colonial' (*AT*, p. 21).[4] Significantly, he includes in this self-exoticizing category the literature of the Negritude movement, which, he claims, attempts to oppose the colonial view of black people without really challenging it: it accepts the image as it is and simply reverses the values attached to it (*AT*, pp. 24–25). Even Césaire's more humorous version of Negritude in his *Cahier d'un retour au pays natal*, characterized by Ménil as 'Ou bien, usant de l'humour, nous assumons hardiment toute l'ignominie de l'image dégradée que les colonialistes conçoivent de nous, en même temps que nous la rejetons du fait même que nous l'exprimons sur le mode de l'ironie', is also condemned by him as 'contradictoire en soi, insuffisante et entachée de fausseté' (*AT*, p. 25).[5]

However, Césaire's use of irony in the *Cahier d'un retour au pays natal* is treated far less negatively in some later articles in *Tracées*; and this is symptomatic of a major difference between Ménil's attitude to double consciousness and Du Bois's original formulation. That is, for Ménil double consciousness, as well as its significance as a form of psychological alienation, also has *positive* manifestations in the domain of literature. Here it comes closer to Mikhail Bakhtin's concept of 'dialogism':

4    I have discussed this in more detail in Chapter 2 of my *Language and Literary Form in French Caribbean Writing*.

5    Aimé Césaire, *Cahier d'un retour au pays natal* (Paris: Présence africaine, 1939). This is a key text for Ménil, who refers to it on numerous occasions in his writing.

the dialogic text is one constituted by two or more discourses of equal status in dialogue with each other, rather than governed by a single 'monologic' authorial voice. His main example is the novels of Dostoevsky, which he characterizes in strongly positive terms as 'polyphonic': 'A plurality of independent and unmerged voices and consciousnesses, a genuine polyphony of fully valid voices is in fact the chief characteristic of Dostoevsky's novels'.[6]

In particular, Bakhtin's definition of irony and parody (among other styles) as 'double-voiced discourse' would seem to provide a means of relating these textual features to the double consciousness of Du Bois.[7] But Bakhtin's conception has none of the sombre tonality of Du Bois's 'two warring ideals in one dark body, whose dogged strength alone keeps it from being torn asunder'; rather, it is a celebratory recognition of the multi-voiced play of the text: 'Language lives only in the dialogic interaction of those who make use of it. Dialogic interaction is indeed the authentic sphere where language *lives*'.[8]

Ménil's writing expresses, as I have shown, the painful splits and contradictions of Du Bois's double consciousness; but it also, and with equal insistence, values the complexity and subtlety that double consciousness produces in literature. Thus, in *Tracées*, his 'conscience antillaise [...] nécessairement parodique' (*AT*, p. 225) is negative in so far as it is a symptom of alienation, but positive in its literary expression as a form of dialogic discourse, as the continuation of the above quotation makes clear: 'Pour une telle conscience divisée et soucieuse, la naïveté dans l'art est interdite. De là, dans nos œuvres, ces dissonances, dont Baudelaire disait déjà au siècle dernier, qu'elles sont agréables aux oreilles modernes' (*AT*, p. 226).

*Tracées* and *Antilles déjà jadis* contain numerous examples of and references to such dialogism. In the long article that closes *Tracées*, 'Dialogues sur une esthétique à faire ou bien', Ménil, as its title suggests, develops his position on a Marxist theory of literature by means of a dialogue, externalized between 'Moi' and 'Lui', in which 'Moi' gradually overcomes the objections put forward by 'Lui'. Also in *Tracées* he finds a similar process implicitly at work in André Breton's preface to Césaire's *Cahier d'un retour au pays natal*, which he sees as Breton arguing with himself ('À mots couverts Breton entame alors un débat avec lui-même', *AT*, p. 203) as to whether the *Cahier* can be considered a surrealist poem since — contrary to their aesthetic — it has a definite subject: 'Breton réplique à un interlocuteur absent et invisible (puisque cet interlocuteur c'est lui-même, Breton)' (*AT*, p. 205).

6    Mikhail Bakhtin, *Problems of Dostoevsky's Poetics*, ed. and trans. by Caryl Emerson (Minneapolis: University of Minnesota Press, 1984), p. 6. On dialogism, see especially pp. 193–203. Bakhtin himself, it should be noted, limited dialogism to the novel, but there seems no reason why it cannot be extended to all types of literary text. His description of one particular type of dialogism is particularly relevant to the concept of double consciousness: 'dialogic relationships are also possible toward one's own utterance as a whole, toward its separate parts and toward an individual word within it, if we somehow detach ourselves from them, speak with an inner reservation, if we observe a certain distance from them, as if limiting our own authorship or dividing it in two' (p. 184).

7    Of 'double-voiced discourse' Bahktin writes: 'discourse [...] has a twofold direction — it is directed both toward the referential object of speech, as in ordinary discourse, and toward *another's discourse*, toward *someone else's speech*' (*Problems of Dostoevsky's Poetics*, p. 185).

8    Ibid., p. 183.

Breton of course was a French rather than a Caribbean writer; but most of Ménil's examples of dialogism concern Caribbean writers, and in particular Césaire. Here it takes the form of irony and parody, i.e. Bakhtin's double-voiced discourse. Thus while 'L'Exotisme colonial' condemned the Negritude of both Senghor and Césaire as a reactionary cultural identity,[9] Ménil's later discussion in *Tracées* of Negritude in 'Le Passage de la poésie à la philosophie' differentiates sharply between 'l'étonnante lourdeur des conceptions' of Senghor and Cesaire's 'légèreté d'esprit', and even goes so far as to claim that Senghor misinterprets the *Cahier* through failing to recognize that Césaire is being ironic much of the time (*AT*, p. 81). Césaire's 'légèreté', in contrast, means that he 'se tient à distance de ce qu'il est et de ce qu'il dit pour produire *l'effet littéraire de la dérision*' (*AT*, p. 82) — internal distance or doubleness now having beneficial literary effects. Ménil goes on to expand on Césaire's ironic double-voiced discourse: 'Dans le "Cahier", il y a Césaire qui parle. Mais le retour constant de Césaire sur lui-même pour se contester, pour contester en lui le colonisé, fait surgir un autre-de-Césaire. Dualité'. In fact, because the text also incorporates the voice of the colonizer, there are actually three discourses in play: 'La parole poétique du "Cahier" n'est pas simple puisque la même parole exprime trois voix' (*AT*, p. 83).

Doubleness in these various forms, in other words, is good for literary style. Ménil finds it in other works by Césaire, such as in his play *La Tragédie du Roi Christophe*,[10] where humour serves to reveal the double consciousness of Christophe's position: 'Le fait que le thème est traité sur le mode bouffon montre bien la double conscience de Christophe romantique et héroïque sur une face, réaliste et critique sur l'autre' (*AT*, p. 186). In addition, the Argentinian Jorge Luis Borges and the Cuban Alejo Carpentier are cited as practising a baroque style of writing that through its use of caricature, parody, and exaggeration also rejoins the idea of double-voiced discourse, and that Ménil claims is typical of the Caribbean and Latin America (*AT*, pp. 224–25); other writers from the region influenced by the baroque aesthetic are Miguel Asturias, Stephen Alexis [*sic*], Bertène Juminer, and Paul Niger (*AT*, p. 201). Valuing this kind of literary complexity thus does not imply a preference for the sophisticated European writers such as Mallarmé for whom Ménil does indeed often express his admiration, but is linked to his view of the necessary 'doubleness' of Caribbean consciousness. Indeed, a very similar version of double consciousness in both its psychological and its literary forms is theorized by another Martiniquan writer, Édouard Glissant, through his concept of the 'poétique forcée' or 'contre-poétique'. Glissant defines this as a constrained discursive strategy arising from French Caribbean writers' lack of an adequate unalienated language, but which is thereby also uniquely able to express the ambiguity of their position: 'Notre perspective est de nous forger [...] un langage par quoi nous poserions volontairement l'ambigu et enracinerions carrément l'incertain de notre parole'

---

9    Cf. *AT*, p. 66: 'dans *Tropiques*, (1940–45) [Césaire] exaltera un anti-intellectualisme qui s'alimente aux même sources philosophiques [que celles de Senghor]. De plus, c'est Césaire qui mettra au point la doctrine de la négritude dans sa fameuse lettre de démission au parti communiste français (1956)'.

10    Aimé Césaire, *La Tragédie du roi Christophe* (Paris & Dakar: Présence africaine, 1963).

(*DA*, p. 283).[11] Far more broadly, the Australian postcolonial theorist Helen Tiffin's concept of 'counter-discourse' extends a similar idea to the whole of postcolonial literature: 'a post-colonial subversion and appropriation of the dominant European discourses' that necessarily involves parody and irony.[12] Postcolonial literature, in this sense, critiques but also capitalizes on the alienation of the colonial subject in order to produce literature characterized by a particular kind of complexity.

In the specific case of Ménil, this promotion of double-voiced irony and dialogic forms can be seen as one part of a general preference for complex, ambiguous texts that he felt he had to defend against accusations that it went against the Marxist conception of good literature ('Dialogues sur une esthétique à faire ou bien' is concerned to rebut precisely these accusations). He argues against the view held by many in the Communist Party that literature must be simple in order to be accessible to the masses; and in this context his own liking for Mallarmé expressed in *Antilles déjà jadis* (*AT*, pp. 303–04) and other such writers could be seen as a provocative sign of bourgeois decadence. 'Le Roman antillais', originally published in the Martiniquan Communist party journal *Action* in 1965 and republished in *Tracées*, tackles this issue vigorously. Ménil starts by attacking the novel *Au fond du bourg* by Léonard Sainville (a Martiniquan communist writer) for subordinating literary value to Marxist propaganda: 'L'impatience pragmatique, le souci du propagandiste, l'urgence politique vont produire ici un effet mécanique. La thèse politique a éclipsé les exigences spécifiques de l'art d'écrire' (*AT*, p. 188). This, Ménil argues, corresponds to 'une esthétique marxiste naïve' which in reality is not Marxist at all ('esthétique naïve parce que les prétendus impératifs ne sont pas marxistes du tout', p. 188), but derives instead from a 'matérialisme vulgaire' (p. 198) — because it is not *dialectical*. This aesthetic is a simple naturalism ('le naturalisme, la platitude dans l'art', p. 190) in the sense that it provides merely a mechanical and superficially accurate representation of its diegetic reality, without attempting to 'résoudre les vivantes contradictions inhérentes à l'activité littéraire et artistique. Et c'est là qu'elle révèle qu'elle n'est pas marxiste, faute d'être dialectique' (p. 190). A genuinely Marxist representation of reality necessarily reveals that reality's underlying contradictions, which are to be dynamically resolved by the dialectic — and double consciousness is certainly one of these contradictions. Similarly, naturalism's relegation of 'style' to superficial decoration fails to recognize the dialectical relation between style and content: 'la conception dialectique d'un style qui est un processus actif et qui entretient avec le fond du roman un rapport réel, fonctionnel, efficace' (p. 197).

In developing this argument, Ménil appeals to the Marxist notion of the 'relative autonomy' of art: 'Mais Marx n'a-t-il pas assez insisté sur la complexité de la création artistique, sur *l'autonomie relative* de l'art [...]' (*AT*, p. 189, my emphasis); and he returns to this concept in the 'Dialogues sur une esthétique à faire ou bien',

11    I have discussed the 'contre-poétique' in more detail in *Édouard Glissant and Postcolonial Theory* (Charlottesville & London: University Press of Virginia, 1999), pp. 30–34.

12    Helen Tiffin, 'Post-Colonial Literatures and Counter-Discourse', in *The Post-Colonial Studies Reader*, ed. by Bill Ashcroft, Gareth Griffiths, and Helen Tiffin (New York & London: Routledge, 1995), pp. 95–98 (p. 95).

referring to 'l'autonomie relative de l'esthétique et de la politique en même temps que leur intrication réciproque', and going on to explain that:

> Cette autonomie, il faut le rappeler, n'est pas absolue mais relative. Ce qui veut dire que les activités littéraires et artistiques se développent [...] en relation, corrélation, contradiction et détermination réciproque avec les autres activités parmi lesquelles les activités politiques [...]. Une dialectique est à envisager dans l'actuelle crise de notre société telle que la politique peut se trouver bousculée par l'esthétique et réciproquement. (*AT*, p. 229)

The concept of relative autonomy is clearly taken from the work of Louis Althusser, a French Marxist who was very influential from the mid-1960s through to the end of the 1970s. It arises from his critique of earlier 'reflectionist' Marxism, in which the economy directly determines all political, ideological, and cultural forms, so that these are mere 'reflections' of the economic base. Relative autonomy, on the other hand, enables Althusser to construct a more multi-dimensional structural model in which culture etc. can in some cases be determining within the overall structure of society — so that it may indeed happen that 'la politique peut se trouver bousculée par l'esthétique'. The economy remains the ultimate determining force but on a far more general scale; it does not directly determine particular cultural forms.[13] The structuralist Marxism of Althusser, in other words, is used by Ménil to refute the vulgar Marxism of the Martiniquan Communist Party.

For Althusser, then, literature is not directly determined by the economic base of society, since its relative autonomy allows for multiple reciprocal determinations. But in the relatively few articles that he wrote on the subject, Althusser in his early work also views the literary text, and indeed art in general, as having a particular relation to ideology — and one that can be interpreted as strikingly consonant with the idea of double consciousness. Rather than serving as a mere vehicle for ideology, art has the ability to make it visible *as* ideology; and it does this by a kind of internal distancing: the novels of Balzac and Solzhenitsyn, for instance, 'make us "perceive" [...] in some sense from the inside, by an internal distance, the very ideology in which they are held'.[14] By thus implicitly designating its own representation of reality *as* ideological, in other words, the literary text distances itself from its ideology by a kind of internal split that, while not exactly parody, is close to Bakhtin's notion of double-voicing.

Ménil's 'Le Roman antillais' argues forcefully that the literary text is constituted by its writing rather than by the content of its representation: 'c'est l'écriture qui fait le roman fond et forme ensemble' (*AT*, p. 197); and does so by appealing to another Althusserian concept, that of 'practice'[15] — Marxist aesthetics must 's'arracher aux séductions grossières du matérialisme vulgaire qui ne comprend pas que notre vision

13   See Louis Althusser, *Pour Marx* (Paris: François Maspéro, 1965); *For Marx*, trans. by Ben Brewster (Harmondsworth: Allen Lane, 1969).

14   Louis Althusser, 'Lettre sur la connaissance de l'art', *La Nouvelle Critique*, 175 (April 1966), 136–41; 'Letter on art', in *Lenin and Philosophy and Other Essays*, trans. by Ben Brewster (New York: Monthly Review Press, 1971), pp. 203–19 (p. 204). This 'internal distance' recalls Ménil's comment, already quoted, that Césaire 'se tient à distance de ce qu'il est et de ce qu'il dit' (*Tracées*, p. 82).

15   Althusser, *For Marx*, p. 166.

du monde est non pas une contemplation passive, mais une activité conquérante, *une pratique*' (*AT*, p. 198). Writing, then, is a practice; and later in his career Ménil moves even more decisively away from naturalism's privileging of the representational content of a literary work by defining literature as a form of autonomous *production*. Commemorating the death of the Martiniquan Marxist novelist Vincent Placoly, he describes the latter's work as follows:

> Une esthétique qui sait dire non à la banalité du sentiment et du langage pour bien asseoir la liberté et l'indépendance de la création littéraire. Car, ne l'oublions pas, il s'agit ici non pas de reproduire mais de *produire* [...]. Heureusement, ici, la littérature garde son autonomie pour dire ce qu'elle seule peut dire et qu'elle apporte à l'action politique.[16]

This idea of the literary text as a specific type of production is central to the theory of Pierre Macherey, another French Marxist literary theorist who, while deeply influenced by Althusser, arrived at a fuller and rather different conception of literature in his *Pour une théorie de la production littéraire*. Macherey's theory, like that of Althusser, has implications for the idea of literature as double-voiced discourse, but not at all in the same way. For Macherey, the literary text is structured by a number of discrete factors, such as the author's 'ideological project', the general historical situation in which the work is written, and the influence of previous literary forms; and this very Althusserian idea of multiple determinations results in contradictory pulls on the text. Therefore it is characterized by an internal complexity; it is, so to speak, forced to say several different things at once: 'l'accent est mis sur la *diversité de la lettre*: le texte ne dit pas une chose, mais nécessairement plusieurs à la fois'.[17] In other words, to revert to Bakhtin's terminology, it is necessarily dialogic.

Althusser and Macherey thus provide Ménil with a Marxist alternative to the Communist Party's 'vulgar materialism', in sanctioning the importance of style and form as against 'content' and, at least in Althusser's case, by positing that art and literature can in some cases have a determining effect on social reality and politics. Additionally, however, Althusser's 'internal distancing' provides evidence that a kind of dialogic discourse can form part of a Marxist theory of literature, while Macherey's 'diversité de la lettre' more explicitly presents double-voicing as a necessary and integral element of such a theory. Ménil himself does not refer to this aspect of Althusser's and Macherey's work, but it does strengthen his own argument: in integrating dialogic discourse into their overall structuralist Marxist theories of literature, they both clearly oppose the 'platitude' of the naturalism promulgated by vulgar Marxism, which precludes any type of double-voicing.

Another subject on which Ménil wrote a considerable amount and which brings together the two issues of cultural identity and literary style is folklore. In his early surrealist days in the 1940s, on the editorial board of the review *Tropiques*, Ménil along with Aimé and Suzanne Césaire regarded the traditional folklore of their island as a possible source of cultural reintegration: a way in which Parisian-educated

---

16    René Ménil, 'Vincent Placoly s'en va: adieu, frère volcan', *Tranchées. Revue politique et culturelle du Groupe Révolution socialiste* (January 1993), 11–12 (p. 11, my emphasis).

17    Pierre Macherey, *Pour une théorie de la production littéraire* (Paris: François Maspéro, 1966), p. 33.

intellectuals such as themselves could rediscover their roots and as it were plug into an authentically Martiniquan collective unconscious, thereby also acquiring an authentically Martiniquan cultural identity. But even then they were distinctly ambivalent about this kind of surrealist primitivism;[18] and there was certainly never any suggestion that their own writing should mimic the literary style of folklore. Subsequently Ménil rejected surrealism (while, sometimes, making an exception for the work of Césaire). Equally, in 'Problèmes d'une culture antillaise', originally published in *Action* in 1964 and then republished in *Tracées*, he is beginning to feel that folklore cannot provide a basis for cultural identity. Thus although he lists, among the factors that make up unalienated Martiniquan culture, 'les croyances répandues dans nos campagnes et nos villes, [...] ces fêtes et ces danses, ces objets fabriqués par nos artisans' (*AT*, p. 33), by the end of the article we find him stating clearly that folklore lacks the dynamic connection to present-day reality and change that are necessary for the construction of a valid cultural identity:

> Le folklore tend à figer, à fixer la vie dans les gestes du passé et, à cet égard, il n'est pas la culture, il n'est pas la lutte culturelle. Il en est même, sous certain aspects, le contraire si on ne cherche pas à le dépasser en créant les nouvelles formes de la vie de demain. (*AT*, p. 45)

Subsequently, *Antilles déjà jadis* presents a substantial critique of the use later made of folklore by the 'créolité' school of novelists of the 1980s and 1990s (that is, primarily, Patrick Chamoiseau and Raphaël Confiant, although Ménil does not name them). Its introduction castigates those who see 'une donnée naturelle — la créolité' as a goal to be achieved rather than just the already existing starting point for the construction of a world view and a set of moral values; he comments acidly: 'Content de soi devant le miroir, c'est bien vite l'applaudissement à son propre pittoresque' (*AT*, p. 239). This is followed in *Antilles déjà jadis* by 'Une philosophie des racines', which criticizes as reactionary and futile the attempt to rediscover one's roots, and links this to folklore — 'La recherche des racines a donné lieu aux Antilles à une manière de théorisation culturelle sur fond de folklore' — and then to the 'créolité' movement: 'Tout cela aboutit obscurément à un mode de pensée et un courant idéologique que l'on appelle depuis quelques années la créolité'. It is only, he claims, the alienated petty bourgeoisie who feel the need to constantly prove and proclaim their 'créolité': 'Chanson de la mauvaise conscience qu'on n'entendra pas dans la rue car là, chacun sait, sans le dire, qu'il est créole' (*AT*, p. 243). Two further short pieces in *Antilles déjà jadis* ('Sur l'identité et le folklore' and 'Le Folklore dans la littérature') criticize the 'créolité' novelists for their use of folklore on both identitarian and literary grounds. First Ménil accuses them of a kind of identitarian anxiety which compels them to try to prove that they are indeed authentically Creole although they write in French, by filling their narratives up with typical traditional Martiniquan customs: 'Dérapage dans le folkorisme, le régionalisme, l'exotisme paresseux et, en fin de compte, dans une espèce de patriotisme créole' (*AT*, p. 275). Then he dismisses the literary value of their work on the grounds

---

18    I have discussed this in more detail in Chapter 1 of *Language and Literary Form in French Caribbean Writing*.

that the direct importation of folklore results in a naive naturalism similar to that which he earlier condemned in relation to vulgar Marxism, the over-valuing of the representational content — 'Cette esthétique ne croit-elle pas naïvement que la littérature ici pour être valable n'aurait qu'à refléter, décrire, photographier les formes du folklore pour accomplir sa tâche?' — and the accompanying devaluation of language and form: 'Dans ce cadre, on aura une expression de la vie sous forme de clichés [... ] bref, une littérature qui s'annule elle-même' (*AT*, p. 276).[19]

It would appear, therefore, that the kind of literature whose main concern is to promote a particular cultural identity inevitably, according to Ménil, results in a superficial and simplistic literary style that in effect disqualifies it as literature, in contrast to the dialogic literature produced by double consciousness. If, as I have argued, double consciousness is — to put it simplistically — bad for cultural identity but good for literary style, should we then conclude that its opposite, the straightforward promotion in literature of a unitary identity, just reverses the two terms, in other words is bad for literary style but, in principle at least, good for cultural identity? If this were the case, one would have to conclude further that Ménil is prepared to sacrifice the possibility of a viable cultural identity in favour of complex, ambiguous, sophisticated literature, and it is hard to see how this could be compatible with his Marxist position on the importance of the 'lutte culturelle'. But in fact he is not doing this: for reasons that are integral to his Marxist position on cultural identity.

While Ménil never rejects the concept of cultural identity in principle, it is very noticeable that all the examples of it that are discussed in *Tracées* and *Antilles déjà jadis* are distinctly negative: Negritude and 'créolité', as we have seen, but also the phenomena that he analyzes in his Barthesian 'Mythologies antillaises', in *Tracées*.[20] These range from the apparently trivial — a militant T-shirt, Afro hair styles, 'traditional' straw huts for tourists on the beach — to more abstract conceptualizations of the Martiniquan personality; but they are all an attempt to answer the question: 'Être Antillais, c'est quoi?' (*AT*, p. 53). That is, they are all attempts to create a cultural identity by reacting against the current situation of French Caribbean social existence, which is dominated by the ideology of metropolitan France: 'Elles surgissent en général [...] comme *contre-mythologies*, en réaction contre les mythologies de la colonisation'); but, he goes on, 'Réactionnelles, elles le sont en même temps, est-il besoin de le dire, au sens où l'on dit d'un malade qu'il réagit à son mal par la

---

19   Right at the end of *Antilles déjà jadis* he returns to the attack in a letter to Jacqueline Leiner, where naturalism is explicitly linked to the literary incorporation of folklore (p. 304), and Ménil brings in Mallarmé to criticize it: 'Paraphrasant Mallarmé nous dirons que ce n'est pas avec des enterrements, des danses, des comportements humains réels (la matérialité externe du folklore et de la perception exotique) — que l'on bâtit littérairement le roman' (p. 304).

20   Cf. Roland Barthes, *Mythologies* (Paris: Éditions du Seuil, 1957). Barthes draws on concepts from semiology and linguistics to show how we use second-level connotative meanings to send out messages about ourselves, and how these are incorporated into journalism, literature, film, and other cultural forms. For example, instead of stating (denotatively) that a woman is rich, the text will tell us that she is wearing a mink coat: an apparently factual statement that nevertheless connotes wealth. Myth also presents contingent, historically specific realities as natural and therefore asocial, and is thus 'une parole dépolitisée' (p. 216).

fièvre ou la névrose' (*AT*, p. 52). They are, in other words, merely symptoms of the problem rather than solutions to it. Ménil repeats here the criticism he has already made in 'L'Exotisme colonial' of Negritude as adopting the white racist view of the black man and simply reversing the values attached to it, and that he now defines as 'mythologies par inversion dans le miroir' (p. 58). Other attempts to create a Martiniquan identity — which he lists, sarcastically capitalized, as 'Authenticité, Spécificité, Différence, Personnalité et d'autres encore' — are also dismissed as 'Mythologie de la petite bourgeoisie à la recherche de son "essence" imaginaire, faute de pouvoir jouer un rôle réel sur la scène de l'histoire' (p. 60). As this suggests, mythologies arise out of a lack of political power.[21] Thus they try, unconsciously, to cover up this lack by essentializing, or naturalizing, socio-political realities such as colonialism, presenting them as ahistorical and eternal, in which case it is pointless to struggle against them. (This, as Ménil indicates by citing Roland Barthes here, is an important theme of the original *Mythologies*, in which Barthes writes: 'Nous sommes ici au principe même du mythe: il transforme l'histoire en nature'.)[22] The only effective way to free oneself from colonial mythology, Ménil argues, is to break away from mythologies altogether: 'La bonne rupture ne pourrait se faire que dans un *ailleurs non mythologique*' (*AT*, p. 58), and the final section of the article, subtitled 'Une politique sans mythologie', argues that only Marxism can provide this.

Everyone — Ménil, the proponents of Negritude and of 'créolité', the folklorists, the wearers of Afros etc. — agrees that a valid cultural identity cannot be attained without overcoming alienation. But only Ménil also believes that the *only* way to overcome alienation is by engaging in the struggle for political liberation, which in the case of Martinique means independence or at least 'autonomy': Antillean culture, he claims, cannot exist without 'la reprise, la récupération du pouvoir politique dans la société antillaise par les Antillais eux-mêmes — ce qu'aujourd'hui nous appelons l'autonomie' (*AT*, p. 42).[23] (Conversely, Négritude's entrapment in mythologies makes it unable to 'fonder une politique anticolonialiste conséquente', *AT*, p. 61.) Culture, therefore, has to be part of the political struggle, as he states emphatically several times: 'La lutte pour la culture doit donc être intégrée dans la lutte générale pour l'amélioration des conditions de la vie des Antillais' (*AT*, p. 45); 'C'est que la culture en régime colonial a pour condition première la libération du joug colonial' (*AT*, p. 36), and so on. And if this is the function of culture, then it follows that cultural identity also can be achieved only through one's commitment to political struggle.

Equally, the undoubted importance of reclaiming one's history is not simply a matter of finding one's 'roots', as Ménil argues in 'Une philosophie des "racines"', in *Antilles déjà jadis*: 'La pensée végétaliste des racines est une métaphore et il convient

21   *AT*, p. 53: 'C'est de ne rien contrôler et de n'être sûr de rien — ni du passé, ni du présent, ni encore moins de l'avenir — qui fait de la société antillaise le lieu rêvé des mythologies et des névroses passéistes et futuristes pour supporter, dissimuler, fuir un insupportable présent'.

22   Barthes, *Mythologies*, p. 202.

23   There are echoes here of the problematic interdependence of cultural and political autonomy discussed in Chapter 3. The 'vulgar Marxists' of course share this view of the supremacy of political struggle, but they, according to Ménil, are not interested in the 'lutte culturelle'.

de dialectiser cette image analogique, la relativiser avec ses contradictions'. The metaphor of roots implies stability and permanence, whereas a real understanding of our history reveals that we are endlessly, and dialectically, changing: human nature is 'éternellement inachevée dans une histoire sans fin' (*AT*, p. 242).

Two consequences follow from this. Firstly, a fully unalienated cultural identity is possible only once political liberation has been achieved. Therefore, Ménil's fellow Martiniquans should involve themselves in this struggle, rather than prematurely manufacturing identities that will inevitably be inauthentic and merely 'mythological'. The implication is that such political commitment in itself goes some way towards overcoming the contradictions of double consciousness. Secondly, the Martiniquans need, through understanding their history and their ever-changing place in social reality, to realize that cultural identity can never be fixed and permanent, but is itself necessarily fluid and open-ended. Moreover, this constant change is produced dialectically, i.e. by the dynamic resolution of contradictions. And a major example of such contradictions is of course double consciousness: the painful conflict caused by the internalization of the colonial other's view of oneself. Political liberation alone will, by changing social reality as a whole, resolve this split and this contradiction. Double consciousness, from this point of view, is not a fatal or a tragic condition, but a dialectical one: a contradiction that can of itself generate the possibility of its resolution. Equally, the literature that derives from double consciousness, which I have characterized as dialogic, is not merely a form of aesthetic compensation for the psychological distress of alienation, but rather an illustration and illumination of this particular stage in the dialectic. Therefore it is not a question of having to choose between good literature and unalienated cultural identity, because both are products of the same 'lutte culturelle'.

CHAPTER 5

❖

# Globalization and Political Action in the Work of Édouard Glissant

Between the publication of *Le Discours antillais* in 1981 and *Poétique de la Relation* in 1990, Glissant's work undergoes a marked change: of focus, of mood, and of political position. Whereas he had previously concentrated his attention mainly on his own island of Martinique, in the 1990s he broadens his vision to the whole world. The pessimism of *Le Discours antillais* is replaced by exhilaration, and the anticolonial struggle that dominated the earlier texts, in which the *isolation* of Martinique was an important factor, gives way to a view of the world — influenced by chaos theory and the 'nomadology' of Deleuze and Guattari[1] — as a dynamic totality of interacting communities, all aware of each other and all constantly changing.[2] *Poétique de la Relation* and the subsequent *Introduction à une poétique du divers* and *Traité du Tout-monde* all invent a variety of more or less synonymous names for this phenomenon: 'créolisation', 'chaos-monde', 'Tout-monde'.

Another name for it is *Relation*, a concept that has always been central to Glissant's thinking but whose implications now change somewhat. Originally it was an anti-imperialist project, countering the West's imposition of its pseudo-universalist values on the rest of the world with an insistence on diversity and an anti-essentialist, relational concept of human existence. In *Le Discours antillais* he writes 'Le Même requiert l'Être, le Divers établit la Relation. Comme le Même a commencé par la rapine expansionniste en Occident, le Divers s'est fait jour à travers la violence politique et armée des peuples' (*DA*, p. 190). Colonized peoples had to 'enter into Relation' as part of their struggle for liberation (*DA*, p. 29). Now, however, Relation has become a global reality; every culture in the world is a 'relais actif de la Relation' (*PR*, p. 191), and it is no longer a question of 'entering into it'.[3] But Relation was always also a *value* in that it was anti-essentialist and anti-racist, and it defined identity in relational terms rather than as the 'root-identity' that fuelled colonial conquest and still fuels sectarian politics.[4] This dimension persists in the Tout-monde, which includes not only the contemporary world but also our

1     Gilles Deleuze and Félix Guattari, *Mille Plateaux* (Paris: Éditions de Minuit, 1980).
2     *TTM*, p. 23: 'Pour la première fois, les cultures humaines en leur semi-totalité sont entièrement et simultanément mises en contact et en effervescence de réaction les unes avec les autres'.
3     *PR*, p. 186: 'On n'entre pas d'abord en Relation, comme on serait entré en religion'.
4     See Chapters 1 and 6 for further discussion of 'root-identity'.

consciousness of it — 'Notre univers tel qu'il change [...] et, en même temps, la "vision" que nous en avons' (*TTM*, p. 176) — and this consciousness of the Tout-monde preserves the relational diversity and respect for the other, the rejection of fixed ideological positions, that has not yet been fully realized in the Tout-monde qua objective reality. Because, although Glissant's enthusiasm for it may at times suggest otherwise, he is in fact clear that the Tout-monde has not eliminated oppression, inequality, and racism: 'Je pense que la Relation n'est pas vertueuse ni "morale" et qu'une poétique de la Relation ne suppose pas immédiatement et de manière harmonieuse la fin des dominations' (*IPD*, p. 106)

It has, however, increased the chances of their elimination, in various ways. First, Glissant emphasizes how global mediatization means that even local conflicts now resonate around the world: 'Nous acceptons maintenant d'écouter ensemble, sachant aussi que, l'écoutant, nous concevons que *tous l'entendent désormais*' (*TTM*, p. 17). Second, the unpredictability that, given the huge number of variables involved, is one of the main features of the 'chaotic' Tout-monde ('la *terra incognita* devant nous est le champ inépuisable des variations nées du contact des cultures', *PR*, p. 69), makes it harder for domination to become entrenched (*IPD*, p. 104). Third, Glissant claims that although oppression continues in the Tout-monde, the movement away from 'root-identity' has destroyed the basis of the claim to legitimacy which bolstered colonialism, for instance. (*IPD*, pp. 68, 77).

Conversely, other aspects of Glissant's work would appear to problematize the possibility of political action in a globalized world. It is not just that his optimistic tone contrasts disconcertingly with the embattled stance of *Le Discours antillais*; more substantively, his writing often gives the impression that this chaotic, dynamic totality is not susceptible to deliberate intervention. Change happens constantly, but, as it were, automatically, through 'les mécanismes indémontables de la Relation' (*PR*, p. 234). This, together with the devaluing of ideological positions that its ethical relativism requires, might seem to suggest that in the Tout-monde political comment and action have become irrelevant, that in turning from Martinique to the world as a whole Glissant has also turned his back on politics. In the final section of this chapter I will argue that this is not in fact the case. But because this phase of his work coincides with his becoming much better known, particularly in the United States, I want to approach the issue via the reception of Glissant in the world outside Martinique by discussing two North American critiques that compare the early and late stages of Glissant's work and evaluate them very differently.

Chris Bongie's *Islands and Exiles* is a wide-ranging study of colonial and postcolonial texts that takes Glissant's concept of creolization as the 'central theoretical point of reference' of its enthusiastically post-modern analysis of 'post/colonial' literature.[5] For Bongie, both colonialism and anticolonial struggle belong to the modernist era of belief in essentialist identity and historical progress towards liberation that has now been superseded by postmodernism. Postmodernism has deconstructed the opposition between colonialism and decolonization, revealing

---

5    Chris Bongie, *Islands and Exiles: The Creole Identities of Post/Colonial Literature* (Stanford, CA: Stanford University Press, 1998); hereafter referred to as *IE*.

them to be virtually identical ('the colonial project and its anticolonial double', *IE*, p. 13); the slash in 'post/colonial' expresses the lack of any clear distinction between the colonial and the postcolonial. Within this framework, Bongie presents Glissant's trajectory from anticolonial engagement to worldwide Relation and creolization as a journey of enlightenment. The early Glissant was caught up in the delusion of the struggle for national independence for Martinique; this was followed by a period of pessimism in the 1970s (*Malemort*, *La Case du commandeur*, *Le Discours antillais*), which led in turn, with *Mahagony* and *Poétique de la Relation*, to a rejection of his previous ideals in favour of a postmodern 'creolizing' stance that accepts the world as it is — a world to which ideological conflict is irrelevant.[6]

However, just as the colonial is still present in the postcolonial, so, in Bongie's deconstructivist view, the new intellectual positions are unable in principle to break completely free of the earlier positions that they oppose; therefore, traces of early Glissant remain in his later work. For Bongie early Glissant is simply wrong and the persistence of the theme of resistance in his later work merely regrettable ('Glissant's work is, from start to finish, committed to any number of ideological errors made in the name of structuring resistance', *IE*, p. 143), albeit inevitable (pp. 68–69). His analysis of Glissant is concerned 'with the way that this vision [of creolization] is inextricably tangled up with other ideological commitments' (p. 137), central to which is 'a Fanonesque politics of national identity and anticolonial resistance — an ideological position to which [...] Glissant once seemed wholeheartedly committed' (p. 138), and Bongie asks how this can 'fit in with the anti-ideological poetics of *inter*national creolization that he has so productively pursued [...] especially over the course of the last decade' (p. 138).

Bongie is therefore keen to emphasize the extent to which Glissant has 'recanted' his commitment to anticolonial resistance (*IE*, p. 135). But, even allowing for the ambiguities inherent in its inevitable persistence, his argument suffers from a scarcity of textual evidence and leads him into what are in my view misreadings of the later texts. For instance, he claims that Glissant's depression in the 1970s stems not only from Martinique's continued dependence on France (as is amply attested throughout *Le Discours antillais*) but equally from his disillusionment with the new nation-states that have been established through decolonization elsewhere (*IE*, p. 150); but he produces no evidence at all for this view. Similarly, he interprets *Mahagony*'s attack on the single, authoritative narrative voice (in which Mathieu, a character in the earlier novels, intermittently assumes the role of narrator in order to criticize the author's previous representations of him) in very narrow terms (*IE*, pp. 174–79), as Glissant distancing himself from his earlier anticolonial exhortations, while at the same time 'skeptically' reaffirming them.[7] But *Mahagony*'s undermining of narrative authority is never linked to attitudes towards decolonization; its shift

---

6    Édouard Glissant, *Malemort* (Paris: Éditions du Seuil, 1975); *La Case du commandeur* (Paris: Éditions du Seuil, 1981).

7    *IE*, p. 180: 'The Glissant of *Mahagony* is committed both to relativizing and affirming those beliefs of his that have been put into question by the historical trajectory of "national disenchantment", the collapse of that radically different and truly post-colonial future to which the modernist literature of decolonization looked forward'.

from the collective 'we' of *Malemort* and *La Case du commandeur* to the singular 'I', which is the only evidence Bongie adduces (*IE*, p. 174), is hardly conclusive. More generally, while in his later works Glissant does, certainly, at times state that anticolonial struggle required the 'root-identity' that he now rejects, to give these occasional comments the prominence that Bongie does and thereby to imply that these texts are *primarily* an (ambivalent) rejection of decolonization is a serious distortion of their overall thrust.[8] Relation and creolization constitute a critique of essentialist notions of identity in general, and their principal target is the West rather than newly independent third-world nations.

On the question of whether *any* kind of political action is possible in this creolized, postmodern world, Bongie is more equivocal. On the one hand, he argues that postmodernism is not a simple disengagement from ideology; rather, it 'distances' it in a way that permits an ambivalent, problematizing, relativizing, sceptical re-engagement with it: 'the (dis)engagement of the postmodern' (*IE*, p. 172). On the other hand, elsewhere, while he recognizes that there are still political battles to be fought, he implies that fighting them goes against the tenets of postmodernism: it places 'limits' on the 'relational thinking' of creolization (*IE*, p. 142). In this view, postmodern reality excludes any notion of radical difference, either between social groups or between the present and the future; it therefore rules out both the 'taking sides' that is basic to political action and the possibility of a revolutionary future that will be radically different from the present.[9] Political action therefore necessitates the adoption of Gayatri Spivak's 'strategic essentialism', which Bongie appears to endorse.[10] But when on the last page of his book he cites Glissant doing exactly this, it is in tones of patronizing disapproval:

> Glissant blandly informs us that 'blacks in the United States *naturally* need Afrocentrism in order to struggle against their condition, and one cannot ask a black homeless person in New York to rise up in the name of creolization' [*IPD*, p. 105]. If yet further proof were needed that, as Glissant himself once

8    For instance, Bongie runs together two quotations from *Poétique de la Relation*: '"Most of the nations that liberated themselves from colonization," [Glissant] points out in the *Poétique*, "have tended to form themselves around the idea of power, the totalitarian drive of the single root, rather than in a founding relation with the Other" (pp. 26–27). "Identity for colonized peoples", he continues, "will in the first place be an 'opposed to', that is to say at the outset [au principe] a limitation". "The real work of decolonization", he concludes, 'will have been to go beyond this limit" (p. 29)' (*IE*, pp. 61–62; Bongie's translations, with his page references to *PR*). But the first quotation occurs in the middle of a paragraph that is about the historical force of the 'root-identity' in Western nations, and the 'liberation' referred to is *of* these nations *from* the Roman Empire; while the second quotation, in contrast, makes an explicit distinction between the root-identity of (contemporary) *colonized* peoples, and the work of decolonization, precisely, in moving beyond this.

9    *IE*, p. 410: 'Lacking the grounds for a belief in radical difference, the postmodern sensibility is unable to accredit [...] the possibility of a truly revolutionary future: it locates us in a confusing and complicitous present in which differences have become (un)likenesses'.

10    *IE*, p. 11: 'Provisional affirmations of identity are often politically necessary, notwithstanding the fact that they are theoretically "unviable" (to echo Gayatri Spivak)'. For Spivak on strategic essentialism, see for example her interview with Elizabeth Grosz, 'Criticism, Feminism and the Institution', in Gayatri Spivak, *The Postcolonial Critic: Interviews, Strategies, Dialogues*, ed. by Sarah Harasym (New York & London: Routledge, 1990), pp. 10–11.

put it, there are no guarantees against the 'many mistakes that resulted from the old ideological ways of thinking', then this anxiously 'commonsensical' remark would supply it. (*IE*, p. 434)

While Bongie at one point asks, 'Are there not different ethicopolitical arguments that might take us *beyond* community and identity as it has been traditionally defined?' (*IE*, p. 415), he does not pursue this possibility. Nor does he comment on the fact that the quotation from *Introduction à une poétique du divers* that prefaces his main section on Glissant, and which he uses to instantiate Glissant's rejection of the politics of decolonization, begins with the statement: 'I think that in the context of globalization the modalities of resistance *will change*' (*IE*, p. 34, my emphasis; see *IPD*, p. 106). It is precisely the possibility of such new modes of resistance that is central to my argument here, and I will return to it in the final section of this chapter.

Peter Hallward's *Absolutely Postcolonial: Writing between the Singular and the Specific* reproduces Bongie's characterization of early and late Glissant, but reverses Bongie's evaluation of them. For Hallward the early anticolonial phase of commitment to national resistance is positive, and the later Tout-monde is negative because, he claims, Glissant now abandons any kind of political commitment. In Hallward's terminology, Glissant moves from a 'specific', grounded engagement with a dialectic of national liberation to a 'singular' — that is, self-sufficient and non-relational — vision of the world as an immanent totality, impervious to conscious political intervention.[11] Late Glissant is, in Hallward's view, typical of postcolonial theory in general, with its fondness for hybridity and ambivalence and its suspicion of clear-cut oppositions (*AP*, p. xiv).[12]

Hallward produces a philosophically sophisticated account of both these stages in Glissant's trajectory. But he never squarely addresses the question of *why* the shift from the specific to the singular happens. The key text here is *Le Discours antillais*, and Hallward's positioning of it is somewhat confused. That is, he splits Glissant's theoretical texts into two groups, 'early' and 'late', with *Le Discours antillais* assigned unambiguously to the early phase (*AP*, p. 69). The novels, however, are (as in Bongie's formulation) divided into *three* phases: '*La Lézarde* (and *Le Quatrième Siècle*) as affirmative of the initial national programme, *Malemort* and *La Case du commandeur* as more or less despairing of it, and *Mahagony* and *Tout-monde* as broadly affirmative of the new, post-national or 'chaotic' alternative' (p. 69).[13] But if *Malemort* in 1975 is already 'despairing' of the national project, it is hard to see how in 1981 *Le Discours antillais* could still simply 'affirm' it; and indeed, the 'dialectical energy' of *Le Discours* mutates, further down the same page, into *Le*

---

11   Hallward, *Absolutely Postcolonial*, p. 5; hereafter referred to as *AP*.
12   In this sense postcolonial theory is perfectly exemplified by Bongie. Hallward's conception of late Glissant also seems clearly influenced by *Islands and Exiles*; although Hallward, curiously, does not mention Bongie, the Glissant he is attacking is the Glissant whom Bongie created — and who, I argue, has never really existed. In a further twist, Bongie later adopted Hallward's position on Glissant: see Bongie, *Friends and Enemies*, Chapter 7.
13   Édouard Glissant, *La Lézarde* (Paris: Éditions du Seuil, 1958); *Le Quatrième Siècle* (Paris: Éditions du Seuil, 1964), hereafter referred to as *QS*.

*Discours* as illustrating and diagnosing 'the dialectic en panne' that sums up *Malemort* (*AP*, p. 87). In other words, *Le Discours antillais* cannot fit neatly into Hallward's periodization of Glissant's theoretical work because it is in fact a deeply ambiguous text. But Hallward's reductive reading of it cannot acknowledge this — perhaps as a consequence of his general intolerance of ambiguity, which he associates with postcolonialism's desire to sideline opposition in favour of complacently free-floating ambivalence. But the ambiguity that is fundamental to *Le Discours antillais* is of a very different kind. Far from being the expression of a choice not to take sides, it is the result of an extremely constrained, compromised situation in which political resistance is drastically limited; it is ambiguous because it both campaigns for independence and analyzes, in depth, the obstacles that make independence virtually impossible.

Hallward, however, does not adequately recognize this. He comments on 'the abjectly passive form of neo-colonial dependency' (*AP*, p. 87) afflicting Martinique in the 1970s, but does not identify this as the reason for Glissant's abandoning of the national project. In particular, he ignores the importance of departmentalization in creating a 'blocked' political situation in which those who might otherwise fight for independence are bought off by an illusory equality with France; and yet this is the problematic that dominates *Le Discours antillais*.[14] Hallward refers to departmentalization only to say that it has ruined the local economy (*AP*, p. 87) and while this is true, departmentalization also in fact brought to Martinique a higher standard of living than that of the independent Caribbean islands, thus providing a further reason not to seek independence. It encouraged Martiniquans to identify with France (Glissant's 'pulsion mimétique [...] une violence insidieuse', *DA*, p. 31), camouflaged the distinctions between colonizer and colonized, and was thus responsible for the ambiguous situation to which *Le Discours* responds. Throughout this text, Glissant emphasizes the difficulty of resisting domination that is not local and brutally obvious but operates at arm's length, in a concealed fashion.

For instance, it is in this context that his concept of 'detour' must be understood. A detour is a confused, often desperate, sometimes irrational form of resistance: it is 'le recours ultime d'une population dont la domination par un Autre est occultée' (*DA*, p. 32).[15] But Hallward sees it very reductively as a type of folklore, as 'primitive' (*AP*, pp. 79–80), and above all as a simple evasion of responsibility.[16] The detour, he claims, is a mere 'obstacle to be overcome in the constitution of a *national* consciousness', and Glissant is 'generally dismissive of it' (*AP*, p. 71). While Glissant does indeed regard it as a transitional stage in the dialectic of national liberation, it does not follow that his view of it is dismissive or condemnatory.[17]

14    See in particular the introduction to *DA*, pp. 11–22.
15    See Britton, *Édouard Glissant and Postcolonial Theory*, pp. 25–29.
16    *AP*, p. 80: 'Detour per se merely encourages evasion of a national responsibility'; and p. 92: 'The result, once again: *détour* and irresponsibility'.
17    In an interview given on the publication of *Le Discours antillais*, Glissant emphasizes that 'the use of the Detour does not in any sense mean an escape from reality. In the Caribbean, one of the traditional forces of opposition in complicated situations is the ruse' (see 'Assimilation ou antillanité?', *Afrique-Asie*, 245 (3 April 1981), 46–47).

Calling it an evasion of responsibility implies that other, more valid, choices could be made, but the detour is the 'ultimate resort' of people who have no other choice open to them; and in a situation in which possibilities for political action are severely limited, those that do exist, however inadequate, cannot simply be rejected. Equally, if as I have argued Glissant abandoned the project of national independence for Martinique because of his growing conviction that the forces of assimilation and departmentalization were such that independence was not a realistic possibility in the foreseeable future, then his move into 'singularity' was itself wholly 'specific', in Hallward's sense of a determinate response to real external factors, and this in turn implies that Glissant has not necessarily rejected other kinds of political action.

But for Hallward this is impossible because he believes that the *only* vehicle for progressive politics is the nation-state, which late Glissant abandons. Hallward cites campaigns for national liberation led in the past (*AP*, p. 128), and argues vigorously that only the nation, 'made up of all those who, whatever their cultural origin or "way of being", collectively *decide* to assert (or re-assert) the right of self-determination' (*AP*, p. 127), can transcend cultural particularities to enact change based on general principles of justice, equality, and liberty. This in itself is a persuasive argument, but Hallward's attempts to defend it against the obvious objection that it is no use extolling the virtues of the nation if globalization has rendered it powerless are less convincing. Those oppressed groups who do not yet have a state of their own may indeed want one, as he remarks (*AP*, p. 131), but his next sentence contradictorily reveals that having one is actually no safeguard against dispossession by external forces.[18] In a world of multinational economies and US neo-imperialism, gaining national independence does not guarantee freedom from oppression; Glissant's later texts repeatedly argue that the non-localized 'invisibility' of the multinationals, situated nowhere and everywhere, eludes conventional resistance and requires us to find new ways of opposing them.[19] Moreover, national liberation is far more difficult to achieve in the first place in a globalized world: the Palestinians, whom Hallward cites as currently engaged in such a struggle (*AP*, pp. 128, 131), would have a far better chance of success if their enemy were solely the state of Israel and not also the supranational hegemony of the United States. And Hallward's claim that globalization has not diminished the sovereignty of 'already-powerful nations' because 'what international business has long pursued and now mainly achieved is clearly not so much an end to the state *per se* as ' "a weak nation-state in relation to capital and a strong one in relation to labour" ' (*AP*, p. 132)[20] — that is, a state that is subservient to the multinationals and oppresses its own workers — will be of little comfort to supporters of the egalitarian democratic nation that he is promoting.

---

18    *AP*, pp. 131–32: 'Having a state of one's own still seems to matter a great deal to those who don't have one. And as often as not, the cause of the eventual reversal or corruption of progressive state-sanctioned change in places such as Guatemala (1954), Chile (1970) and East Timor (1975) has been less the fault of the state *per se* than the violent intervention of another, more powerful state'.
19    See, for example, *IPD*, pp. 102–03.
20    The quotation is from Immanuel Wallerstein, 'Post-America and the Collapse of the Communisms', *Rethinking Marxism*, 51 (1992), 90–102 (p. 99).

It is this refusal to envisage any kind of progressive political action not based in the nation-state that leads Hallward to accuse late Glissant of reneging on the author's commitment to political change. Since national independence has not been realized in Martinique, the Tout-monde cannot constitute a *subsequent* stage in a dialectic whereby the national moment is surpassed in a movement onto the international plane: 'Rather than surpass a dialectical process *through* its resolution, as required in the early work, his later work simply changes criteria' (*AP*, p. 120). In other words, Glissant is guilty of just giving up on national politics, and of, opportunistically, converting a 'problem' into an 'opportunity': 'It is precisely that problem which frustrated a national reconciliation in *Malemort* which now provides the opportunity for the newly global post-national reconciliation' (p. 120). I have argued that the reasons for Glissant's shifts are anyway far more cogent and objective than Hallward can admit, but in this passage he even claims that late Glissant ends up *celebrating* dispossession: 'Glissant's critique of dispossession risks conversion into an elective affirmation of dispossession (however "positively" affected)' (p. 120). This latter is presumably the Deleuzean deterritorialization that has indeed influenced the articulation of the Tout-monde; but to define it as dispossession again reveals the limits of Hallward's position that, politically, only the collective possession of a national territory counts for anything.[21]

The question is, then, does late Glissant's view of the world really exclude political action per se? Hallward's characterization of it as a self-constituting, self-sufficient totality is entirely accurate: this late form of Relation does not relate to anything outside itself.[22] But it does not necessarily follow that it excludes conflict and opposition between its internally related elements — that it is, as Hallward also claims, 'a pre-established harmony' (*AP*, p. 123). In fact, Glissant emphasizes the equal prominence of conflict within Relation; the page of *Poétique de la Relation* from which Hallward quotes to support his assertion that 'related singularities are [...] necessarily compatible, for all express the same totality and nothing else' (*AP*, p. 124) actually starts by defining Relation as 'les retentissements des cultures, en symbiose ou en *conflit* [...] dans la *domination* ou la libération' (*PR*, p. 145, my emphasis).

The main problem that Glissant himself identifies concerns the unpredictability of globalization, which, although it can upset oppressive regimes, also problematizes planned action against them: 'Si l'imprédictibilité est la loi en matière de relations de cultures humaines entre elles, est-ce que nous n'allons pas tomber dans un pessimisme ou un nihilisme totalement ravageurs? [...] si c'est imprévisible, pourquoi

---

21    One of Hallward's main examples of Glissant converting a problem into an opportunity is the 'economy of disorder', which he misreads as the goal of the Tout-monde in general (*AP*, p. 119), but the passage of *Poétique de la Relation* that he references in support of his interpretation clearly defines it as a tactical response to the specifically Martiniquan problem of economic dependence on France: 'Être capable à tout moment de changer de vitesse et de direction sans changer pourtant de nature ni d'intention ni de volonté: peut-être était-ce là le principe optimal pour un tel système d'économie. Les changements de cap y dépendraient d'une analyse sévère du réel' (*PR*, p. 141).

22    *AP*, p. 105: '*La Totalité* become sufficient to itself, immediate to itself, one and the same as end and means'.

agir et pourquoi faire?' (*IPD*, p. 85). We can neither predict nor control the future of the world (*PR*, p. 138). But at the same time, 'La Relation n'implique ou n'autorise aucun détachement œcuménique' (*PR*, p. 45) and Glissant's answer to his own question is to develop a new conception of political action. This depends upon a distinction between two types of action, which he begins to elaborate in *Poétique de la Relation*. While 'il ne peut se développer une stratégie *généralisable* de l'action dans la Relation' (*PR*, p. 192, my emphasis), reactive interventions in *local* situations are both possible and necessary: 'C'est pourquoi une telle intervention "dans la Relation" ne peut vraiment se faire que "dans un lieu"' (*PR*, p. 192). The unpredictability of globalization precludes long-term campaigns to establish political systems or 'grands schémas idéologiques' (*IPD*, p. 132), but these in any case conflict with the values of Relation; local interventions respond immediately to particular existing situations, and so can more easily keep pace with the unpredictable changes of Relation as reality; and they do not invoke substantive ideological convictions other than a defence of human rights and opposition to deprivation and inequality.

But local action must be carried out with an 'imaginaire de la totalité' (*PR*, p. 170), a consciousness of the equality and interrelatedness of all the world's communities (*IPD*, p. 56); in defending a threatened minority language, for instance — a prominent theme in these texts — one must do it in the name of all the other minority languages in danger of disappearing, not as an identitarian battle to promote one's own particular community (*IPD*, pp. 40–41). Glissant argues eloquently that only this global consciousness of Relation can prevent local action from degenerating into sectarian violence, as happened in Rwanda and Bosnia (*IPD*, pp. 90–91). He praises the campaigns led by Nelson Mandela in South Africa and the Roma in Sarajevo: faced with white racism, the African National Congress did not assert a countervailing black identity but worked together with 'Coloureds', Indians, and whites, thus learning 'le sens de la Relation' (*PR*, p. 218). Glissant also cites long extracts from the letter written to the mayor of Sarajevo by the Roma victims of ethnic conflict, in which they proclaim their faith in 'un Sarajevo libre et pluri-ethnique' and define themselves not as Roma but as 'tous ceux qui luttent pour une démocratie pluri-ethnique' (*IPD*, p. 64).[23]

The new form of political action in the globalized world, in other words, is to combine local action with global consciousness of Relation — summed up most recently in Glissant's slogan 'Agis dans ton lieu, pense avec le monde' (*NRM*, p. 150). The importance of local action — 'Il y a des résistance concrètes qu'il faut mener. Dans le lieu où on est' (*IPD*, p. 107) — is emphasized with specific examples: Mandela and the Roma, the defence of endangered languages, and an ecological project for Martinique in which Glissant himself was actively involved. The latter is outlined in a speech given to the Association pour la sauvegarde du patrimoine martiniquais in 1989, in which Glissant campaigns for the development of the local economy, restricting imported goods, and educating people to appreciate local produce (*PR*, pp. 155–71); he returns to this project in *Traité du Tout-monde*,

---

23   See Chapter 6 for more detailed discussion of Glissant's commentary on this letter.

extending it to issues of education and social policy (*TTM*, pp. 226–33).[24] These reactive interventions are not, in fact, necessarily limited to one place; Glissant also describes the creation of the International Writers' Parliament in which he was involved in the late 1990s with Wole Soyinka, which set up a network of 'refuge towns' where writers persecuted by their governments could live (*TTM*, pp. 247–52). He is quite unequivocal on the general need to defend the oppressed in particular situations.

Overall, however, the 'global consciousness' dimension of this synthesis receives rather fuller development in his writing. In defining it as an '*imagination* of the totality' (my emphasis), Glissant stresses its creative, transformative potential: it is not merely an understanding of the present state of affairs but a vision of the force of Relation as a principle that combats the mentality of the 'root-identity'. While it remains sterile unless 'implicated' in a concrete situation ('il nous faut pourtant, non pas seulement imaginer la totalité [...] et non pas seulement approcher la Relation par un déport de la pensée, mais aussi impliquer cet imaginaire au lieu où nous vivons', *PR*, p. 212), it is also, conversely, the necessary condition for any particular action to succeed: 'aucune solution mise en acte ne saurait pourtant ignorer ni mésestimer le mouvement de cette totalité, qui est Relation' (*PR*, p. 217). All these later texts reiterate his belief that all political progress depends, beyond intervention in local situations, on the long-term development of this transformative consciousness of totality — depends, in other words, on 'changing mentalities':

> Ces combats culturels ou politiques [...] s'insèrent dans un contexte mondial tel qu'il faut, en même temps qu'on mène ce genre de combat [...] contribuer à changer la mentalité des humanités, abandonner le 'si tu n'es pas comme moi tu es mon ennemi, si tu n'es pas comme moi, je suis autorisé à te combattre'.
> (*IPD*, p. 56)

Or, in *Traité du Tout-monde*: 'Nos actions dans le monde sont frappées de stérilité si nous ne changeons pas, autant que nous y pouvons, l'imaginaire des humanités que nous constituons' (*TTM*, pp. 29–30).

This idealist position — Glissant believes that consciousness determines social existence rather than the reverse — correlates with the greater emphasis that he places on cultural oppression as distinct from economic oppression; his fundamental opposition of 'root-identity' and 'relation-identity' defines the struggle in cultural, that is identitarian, terms, and he tends to see racism rather than deprivation as the basic form of oppression:

---

24    Nick Nesbitt sees this particular project as evidence against Hallward's assertion of the apolitical nature of late Glissant: 'Were one to stop reading Glissant with *Introduction à une poétique du divers*, we could perhaps join Peter Hallward in detecting an increasing disengagement and aestheticism in Glissant's work. And yet, without returning to the violent engagement of *Discours* and *Malemort*, I think that Glissant's surprising yet convincing call to turn Martinique into a biological nation in *Traité du Tout-monde* (1997) not only recovers a political and ethical dimension seemingly lost in his later thought but is fully coherent with Glissant's life-long project of enlightenment and striving for an intersubjective totalizing consciousness of the *Tout-monde*' (*Voicing Memory: History and Subjectivity in French Caribbean Literature* (Charlottesville: University Press of Virginia, 2003), p. 184).

> Autant que jamais, des masses de Nègres sont menacées, opprimées parce qu'elles sont nègres, des Arabes parce qu'ils sont arabes, des Juifs parce qu'ils sont juifs, des Musulmans parce qu'ils sont musulmans, des Indiens parce qu'ils sont indiens, et ainsi à l'infini des diversités du monde. (*TTM*, p. 21)

To see the world as made up of cultures rather than nations not only reflects the postnational realities of globalization but also (as Hallward points out, *AP*, p. 126) privileges the cultural over the economic.[25] But this does not mean that late Glissant is apolitical; antiracist politics (which, in simple terms, defines Relation) is very different from no politics at all.

Moreover, Glissant's most recent work adopts a markedly less optimistic position on globalization: *La Cohée du Lamentin* (2005) introduces a distinction between *mondialisation*, that is, globalization in its negative form as domination by the multinationals and neo-liberalism, and 'mondialité', a new name for the Tout-monde.[26] Globalization is now seen as responsible for creating massive numbers of immigrants and refugees, whose suffering is described in *Une nouvelle région du monde* (see, for example, pp. 82–86, 122–23, 145–46), and this topic is given a very directly political form in *Quand les murs tombent* (2007), co-written with Patrick Chamoiseau, which consists of an attack on President Nicolas Sarkozy's new ministry of immigration.[27] Finally, *Mémoires des esclavages* (2007) campaigns for the creation in France of a 'national memory' of slavery that will, Glissant argues, require the French to overcome the racism that prevents them from acknowledging their historical participation in slavery and embeds this in the concrete form of a projected national centre.[28] Lack of space prevents me from discussing these recent texts in any detail, but they clearly signal Glissant's return to a more overtly militant political perspective, based now on the 'place' of France rather than Martinique, but, crucially, still on the principles of Relation, creolization, and so on, that he developed in the 1990s. And this in itself is surely evidence that these principles can form the basis for a viable new form of political action in a globalized world.

---

25    More recently, Glissant has given a more balanced formulation of the relation between the two: 'Les principales "raisons" de ces affrontements apparaissent certes de nature économique, il s'agit presque à chaque fois d'exploiter une collectivité, mais une autre dimension s'y ajoute, comme un mystère de la relation entre humanités diverses, un inexplicable état d'intolérance et du sectarisme, dont on ne conçoit pas comment résoudre l'énigme' (*NRM*, p. 205).

26    Édouard Glissant, *La Cohée du Lamentin* (Paris: Gallimard, 2005), p. 15.

27    Édouard Glissant and Patrick Chamoiseau, *Quand les murs tombent: l'identité nationale hors-la-loi?* (Paris: Galaade/ Institut du Tout-monde, 2007).

28    Édouard Glissant, *Mémoires des esclavages: la fondation d'un centre national pour la mémoire des esclavages et de leurs abolitions* (Paris: Editions Gallimard, 2007), hereafter referred to as *ME*.

CHAPTER 6

❖

# Being-in-Common and Relation: The Idea of Community in the Work of Jean-Luc Nancy and Édouard Glissant

Édouard Glissant is the foremost thinker of the French Antilles; he was born in Martinique in 1928. Jean-Luc Nancy, born near Bordeaux twelve years later in 1940, is an eminent French philosopher. Both of them are centrally concerned with the theme of living together; but the different positions from which they are writing — a postcolonial Caribbean and a European Frenchman — result, as one might expect, in different ideas of community; but there are also some striking similarities.

Nancy is working in a European context, with the long historical time-scale that this implies, in contrast to the much newer societies of the Caribbean, which were literally formed by colonialism. He also belongs to a distinctively European philosophical tradition: much of his *La Communauté désœuvrée* consists of a dialogue with Georges Bataille and Maurice Blanchot, in particular the latter's *La Communauté inavouable.*[1] In addition, he comments frequently on the work of earlier European philosophers such as Rousseau, Kant, Heidegger, and Hegel. But Glissant, too, was to a significant extent formed in this tradition, in the course of his studies in philosophy at the Sorbonne in 1946 and his reading thereafter: Hegel, in particular, is a frequent point of reference throughout his writing, as has been extensively discussed by Nick Nesbitt and Alexandre Leupin.[2] Later, he was closely involved in the work of Gilles Deleuze and Félix Guattari, who are referenced from *Le Discours antillais* onwards. Caribbean influences are of course also very present in Glissant's thought: the work of Frantz Fanon, for instance, and that of Derek Walcott and Edward Kamau Brathwaite, who provide the two epigraphs to *Poétique de la Relation*. But like most of the students from France's colonies, his intellectual formation took place in Paris, and this remains apparent throughout his career.

---

1    Jean-Luc Nancy, *La Communauté désœuvrée* [1986], 2nd edn (Paris: Christian Bourgois, 1990), henceforth referred to as *CD*; *The Inoperative Community* trans. by Peter Connor and others (Minneapolis: University of Minnesota Press, 1991). Maurice Blanchot, *La Communauté inavouable* (Paris: Éditions de Minuit, 1984).

2    See, for example, Nick Nesbitt, *Voicing Memory*, and Alexandre Leupin, *Édouard Glissant, philosophe: Héraclite et Hegel dans le Tout-Monde* (Paris: Hermann, 2016). Leupin emphasizes Glissant's immersion in the European philosophical tradition: 'la pensée de Glissant [...] se nourrit d'une anthropologie philosophique concrète dont les sources se trouvent souvent en Occident' (p. 16).

However, Glissant's attitude to European thought is far from uncritical, and his criticisms mainly revolve around its claim of universal validity — in other words, they assert the right of peoples in the rest of the world to reject the philosophical dominance of the West, and thus stem directly from his position as a postcolonial intellectual. But in so far as Nancy is arguing that the traditional European concept of community is inadequate to contemporary *European* reality, he is proposing something far less freighted with the usual European notions of the individual, historical origins, etc., and this lack of cultural specificity facilitates a comparison of his approach with that of Glissant.[3]

Nancy makes a fundamental distinction between 'l'être commun' or 'common being' and 'l'être-en-commun' or 'being-in-common'. In *La Communauté désœuvrée* he critiques the traditional Western ideal of community as common being, i.e. as a self-conscious entity, the 'œuvre' of its individual members, who 'work' to produce it and themselves as a collective identity or essence, which necessarily excludes those who do not belong to it: 'une visée de la communauté des êtres produisant par essence leur propre essence comme leur œuvre, et qui plus est produisant précisément cette essence *comme communauté*' (CD, p. 14). His argument throughout is that it is not relevant to contemporary society, and that our prevalent modern feeling that we have lost such communities does not mean that we are not still living 'in-common'. Indeed, he claims, the traditional ideal of community as common being has *always* been a nostalgic fantasy: 'Il faut soupçonner cette conscience [...] parce qu'elle semble bien accompagner l'Occident depuis ses débuts; à chaque moment de son histoire, il s'est déjà livré à la nostalgie d'une communauté plus archaïque, et disparue' (CD, p. 31).

Instead, we need to recognize that we all, simply, exist 'in common': community is not something created by individuals and added on to their individual existences; rather it is, if the term 'community' is still appropriate,[4] the basic dimension of our existences: 'La communauté n'est pas un prédicat de l'être, ou de l'existence [...] la communauté est simplement la position réelle de l'existence' (CD, p. 203).[5] This, in other words, is 'being-in-common'.

One of his terms for the relations between the 'singular beings' (rather than individuals or subjects) in this community is 'partage': ambiguously a 'sharing' and a distribution or 'spacing', which is not 'une communion, ni une appropriation d'objet, ni une reconnaissance de soi, ni même une communication comme on l'entend entre sujets'; rather, he goes on: 'ces êtres singuliers sont eux-mêmes constitués par le partage, ils sont distribués et placés ou plutôt *espacés* par le partage

3     B. C. Hutchens introduces Nancy's thought by saying that 'His core commitment is to an alternative view of community dissimilar to those normally offered today' (*Jean-Luc Nancy and the Future of Philosophy* (London: Acumen, 2002), p. 1).

4     The French term *communauté* also has the more abstract sense of 'commonality', of interests, etc.

5     Hutchens glosses this as follows, in relation to Nancy's critique of Heidegger: 'Nancy claims that the *Seinsfrage* (the question of being) must be posed in terms of the *Mitseinsfrage* (the question of being-with), in which the "betweenness" of social relations is primary. In general terms, the issue of social relations is the primary form of the ontological question itself' (*Jean-Luc Nancy and the Future of Philosophy*, p. 29).

qui les fait *autres*: autres l'un pour l'autre' (*CD*, p. 64). Or, it is a question of 'exposition': in being-in-common each one's 'self' exists only as its exposition to others (p. 207).

Glissant's *Le Discours antillais* is in many ways an excellent example of the promotion of common being that Nancy castigates. His analysis of Martiniquan society is a basically, if loosely, Marxist one; and Marxism's ideal of community as the conscious 'œuvre' of its individual members 'building' a new society is precisely the conception that Nancy is writing against. The first edition of *La Communauté désœuvrée* was published only five years later than *Le Discours antillais*, in 1986; but Nancy makes it clear from the start that he is writing against the background of the demise of communism: the communist ideal is no longer available to progressive thinkers (*CD*, pp. 11–13). But this perspective was in the 1980s perhaps more charac-teristic of Europe than of postcolonial societies.[6] In *Le Discours antillais*, in line with Marxism, the economy is the determining factor in structuring society;[7] and it is only the absence of a viable economy in Martinique that leads Glissant to propose that the political struggle for independence which is a central theme of *Le Discours* must take the form of what he calls 'cultural action' rather than strikes, for instance.

More generally, he describes how colonial alienation has resulted in a lack of solidarity and community feeling. In particular, in the case of those societies such as Martinique which were created by the transportation of slaves, the coherence of their original African societies was destroyed, and the fact that it was relatively easier for the slaves to be granted or to buy their freedom individually than to gain it through collective struggles — which were always defeated — worked against the development of any such feeling of solidarity. Thus whereas one might perhaps have thought that the anti-individualist position that Nancy is promoting could almost be taken for granted in Third-World societies, the opposite is in fact the case, at least for the colonized societies of Martinique and other Creole communities.

This lack of solidarity, Glissant argues in *Le Discours antillais*, must be consciously remedied: in Martinique, 'l'indispensable équipement du pays resterait lettre morte s'il n'était pensé d'abord par la communauté s'arrachant de son traumatisme et naissant *à sa propre conscience*' (*DA*, p. 93, my emphasis). In other words, community here will not come about as it were naturally, but has to be deliberately 'built', in exactly the sense of Nancy's 'œuvre', as opposed to the 'désœuvrée' form of being-in-common; decolonization and national independence will not be achieved without the construction of, precisely, a national identity. In his earlier *L'Intention poétique* Glissant explains how this conscious construction is particularly characteristic of Martinique:

> Qu'une conscience précède l'état (le corps, collectif, dans sa manifestation et ses patentes) qui l'assumera, c'est là une des caractéristiques de notre situation, et qui est rendue possible tant par les manques et les vicissitudes de notre histoire

6    In *La Communauté désœuvrée* Nancy writes that our general conception of community has not changed much since the Second World War, and that 'La venue au jour et à la conscience des communautés décolonisées n'a pas modifiée en profondeur cet état de choses' (p. 58); but he himself does not explore the question in any depth.

7    See Chapter 1.

[...] que par les progrès de la connaissance. Plus tardifs (plus 'construits' et plus contraints) que les autres peuples, nous ne naissons pas d'un lent travail d'agré-gation, mais littéralement dans la conscience de notre nécessité. (*IP*, p. 187)

Another relevant concept here is 'opacity', which in *Le Discours antillais* designates a way in which the colonized can protect themselves from the master, who was able to command the slaves who greatly outnumbered him only through surveillance and intelligence, in other words by seeing and understanding what they were doing. Opacity — outwitting the 'regard du maître' through the impenetrability of their presence — enabled the slaves to protect themselves to some extent against the master. Therefore, it was a tactic that operated mainly between master and slaves: neither the colonizers nor the colonized needed it in their relations within their own groups. Later, on a more abstract but equally relevant level, opacity also protected the colonized against the French policy of assimilation, that is, the instilling of 'Frenchness' in France's colonial subjects, where the capacity to resist such appropriation becomes particularly important.

This divergence between Glissant's position and that of Nancy is surely attributable to the very different situations in which they are writing: the colonized intellectual who is involved in the struggle for political independence from France, and the metropolitan French philosopher who is, certainly, sympathetic to such anticolonial struggles but for whom they are not the main focus of his thought. In his later work, however, Glissant gives up on the struggle for political independence for Martinique and instead broadens his focus to the 'whole world', the 'Tout-monde', and the world-wide impact of creolization.[8] This has the effect of bringing Glissant's and Nancy's conceptions of community much closer together, as I will discuss later in this chapter. Nevertheless, two important differences remain in the later texts: they concern *culture* and *change*.

Creolization is explicitly concerned with cultures. While Glissant extends it to the world as a whole ('*le monde se créolise*', *IPD*, p. 15), he recognizes that it originates in geographically specific areas — mainly the Caribbean, the southern states of the US, and the Indian Ocean — where it defines culturally specific Creole communities:

> Ce qui se passe dans la Caraïbe pendant trois siècles [...]: une rencontre d'éléments culturels venus d'horizons absolument divers et qui réellement se créolisent, qui réellement s'imbriquent et se confondent l'un dans l'autre pour donner quelque chose d'absolument imprévisible, d'absolument nouveau et qui est la réalité créole. (*IPD*, p.15)

*Traité du Tout-monde*, similarly, seems to recognize the privileged status of the Caribbean as regards creolization when Glissant recommends 'que la Caraïbe créole parle au monde qui se créolise' (*TTM*, p. 233). And although he stresses that his use of the term is 'contentless', describing a process rather than a particular set of characteristics ('La créolisation [...] n'a d'exemplaire que ses processus et certainement pas les 'contenus' à partir desquels ils fonctionneraient', *PR*, p. 103), it is still the case that

---

8    See Chapter 1.

the elements that interact in creolization are not 'people' but primarily cultures: the interaction takes place in 'le champ inépuisable des variations nées du contact des cultures' (*PR*, p. 69). For Glissant it is a question of cultural mixing; hence the term creolization, with its reference to Creole cultures that are fundamentally mixed (or, as he calls them, composite). The importance of culture is also due to the fact that for Glissant it is now the main arena in which political struggle can take place: 'Le culturel a rencontré le politique, et les affrontements majeurs de notre temps en sont empreints' (*TTM*, p. 247).[9]

Nancy, in contrast, presents a distinctively abstract vision of community, which corresponds to his singular beings, stripped down to the bare bones of their finite existence, and seems to exist in a social and cultural void: 'La communauté est faite de l'interruption des singularités, ou du suspens que *sont* les êtres singuliers [...] elle est simplement leur être — leur être suspendu sur sa limite' (*CD*, p. 79). Indeed, this is in a sense the whole point of his theorization. But one of its consequences is that he has little to say about culture.

One exception, however, is Nancy's text 'Eloge de la mêlée' in *Être singulier pluriel*, originally written in 1993 and dedicated to the people of Sarajevo.[10] It consists of a denunciation of ethnic cleansing and, as its title implies, a eulogistic defence of mixed cultures; as such, the term 'culture' appears frequently (albeit often enclosed in inverted commas). But Nancy does question its usefulness: 'ce mot n'identifie rien. Il se contente de court-circuiter toutes les difficultés qui se presseraient en masse si l'on essayait de dire: "peuple", "nation", "civilisation", "esprit", "personnalité"' (*ESP*, p. 177). Also, the article is not really focused on Sarajevo; apart from the first two paragraphs and the last sentence, there is just one brief reference to 'le Croate [...] le Serbe [...] le Bosniaque' (p. 172) and one to the rape of Bosnian women (p. 179). He also recognizes that ethnic cleansing requires us to engage with the conception of cultural identities, while being careful to steer clear of 'leur délire, [...] leur présomption d'être, substantiellement, des identités' (p. 173). But, in a move away from the specificity of the Bosnian situation, he affirms that *all* cultures, from classical Greece onwards, are mixed, and 'le geste de la culture est lui-même un geste de mêlée' (pp. 176–77). (This idea is of course very reminiscent of Glissant's 'créolisation', as when Nancy writes, 'Les cultures [...] se rencontrent, se mêlent, s'altèrent, se reconfigurent' (*ESP*, p. 176).) The main thrust of the article is the defining and characterizing of what he calls the 'mêlée', and explaining why he prefers this term to 'mélange' because it is an action rather than a substance; and this in itself, together with a reiteration of his constant emphasis on difference and separation alongside togetherness, tends to distance him from any substantial analysis of culture.[11] I am not suggesting that Nancy in any sense exploits the tragedy of Sarajevo in order to develop his general ideas, but his treatment of the question is extremely abstract.

9    See Chapters 1 and 5 for a fuller discussion of this.
10    Jean-Luc Nancy, *Être singulier pluriel* (Paris: Galilée, 1996), hereafter referred to as *ESP*.
11    See, for example, *ESP*, p. 180: 'Ce que nous avons en commun, c'est toujours aussi ce qui nous distingue et nous différencie. J'ai en commun avec un Français de *ne pas* être le même français que lui, et que notre "francité" ne soit nulle part, en aucune essence, en aucune figure achevée'.

Coincidentally, Glissant also refers to the siege of Sarajevo, in *Introduction à une poétique du divers*. In a passage from the chapter 'Culture et identité', he explains how the Roma people of Bosnia are organizing a conference in Sarajevo on the possibility of peace, and how they have written to the mayor of Sarajevo asking him to welcome the conference and describing their current situation to him. Right from the start, in other words, we are involved in a specific current situation and a political initiative. Moreover, the bulk of the three pages that Glissant devotes to the topic consists of quotations from the Roma's letter to the mayor, i.e. their words rather than his. The reason that the letter is relevant to Glissant's concerns is that, despite listing all the attacks and persecution to which they *as Roma* have been subject during the war, they argue passionately for the rights of all the ethnicities in the region: they are organizing the conference because 'nous croyons à un Sarajevo libre et pluri-ethnique' (*IPD*, p. 64) and go on to explain that:

> Si l'Union Romani appelle à ce congrès, ce n'est pas pour reproduire une historique distinction entre les Roma et les autres, mais au contraire parce que seule la paix rendra à tous une citoyenneté pluri-culturelle dans la diversité des cultures et l'égalité des droits. (*IPD*, p. 65).

In other words, rather than trying to defend their own specific cultural identity as Roma, their aim is to reinstate and strengthen a community based on the principles of creolization that Glissant himself is putting forward. They are an example, he comments, of '"créolisation", s'agissant de la totalité-monde' (*IPD*, p. 66); in their letter he finds 'l'idée de l'ouverture au monde, et enfin l'idée que tout ceci n'est pas contradictoire de la singularité ni de l'identité' (p. 66). Equally, he concludes, they demonstrate how one must always both engage in concrete political and social struggles in one's own 'place' and also 'ouvrir l'imaginaire de chacun sur quelque chose d'autre, qui est que nous ne changerons rien à la situation des peuples du monde [...] si nous ne changeons pas l'idée que l'identité doit être une racine unique, fixe et intolérante' (p. 66) — in other words, the Roma illustrate his slogan: 'Agis dans ton lieu, pense avec le monde'.[12]

The contrast between these two perspectives on Sarajevo is thus a very good example of the differences between Glissant's and Nancy's approaches to culture, and to community.[13] It is fair to say that Glissant is far more interested in the concrete realities of particular situations. In his view, the differences between both people and communities are more substantive, and result from their different cultures, rather than being a matter of philosophical principle as they are in Nancy's conception. Unlike Nancy, he positions himself throughout his work explicitly within a postcolonial and international perspective, and this in itself means that he is almost by definition fundamentally concerned with the phenomenon of

12   See Chapter 5.
13   They do however hold similar views on the inadequacy of conventional views of multiculturalism: in Nancy's 'Eloge de la mêlée' (*ESP*, p. 173) and Glissant in *Traité du Tout-monde* asking whether 'une théorie moderne du multiculturalisme ne permettrait-elle pas en réalité de mieux camoufler le vieux réflexe atavique, en présentant le rapport entre cultures et communautés [...] comme une juxtaposition rassurante et non comme une imprévisible (et dangereuse) créolisation' (*TTM*, p. 39).

cultural difference, because these cultures are simply so different from each other that the question can hardly be avoided; it also means, of course, that he is more 'political', in an orthodox sense, than Nancy is. It is perhaps revealing that although Nancy prefaces *Être singulier pluriel* with a long list of the conflicts and struggles that dominate the world in 1995 (when he is writing this text), his conclusion is simply to claim that they all demonstrate that our world is 'singulièrement pluriel et pluriellement singulier' (*ESP*, pp. 11–12).

Another consequence of the primacy of creolization, and hence culture, in Glissant's work of the 1990s has to do with *change*. In so far as identities are formed through contacts with different cultures — whether such contact takes the form of straightforward influence by or reaction against the other culture — the resulting identity is shaped by the particularities of the cultures involved. And since the latter are always changing, in the process of creolization, so equally are the identities.

Nancy does represent being-in-common as an endless process with no fixed end-point: the 'désœuvrée' community is that which 'n'a plus à faire [...] avec l'achèvement, mais qui rencontre l'interruption, la fragmentation, le suspens' (*CD*, p. 79). But this is a very different conception of change from the dizzying unpredictability that we find emphasized throughout *Poétique de la Relation* and *Traité du Tout-monde*: distinguishing creolization from the orthodox conception of hybridity, for instance, Glissant says, 'la créolisation nous apparaît comme le métissage sans limites, dont les éléments sont démultipliés, les résultantes imprévisibles' (*PR*, p. 46). He is fascinated by the bizarre and unexpected transitions between entirely different — sometimes politically opposed — cultures that creolization produces:

> Est-il significatif, pathétique ou dérisoire, que les étudiants chinois se soient fait massacrer devant une reproduction en carton-pâte de la statue de la Liberté? Ou que, dans une maison roumaine, les portraits détestés de Ceausescu aient été remplacés par des photos, découpées dans des magazines, des personnages de la série télévisée *Dallas*? Poser seulement la question, c'est imaginer l'inimaginable turbulence de la Relation. (*PR*, pp. 152–53)

In other words, to the extent that it is more closely implicated in particular, concrete socio-political situations, Relation is always fundamentally dynamic, 'turbulent' in a way that Nancy's being-in-common is not; expressing Glissant's constant engagement with issues of social evolution, it works on 'ensembles, dont la nature est de varier prodigieusement dans la Relation' (*PR*, p. 156).

This concept of Relation, however, is in fact the starting point for a consideration of the *similarities* between Glissant's and Nancy's conceptions of community. It occurs in *Le Discours antillais*, where the emphasis is usually on its insistence on the equality of its constituent elements, for example: 'la Relation: c'est l'implication moderne des cultures, dans [...] leur revendication "structurelle" d'une égalité sans réserve' (*DA*, p. 191). But in the texts of the 1990s — as the title of the first of these, *Poétique de la Relation*, implies — it grows far more prominent, expands its meaning, and also becomes extremely close to Nancy's being-in-common. Just as Nancy claims that 'La communauté n'est pas un prédicat de l'être, ou de l'existence [...] la communauté est simplement la position réelle de l'existence' (*CD*, p. 203), so

Relation is the condition of relatedness in which we all, in contemporary society, live and move; it is not an adjunct of individual existences, which do not pre-exist it: 'La Relation [...] ne joue pas sur des éléments premiers, séparables ou réductibles [...]. Elle ne se précède pas dans son acte, ne se suppose aucun a priori [...]. On n'entre pas d'abord en Relation, comme on serait entré en religion' (PR, p. 186).

Globalization has lessened the differences between European and Antillean society, and in so far as this phase of Glissant's thought reflects these new realities it is not surprising that many of the differences between his position and that of Nancy are greatly diminished. More specifically, an important aspect of the oppression of the colonized in Martinique, and hence of the motivation for the independence struggle, had been their isolation, from slavery onwards — 'l'esclavage comme combat sans témoin' (DA, p. 277), 'l'implacable univers muet du servage' (DA, p. 238) — and this has now given way to a new global reality in which 'nous acceptons maintenant d'écouter ensemble le cri du monde, sachant aussi que, l'écoutant, nous concevons que tous l'entendent désormais' (TTM, p. 17). Equally, Le Discours antillais's opposition of 'le Même et le Divers' had been primarily an attack on the West's assumption of its universality, whereas now 'le Divers' expands into a more powerful generative force of difference that informs the new formulation of Relation, transforming it into a global reality based on interdependence; and this brings it much closer to being-in-common. There is no longer any need to 'build' communities through an effort of will, because they are now so to speak automatically formed and re-formed in Relation.

In Relation, also, the opposition between self and other disappears: 'Pensée de soi et pensée de l'Autre y deviennent caduques dans leur dualité [...] Ce qui ici est ouvert, autant que ce là [...] L'ici-là est trame, qui ne trame pas frontières' (PR, p. 204); and this, once again, resonates with Nancy's remark in Être singulier pluriel that 'Les autres "en général" ne sont ni le Même, ni l'Autre. Ils sont les-uns-les-autres, ou les-uns-des-autres, une pluralité primordiale qui com-paraît' (ESP, pp. 89–90). As the title of this book implies, 'singular' is also 'plural'.

Equally, Relation is the opposite of a common identity; it does not assume any similarity between the 'beings' that are related in it, but respects their differences, or, in Nancy's terms, their 'spacing', their 'écarts déterminants', as the title of a chapter of Poétique de la Relation formulates it. In this chapter, Glissant distinguishes two conceptions of identity, rejecting the traditional essentialist 'identité-racine' in favour of an 'identité-relation' that emerges from the 'vécu conscient et contradictoire des contacts des cultures' and 'est donnée dans la trame chaotique de la Relation' (PR, p. 158).[14]

This binary opposition between 'identité-relation' and 'identité-racine' has significant parallels with that between the community 'désœuvrée' and the community as 'œuvre'. For Glissant, identity is actually formed through our contacts

14    For a fuller discussion of these concepts, see Chapter 1. Glissant also often refers to 'identité-relation' as 'identité-rhizome': the 'rhizome' is perhaps the concept taken from Deleuze and Guattari that he uses most extensively (see, for example, PR, p. 23). See the 'Introduction' to Deleuze and Guattari, Mille Plateaux.

with others in Relation; thus his 'identité-relation' recalls the 'exposition' of the 'communauté désœuvrée' in which each one's 'self' exists only as its exposition to others (*CD*, p. 207). In his preface to the English translation of *La Communauté désœuvrée*, Nancy expands on this:

> 'To be exposed' means to be 'posed' in exteriority, according to an exteriority, having to do with an outside *in the very intimacy* of an inside. Or again: having access [...] to the proper of *one's own existence*, only through an 'expropriation' whose exemplary reality is that of 'my' face always exposed to others, always turned towards an other and faced by him or her, never facing myself.[15]

Thus in their common rejection of the notion of the individual as the primary unit of being, their insistence that we exist first and foremost 'in common' or in Relation, and that our 'identity' (although Nancy would reject this term) is not something that develops 'inside' us to make us unique and special, but is rather the almost accidental result of our contacts with others, Nancy and Glissant are extremely similar, and both make a major and distinctive contribution to twentieth-century thought.

But one could also argue that Glissant's conception is less radical than that of Nancy. Glissant is anxious to stress that 'identité-relation' does not mean that the self is 'denatured' or 'diluted'.[16] Also, even in his later work, Glissant admits that 'composite' cultures tend, in the course of their liberation struggles, to revert to atavistic conceptions of identity (i.e. 'identité-racine') which:

> sembleraient nécessaires à toute culture pour qu'elle soit sûre d'elle-même et pour qu'elle ait l'audace et l'énergie de se dire. Elles le font en général sous la pression des nécessités de leur libération [...] qui exige l'ardente certitude d'être soi et non un autre' (*TTM*, p. 195).

But he sees this just as a necessary stage — similar perhaps to Spivak's influential concept of 'strategic essentialism' — which must not become permanent; in *Poétique de la Relation* he argues that this 'tragic' version of identity constructed in opposition to the oppressor is a limitation and that 'Le vrai travail de la décolonisation aura été d'outrepasser cette limite' (*PR*, p. 29). (Indeed, he also stresses that that for 'identité-relation' to become possible, the struggles for independence must have been successfully concluded: 'Mais [cette interdépendance] suppose absolument que les indépendances soient définies au plus près et réellement conquises ou soutenues' (*PR*, p. 157).)

'Identité-relation' is also a more substantive form of connectedness than Nancy's partially equivalent notion of the 'partage' of singular beings.[17] 'Partage' and 'singularité' imply relation — 'le singulier, c'est d'emblée *chaque* un, et donc aussi

---

15   Nancy, *The Inoperative Community*, pp. xxxvii–xxxviii. This edition does not give any indication of an original French version of the 'Foreword'.

16   See Chapter 1 for more detailed discussion of this.

17   Although some of Glissant's comments come closer to Nancy's idea that in 'partage' the singular being becomes 'other', as for instance when he writes that 'la conscience de la Relation' allows us to 'know' 'que l'Autre est en nous, qui non seulement retentit sur notre devenir mais aussi sur le gros de nos conceptions et sur le mouvement de notre sensibilité' (*PR*, p. 39).

chacun *avec* et *entre* tous les autres. Le singulier est un pluriel' (*ESP*, p. 52) — but also, and equally, *separation*: singularity 'assemble [les êtres singuliers] en tant qu'elle les espace, ils sont "liés" en tant qu'ils ne sont pas unifiés' (*ESP*, p. 53).[18] For Glissant, 'identité-relation' means that our identities are constructed solely through our contacts with others who may be very different from ourselves; they are thus more 'liés' than they are separated. Where Nancy stresses the general principle of separation, Glissant's emphasis is rather on the concrete and particular differences between people, and on how we are fundamentally and directly affected by them.

However, Glissant's later version of *opacity* does provide an equivalent to separation. Whereas in *Le Discours antillais*, as I have described, it functions purely as a tactic of resistance against the colonizer, in the later texts such as *Poétique de la Relation* (as with Relation and 'le Divers') it acquires a much broader significance: here it defines a relation with the other in general that recognizes the other's unknowability (cf. Nancy's 'étrangeté irréductible' of the other, *ESP*, p. 24), that refuses to appropriate or objectify the other, and inaugurates instead a relationship that, to borrow Nancy's formulation again, takes place at the limit between singular beings: 'le geste indéfiniment repris et indéfiniment suspendu de toucher la limite, de l'indiquer et de l'inscrire, mais sans la franchir, sans l'abolir dans la fiction d'un corps commun' (*CD*, p. 172). Some of Glissant's descriptions of opacity in his later texts echo this idea of 'touching the limit but without abolishing it', for instance:

> L'opacité, qui n'est pas l'enfermement dans une autarcie impénétrable, mais la subsistence dans une singularité non réductible. Des opacités peuvent coexister, confluer, tramant des tissus dont la véritable compréhension porterait sur la texture de cette trame et non pas sur la nature des composantes. (*PR*, p. 204).

And, finally, opacity is now seen as the only possible basis for any community; a few pages later Glissant writes: 'C'est aussi que cette même opacité anime toute communauté: ce qui nous assemblerait à jamais, nous singularisant pour toujours. Le consentement général aux opacités particulières est le plus simple équivalent de la non-barbarie' (*PR*, pp. 208–09). Thus although *Poétique de la Relation* still considers the West to be a less than enthusiastic participant in Relation, the original notion of opacity as a defensive strategy *against* the West is now replaced by the hope that it will eventually inform all human relations. Whereas on the first page of *Le Discours antillais*, Glissant wrote, referring specifically to Martinique, 'Nous réclamons le droit à l'opacité' (*DA*, p. 11), he now states, 'Nous réclamons *pour tous* le droit à l'opacité' (*PR*, p. 209, my emphasis).[19]

Another area of comparison between Glissant and Nancy concerns the critiques that both make of the interlinked notions of origin and myth. Glissant's 'identité-

---

18   cf. Hutchens: 'There is something foreign in us all, and in this respect we are each equally exposed to our shared strangeness' (*Jean-Luc Nancy and the Future of Philosophy*, p. x).

19   See Patrick Crowley, 'Edouard Glissant: Resistance and Opacity', *Romance Studies*, 24:2 (2006), 105–15, for a detailed and persuasive account of how in Glissant's later work opacity extends beyond its function as a means of anticolonial resistance to a far more general critique of Western thought: 'Glissant writes about opacity in ways that open it up to a broader cultural dimension that foregrounds the capacity of poetic languages to act as conduits of exchange in a world that has been dominated by a form of Western thought that has privileged transparency' (p. 107).

racine' — 'l'identité comme racine unique et exclusive de l'Autre' (*TTM*, p. 196) — is, as its name suggests, part of a critique of the privileging of origin that resonates closely with Nancy's thought; and both thinkers link origin with myth in very similar ways. For Nancy the fundamental myth recounts the origin of a community: he describes a scene — 'peut-être la scène essentielle de toute scène, de toute scénographie ou de toute scènerie' (*CD*, p. 112) — in which a story-teller addresses a group of people and brings them together by recounting the origin of their community, and then comments, 'Nous savons aussi, désormais, que cette scène est elle-même mythique' (*CD*, p. 113). Myth and origin, the myth of origin, are thus the foundation of the traditional conception of community that he is opposing to 'being-in-common'. At times Nancy's arguments seem to apply to all communities; at other times, more specifically to Western civilization (with which, of course, he is primarily concerned):

> L'idée du mythe concentre peut-être à elle toute seule toute la prétention de l'Occident à s'approprier sa propre origine [...] pour pouvoir s'identifier enfin, absolument, autour de sa propre profération et de sa propre naissance. L'idée du mythe présente peut-être à elle seule l'Idée même de l'Occident, dans sa représentation et dans sa pulsion permanentes d'une remontée à ses propres sources pour s'y réengendrer comme le destin même de l'humanité. (*CD*, pp. 117–18)

Glissant, in contrast, although he would certainly concur with the idea that Western civilization sees itself as representing the destiny of all humanity, makes a much clearer distinction between two types of culture: 'atavistic' cultures and 'cultures composites, c'est-à-dire [...] cultures dans lesquelles se pratique une créolisation' (*IPD*, p. 60). In other words, 'la culture atavique, c'est celle qui part du principe d'une Genèse et du principe d'une filiation' (*IPD*, p. 59); and it is only this kind of community that employs 'mythes fondateurs' whose function is 'de consacrer la présence d'une communauté sur un territoire, en rattachant par filiation légitime cette présence, ce présent à une Genèse, à une création du monde' (*IPD*, p. 62). Thus 'filiation', he argues, is the basic structure of the Old Testament, and of classical Greek epics such as the Iliad and the Odyssey (*PR*, p. 62). All of these 'mythes méditerranéens' express a community 'comme transparence naïve pour soi, opacité menaçante pour l'autre' (*PR*, p. 61), and therefore:

> Il y a donc dans le Mythe une violence cachée, qui se prend aux mailles de la filiation et qui récuse en absolu l'existence de l'Autre comme élément de relation. Il en est de même pour l'Epique, lequel singularise une communauté par rapport à l'Autre, et ne pressent l'être que comme en-soi, parce qu'il ne l'envisage jamais comme relation. (*PR*, p. 62)

Composite (i.e. Creole) cultures, conversely, are founded in historical events rather than myth, and they lack a single origin: rather than a 'genèse' they have a 'digenèse', that is to say a double or multiple origin: 'Ces cultures ne génèrent pas de Création du monde, elles ne considèrent pas le mythe fondateur d'une Genèse. Leurs commencements procèdent de ce que j'appelle une digenèse' (*TTM*, p. 195).

But Nancy's rejection of the idea that the world has a single origin is far more general, and far more radical: in *Être singulier pluriel* he writes that our contact with every other singular being is a contact with an origin, 'Tu es absolument étranger parce que le monde commence *à son tour à toi*' (*ESP*, p. 24). Thus, 'nous savons que le monde n'a pas d'autre origine que cette singulière multiplicité d'origines' (p. 27); in other words, origin is 'irréductiblement plurielle [...] l'intimité indéfiniment dépliée et démultipliée du monde' (p. 31). This is one example of the general sense in which Glissant's thought, despite its quite frequent vagueness, tends to remain in closer touch with concrete social realities, whereas that of Nancy is more purely philosophical.

To sum up, therefore, we can conclude that there are many points on which Nancy's and Glissant's conceptions of community diverge. As far as *Le Discours antillais* is concerned, indeed, they have virtually nothing in common: here, Glissant's position as a politically committed, anticolonial intellectual concerned with the situation of the French Antilles results in a view that is diametrically opposed to that of Nancy. But even in his later work, which moves beyond Martinique to the 'Tout-monde' and in which Relation and opacity are reformulated in ways that align them much more closely with Nancy's 'être-en-commun' and 'être singulier pluriel', Glissant's work retains an engagement with concrete cultural and political issues that is distinctly foreign to Nancy's radically abstract and generalizing treatment of his themes. Glissant distinguishes between types of culture and Nancy does not. Nancy stresses the separation of singular beings as part of their relatedness, whereas Glissant emphasizes the contacts between different cultures. Nancy's 'désœuvrée' community is an ever-evolving process, marked by incompletion and suspension, but it lacks the unpredictability and 'turbulence' of Glissant's world-wide creolization.

Nevertheless, the basic features of Nancy's being-in-common and Glissant's Relation as formulated in his later texts are remarkably similar. For both, the individual in the classic humanist sense is a secondary and even dubious construction: we exist primarily in common/in Relation and it is from this that our 'identities' are derived; but at the same time Nancy's 'partage' and 'exposition' work in the same way as Glissant's 'opacity' to prevent us being amalgamated into a common identity. Also, their respective presentations of myth and origin have much in common. Ultimately it is the similarities between the theorizations of these two very different thinkers, rather than the divergences, that are not only the more unexpected but also the more important.

# CHAPTER 7

❖

# Hiding from Others,
# Hiding from Oneself:
# The Obscurity of Language in the
# Work of Édouard Glissant

Opacity is one of the major concepts in Glissant's thought. It functions on several levels: psychological, in the reflexes of the colonized in the presence of the colonizer; literary, in the rejection of a simplistic naturalism; and, especially, ethical, in its promotion of a free and non-reductive relationship to the other. These different levels do not exist in isolation from each other: in the course of his article 'Poétique et inconscient', for example, Glissant juxtaposes the psychological and the ethical — and also the terms 'opacity' and 'obscurity' — in a single sentence describing the Martiniquans' reactions to the French Other: 'sa transparence mortellement proposée en modèle, d'où nous est peut-être né un *goût de l'obscur*, et pour moi comme une *nécessité*, qui est de provoquer l'*opaque*, le non-évident, de revendiquer pour chaque communauté le *droit* à l'opacité mutuellement consentie. (*DA*, p. 277, my emphasis).

Opacity, moreover, also has a linguistic dimension: not only in so far as its psychological, ethical, and literary manifestations are necessarily expressed in language that reflects their characteristics, but also because the Antilleans' situation with regard to their language creates its own obscurities. Glissant's own reputedly 'difficult' style is one manifestation among others of a collective cultural situation in which *hidden meaning*, whether in literature or the Creole folktale, or everyday speech (in both French and Creole), is the result of various different factors and takes diverse forms. Accepting his invitation to us 'd'être mes complices dans l'obscur' (*DA*, p. 276), I propose to track the evolution of these forms through *Le Discours antillais*, *Poétique de la Relation*, *Faulkner, Mississippi*, and *Mémoires des esclavages*.[1] As always when one tries to define the relationships between Glissant's texts, it is not a question of systematic coherence or clear chronological progression: there are some ideas which remain more or less the same throughout, others which occur only in the more recent texts, others which evolve significantly, and others which disappear — only to later reappear, sometimes, in different forms.

---

1   Édouard Glissant, *Faulkner, Mississippi* (Paris: Stock, 1996), hereafter referred to as *FM*.

Opacity is not only relevant to relations with others. It also plays a role within the self: the unconscious, both individual and collective, is a major factor in some of Glissant's writing, perhaps particularly in *Le Discours antillais* and *Mémoires des esclavages*. In other words, hidden meanings can either be meanings consciously hidden from others or repressed meanings, meanings that we hide from ourselves. This distinction will serve as an organizing principle throughout this chapter, but mainly in order to foreground the extent to which the two domains of the conscious and the unconscious overlap and interpenetrate.

In *Le Discours antillais* Glissant distinguishes between those colonized peoples who possess an indigenous language that is inaccessible to the colonizer, in Africa and Asia, and the Caribbean or American descendants of transported slaves who have no such language because their original indigenous languages were soon lost and replaced by Creoles, which developed as languages common to both slaves and their masters. This situation produces two different types of hidden meaning.

The first type specifically concerns the Creole language. Glissant analyzes what he calls 'les ruses du créole' in the period of slavery; that is, he claims that the slaves developed, within the common Creole language, a particular way of using it that replicated the indigenous language's function of being incomprehensible to the master:

> Ainsi le sens de la phrase est parfois comme dérobé dans ce non-sens accéléré où cahotent des sons. Mais ce non-sens charroie le sens véritable, qui est soustrait à l'oreille du maître. Le créole est à ses origines comme une sorte de pacte, secret sous la publicité de son cri [...] cette forme de non-sens qui déroberait et révélerait en même temps un sens *caché*. (*DA*, p. 239)

Later, the chapter of *Poétique de la Relation* entitled 'Lieu clos, parole ouverte' returns to the idea of the ruses of Creole in the context of the oral literature of the plantations: these stories, songs, and so on were in effect a collective act of survival for the slaves, and were characterized by using camouflage in the same way as everyday speech; this is an oral literature that '[s'efforce] d'exprimer ce qu'il est interdit de désigner', through its indirect, figurative language, 'Comme si ces textes s'efforçaient de déguiser sous le symbole, de dire en ne disant pas. C'est ce que j'ai appelé ailleurs une pratique du détour' (*PR*, p. 83). Whether through the ultra-rapid delivery of the 'cri' or the use of opaque images, the 'ruse' of Creole originated as an entirely conscious tactic, an act of survival with a clear and simple purpose: to hide the meaning from the master.

However, Glissant also argues that Creole has retained its camouflaged, clandestine character into the twentieth century, in other words in conditions in which its original purpose is no longer so relevant. At the point at which it should have developed in a more 'normal' fashion, it found itself increasingly marginalized in a new economic situation in which the plantations were largely replaced by tourism, which requires the Antilleans to speak French, and by French social security systems. As a result, Creole is subjected to 'un mode nouveau de la structuration linguistique qui serait "négative" ou "réactive", différente de la structuration "naturelle" des langues traditionnelles' (*DA*, p. 241). It has even lost its skilful manipulation of 'le détour imagé' and has not been able to replace it with a clear system of abstract concepts. Glissant concludes: 'C'est là une condition de stagnation qui fait du créole une langue dramatiquement menacée' (*DA*, p. 241). In contrast to such defenders of Creole as Patrick Chamoiseau, Raphaël Confiant, and Jean Bernabé in their *Éloge de la créolité*, Glissant — at this stage of his thought — judges that 'Prétendre que le créole a de tous temps été notre langue nationale, c'est obscurcir un peu plus, sous le triomphalisme, le lancinant questionnement où sourd notre mal-être mais où s'enracine aussi notre présence' (*DA*, p. 282).

A well-attested phenomenon among postcolonial intellectuals is the malaise that they feel towards the colonial language that they are obliged to use in their professional lives, but in which they find it difficult to express the subjective realities of their existence. This phenomenon can be found all over the postcolonial world; thus the Indian Raja Rao protests that 'One has to convey in a language that is not one's own the spirit that is one's own'; while the Nigerian Chinua Achebe asks: 'Is it right that a man should abandon his mother tongue for someone else's? It looks like a dreadful betrayal and produces a guilty feeling. But for me there is no other choice'.[2] The situation of the Antilles, however, is even more problematic. Rao and Achebe are torn between their mother tongue and the colonial language, but for contemporary Antilleans, according to Glissant, a language that could fulfil the 'maternal' role does not even exist, since Creole, which is objectively their first language, has lost its capacity to articulate all their thought and emotions. Therefore, 'la langue maternelle, le créole, et la langue officielle, le français, entretiennent chez l'Antillais un même insoupçonné tourment' (*DA*, p. 236). Moreover, the difficulty does not affect only literary or theoretical discourse, as is the case for Rao and Achebe, but also everyday speech and other forms of orality.[3]

Glissant's solution to this problem seems at first to be entirely a matter of deliberate will: a *work* that must be carried out on both languages: 'Il nous faudrait déstructurer la langue française, pour la contraindre à tant d'usages. Il nous faudra structurer la langue créole pour l'ouvrir à ces usages' (*DA*, p. 278). This is what he calls 'poétique forcée' or 'contre-poétique'. It lacks the ease that characterizes a 'natural' poetics that springs spontaneously from a culture in which one can express oneself freely; rather, 'Ce caractère contraint fait toute la force (le rêche, le dramatique) d'une telle poétique forcée' (*DA*, p. 245). 'Counter-poetics' is based

---

2    Raja Rao, 'Language and Spirit', in *The Postcolonial Studies Reader*, ed. by Bill Ashcroft, Gareth Griffiths, and Helen Tiffin (London: Routledge, 1995), pp. 296–97 (p. 296); Chinua Achebe, 'The African Writer and the English Language', in *Morning Yet on Creation Day* (London: Heineman, 1975), p. 62.

3    Roger Toumson suggests that the original African languages continue to occupy the phantasmatic position of the maternal language for Antilleans, thus relegating Creole to the status of 'pseudo-maternal language': 'Langue "première" — langue perdue — , la langue maternelle est une sorte de forme sans contenu, vide. Non attestée, elle n'a pour expression que la nostalgie. Véhicule de la communication directe, [...] cette langue est éprouvée comme ayant été "signifiant intégral" et "signifié pur". La nostalgie de l'"Africa mater", telle que la confesse les auteurs de la Négritude est, pour beaucoup, une nostalgie du paradis de cette première parole. C'est en raison du vide ainsi créé que le créole intervient en qualité de langue "pseudo-maternelle"' (*La Transgression des couleurs: littérature et langage des Antilles*, 2 vols (Paris: Éditions caribéennes, 1989), I, 79).

on the distinction that Glissant makes between *langue* and *langage*, the latter being a subjective attitude towards the *langue* as materialized in a practice of that *langue* that is particular to the community in question (*DA*, p. 236); it is thus a question of building a *langage* on the basis of an aggressive or subversive relation with the *langue* that one is nevertheless forced to use:

> Il faut frayer à travers la langue vers un langage, qui n'est peut-être pas dans la logique interne de cette langue. La poétique forcée naît de la conscience de cette opposition entre une langue dont on se sert et un langage dont on a besoin. (*DA*, p. 237).

However, this project of 'forcibly' creating a mode of expression through will-power is always to a significant extent undermined by the conflict between counter-poetics and the *langue*, with the result that counter-poetics is always structured above all by lack and impossibility: 'J'appelle poétique forcée, ou contrainte, toute tension collective vers une expression qui, se posant, s'oppose du même coup le *manque* par quoi elle devient impossible, non en tant que tension, toujours présente, mais en tant qu'expression, jamais accomplie' (*DA*, p. 236). This is why counter-poetics is also an obscure language. But in this case the obscurity does not derive from the conscious desire to hide the meaning from the other (the master), but rather from counter-poetics' inability to express the speaker's meaning easily and 'naturally'; the speaker, in other words, is unable to control his *langage* completely.[4]

Glissant also goes further. In 'Poétique et inconscient' he places greater emphasis on the *unconscious* determinations of counter-poetics. He gives a new definition of the latter: 'Cette poétique trame [...] par à-coups une sorte de non-savoir à travers quoi est tenté l'effort de nier l'avoir totalisateur et corrodant de l'Autre' (*DA*, p. 276), in which 'non-savoir' is to be understood as repressed knowledge rather than the mere absence of knowledge, since Glissant goes on to list the social and historical realities (transportation, slavery, the loss of collective memory, etc.) which he claims structure the collective unconscious of the Martiniquans (*DA*, pp. 277–78).[5] Moreover the collective unconscious in turn structures the *langage*, i.e. the counter-poetics:

> La contre-poétique [...] ne jaillit donc pas spontanément et comme innocemment du langage quotidien de communication. Elle en est à la lettre l'inconsciente cadence. C'est pourquoi je la dis une contre-poétique. Elle marque le déni instinctif, qui ne s'est pas encore organisé en refus collectif conscient. (*DA*, p. 279)[6]

4    In his novel *Malemort*, Glissant gives an eloquent illustration of the difficult beginnings of this 'neuf langage' (see, for example, p. 161).
5    Glissant explains his conception of the collective unconscious in terms reminiscent of Fanon's definition in *Peau noire, masques blancs* (pp. 120, 156), but with greater caution: 'Nous n'entreprenons pas ici une illustration du point de vue jungien, et ne défendons pas l'existence déterminante d'archétypes universels. Mais nous croyons à la répercussion des données socio-historiques non seulement sur les croyances, les mœurs, les idéologies [...], mais aussi, *dans certaines conditions*, sur la formation d'un champ de pulsions "communes" qu'on pourrait alors appeler l'inconscient d'une collectivité' (*DA*, p. 285).
6    It is interesting to note that Fanon, Glissant's Martiniquan compatriot and comrade, also

The differences between the two types of hidden meaning that arise from the transported slaves' lack of an indigenous language thus become clear. The 'ruses du créole' are conscious and pragmatic, whereas counter-poetics consists of a far more ambiguous synthesis of a conscious project and elements belonging to the collective unconscious of Antillean society. However, both are manifestations of the 'détour': an important concept throughout *Le Discours antillais,* whose principal effect is to problematize the distinction between conscious acts of resistance and compulsive, irrational reactions.[7] Thus counter-poetics as a 'déni instinctif, qui ne s'est pas encore organisé en refus collectif conscient' is absolutely typical of the detour; but Creole speech is also 'une pratique du détour' in so far as 'on ne sait jamais si ce discours, en même temps qu'il livre un signifié, ne se développe pas précisément pour en cacher un autre' (*DA,* p. 355). Moreover, the detour as a whole belongs to the domain of obscurity, because it constitutes the only possible tactic of resistance in a political situation (i.e. departmentalization and assimilation) in which domination is not obvious but 'occultée' and 'camouflée'.[8] It is thus not surprising that it results in a use of language that is also 'occulté'.[9]

The texts published after *Le Discours antillais* contain no further references to counter-poetics. The ruses of Creole do reappear in *Poétique de la Relation,* as we have seen, but now without the negative aspects that previously formed an obstacle to Creole's development outside life on the plantations where its ruses had a clear and legitimate purpose. In 'Lieu clos, parole ouverte' (*PR,* pp. 77–89) the periodization is quite different; Glissant distinguishes three stages in Creole oral/ literary production: the 'acte de survie' (Creole orality with its ruses, detours, and opaque images); then the 'leurre', elite literature modeled according to French norms; and finally 'la mémoire', written literature which takes up the stylistic features of the oral 'contes' of the first period. The degeneration of the Creole language, its deficiencies and marginalization, which would logically be contemporaneous with the period of the 'leurre', are not mentioned at all: Creole just disappears, and resurfaces only at the point at which it can be recovered and integrated into a new kind of literature that proclaims its origin in the oral culture of the plantations. This different position can to some extent be explained by the

emphasizes the role of the unconscious in what he calls 'le style des intellectuels colonisés': 'Style heurté, fortement imagé car l'image est le pont-levis qui permet aux énergies inconscientes de s'éparpiller dans les prairies environnantes. Style nerveux, animé de rythmes, de part en part habité par une vie éruptive' (Frantz Fanon, *Les Damnés de la terre* [1961], 2nd edn (Paris: Gallimard, 1991), p. 266.

7    See Chapter 5 for a fuller discussion of 'le détour'.

8    *DA,* p. 32: 'Le détour est le recours ultime d'une population dont la domination par un Autre est occultée [...] le mode de domination (l'assimilation) est le meilleur des camouflages'.

9    Carine Mardorossian compares this situation of concealed domination with Fanon's theorization of Martiniquan alienation in *Peau noire, masques blancs;* but she also stresses the distance between the solutions proposed by the two authors, and foregrounds the status of language in Glissant's work as the determining factor: 'Whereas for Fanon, of *Damnés,* the only solution to the psychological alienation experienced by the black man is violence, Glissant finds an alternative in the very workings of language and speech that he (like Fanon) identified as a symptom of the profound alienation of the Antillean' ('From Fanon to Glissant: A Martinican Genealogy', *Small Axe,* 13:2 (2009), 12–24 (p. 21).

fact that 'Lieu clos, parole ouverte' is concerned exclusively with literary language (oral or written), rather than the possible adaptation of Creole to modern daily life that was a central theme in *Le Discours antillais*. But it is also true that Creole is seen in a much more — indeed, entirely — positive light throughout all Glissant's essays of the 1990s, in which he is formulating the new concepts of the 'Tout-monde' and creolization. This passage, also from *Poétique de la Relation*, is a typical example:

> La créolisation nous apparaît comme le métissage sans limites, dont les éléments sont démultipliés, les résultantes imprévisibles. [...] Son symbole le plus évident est dans la langue créole, dont le génie est de toujours s'ouvrir, c'est-à-dire peut-être de ne se fixer que selon des systèmes de variables que nous aurons à imaginer autant qu'à définir. La créolisation emporte ainsi dans l'aventure du multilinguisme et dans l'éclatement inouï des cultures. (*PR*, p. 46)

It would seem from this that it is the new concept of creolization that has led to this re-evaluation of the Creole language. Creole is no longer marginalized, stunted, always concealing the furtive meanings that it conveys; rather, it is now endowed with all the qualities of openness, dynamism, and infinite relation that characterize creolization. More generally, the ideas of obscurity and opacity in language feature far less prominently in the texts of the 1990s, such as *Poétique de la Relation, Introduction à une poétique du divers,* and *Traité du Tout-monde*.[10]

There is however a third type of hidden meaning, discussed originally in *Le Discours antillais*, that is developed and amplified in the later texts. This occurs only in literary language, and, unlike the first two types, is motivated neither by the difficult relationship with the French language nor by the linguistic limitations of Creole. Instead, it stems from the equally tormented relationship with *history*. Antillean history, confused and partially unknown, is experienced essentially as lack; this is a constant theme in *Le Discours antillais*, where one of the consequences of slavery — that 'combat sans témoins' (*DA*, p. 278) — is that 'l'histoire n'est pas seulement pour nous une absence, c'est un vertige' (*DA*, p. 278). In 'Lieu clos, parole ouverte' this vertiginous absence is linked to the problematic identity of contemporary Antilleans:

> C'est dans les prolongements de la Plantation, dans ce qu'elle a enfanté au moment même où elle disparaissait comme entité fonctionnelle, que s'est imposée pour nous cette recherche de l'historicité, *cette conjunction de la passion de se définir et l'obsession du temps,* qui est aussi une des ambitions des littératures contemporaines. (*PR*, p. 89, my emphasis).

But this is not all. By situating this lack of history in the spatial and temporal framework of the Plantation (rather than Martinique or the Antilles) Glissant defines an enlarged but still specific geographical area: namely, that of all societies that are historically founded on plantation slavery. Elsewhere he calls it 'la Néo-América': 'elle est constituée de la Caraïbe, du nord-est du Brésil, des Guyanes et de Curaçao, du sud des États-Unis, de la côte caraïbe du Venezuela et de la Colombie, et d'une grande partie de l'Amérique centrale et du Mexique' (*IPD*, p. 13). It is

---

10   Glissant's *Faulkner, Mississippi* is an exception here.

this American-Caribbean region that is in question in the chapter 'Roman des Amériques' in *Le Discours antillais*, where Glissant claims that it has its own literature with common themes, of which the most important is this 'hantise du passé [...] il semble qu'il s'agisse de débrouiller une chronologie qui s'est embuée, quand elle n'a pas été oblitérée pour toutes sortes de raisons, en particulier coloniales' (*DA*, p. 254).

Moreover, it also has a common *langage*:

> Nous partageons ainsi un même langage. [...] Je crois que, par-delà les langues utilisées, il y a un langage du roman américain qui est fait à la fois d'une réaction de confiance aux mots, d'une manière de complicité avec le mot, d'une conception opératoire de la durée (par conséquent de la durée syntaxique) et enfin d'une liaison très tourmentée entre écriture et oralité. (*DA*, p. 256)

Based on this concept of *langage* that he has already introduced but now extends beyond the relationship to a single *langue*, Glissant posits, alongside the French, Creole, English, Spanish, etc., *langues* of the American-Caribbean region, a single *langage* adopted by all its writers to express the realities particular to their region and their common history.[11] This is an idea that often recurs in the later essays.[12] Also, the main features of this *langage* remain, with a few exceptions, constant from one essay to another. On the one hand Glissant criticizes European literary realism as inadequate to express the obscure historical realities of the American-Caribbean region. This idea already occurs in the section 'Techniques':

> Le réalisme occidental n'est pas une technique 'à plat', hors profondeur, mais le devient quand il est adopté par nos écrivains. La misère de nos pays n'est pas seulement présente, patente. Elle comporte une dimension d'histoire (d'histoire non évidente) dont le seul réalisme ne rend pas compte. (*DA*, p. 198)

Thus in 'Roman des Amériques' he rejects this realism ('le réalisme, c'est-à-dire le rapport logique et consécutif au visible, plus que partout ailleurs trahirait ici la chose signifiée', *DA*, p. 255), in favour of a style that would allow the writer to evoke phenomena that are hidden or 'souterrains'.[13] For this he chooses 'une voie allégorique' (*DA*, p. 257), a baroque style that favours indirect meanings: 'Ainsi les littératures de la Caraïbe, qu'elles soient de langue anglaise, espagnole ou française, introduisent-elles volontiers des épaisseurs et des cassures — comme autant de détours — dans la matière dont elles traitent' (*PR*, p. 85).[14]

11    *PR*, p. 231: 'Il est des communautés de langage qui outrepassent les barrières des langues'.

12    Thus in *Introduction à une poétique du divers* Glissant quotes Alejo Carpentier telling him: 'Nous autres Caraïbéens nous écrivons en quatre ou cinq langues différentes mais nous avons le même langage ' (*IPD*, p. 43); and in *Poétique de la Relation* Glissant says of himself: 'Je me sens plus proche des écrivains de la Caraïbe anglophone ou hispanophone, ou bien entendu créolophone, que de la plupart des écrivains français. [...] Nos langues diffèrent. Notre langage (à commencer par la relation aux langues) est le même' (*PR*, p. 231).

13    In fact this 'langage' characterizes not only Glissant's novels but also his essays. René Ménil, in an article on *Le Discours antillais*, describes the book's project as 'une quête de courants souterrains' which allows Glissant to 'écrire les Antilles d'une écriture rusée, grâce à quoi des zones interdites se révèlent qui n'avaient pas été dites' ('Une quête de courants souterrains', CARÉ, 10 (April 1983), 27–31 (p. 30)).

14    This conception of Caribbean-American literature resonates with René Ménil's characterization of it, as discussed in Chapter 4.

On the other hand, this *langage* is inspired by the discursive features of the Creole folktale, which itself shares the ruses and detours of the Creole language. The passage of 'Lieu clos, parole ouverte' that I have just quoted continues: 'mettant en pratique, à la manière du conte des Plantations, des procédés de redoublement, d'essoufflement, de parenthèse' (*PR*, p. 85). As well as its preference for figurative rather than literal meanings ('La symbolique des situations y prévaut sur le raffinement des réalismes', *PR*, p. 85), the obscurity stems from the way in which these texts reject linear narrative in favour of constant parentheses and a stylistic redundancy which, unlike the kind of pedagogical repetition that aims at maximum clarity, actually disorientates the reader because it is never exact but allows for a slippage of meaning across slightly different versions.

The obscurity of this literary practice is completely conscious. The writers choose to return to the techniques of their traditional oral culture in order to create a new literature that will be capable of representing their contemporary situation. In the old Creole culture of 'ruse' the purpose was to hide the meaning from the master; in the case of the American-Caribbean novel it is the reader who occupies the position of the Other who does not understand. But the reader is not an enemy; so why would the writer want to conceal from him or her the meaning of the text? Much has been written about the effect on the reader of the textual opacity that typifies American-Caribbean novels such as those of Glissant.[15] But one can assume that its basic motive is not to block the reader's access to the fictional world that is evoked, but to make us experience as directly as possible the obscurity — both phenomenological and epistemological — of this world, by immersing us in a text that, through its structure and language, is in some sense the equivalent on the literary level. One could also observe that it is sometimes less a case of an obscure language than of a language which *connotes* obscurity. Far from being an enemy, the readers are, at least are invited to become, the author's 'complices dans l'obscur' (*DA*, p. 176).[16]

Among the authors of the 'roman des Amériques', Glissant includes the great novelist of the American South, William Faulkner (*DA*, p. 258). Fifteen years later, he publishes *Faulkner, Mississippi*, in which he highlights the striking similarities between the American South and the Caribbean (*FM*, pp. 46–47, 148–49, 334)

15    As far as Glissant is concerned, see for example Daniel Aranjo, 'L'Opacité chez Édouard Glissant ou la poétique de la souche', in *Horizons d'Édouard Glissant*, ed. by Yves-Alain Favre (Pau: J & D Éditions, 1992, pp. 93–112); Crowley, 'Édouard Glissant: Resistance and Opacity'; François Noudelmann, 'La Trame et le tourbillon', in *Autour d'Édouard Glissant,* ed. by S. Hassab-Charfi and S. Zlitni-Fitouri (Bordeaux: Presses universitaires de Bordeaux, 2008), pp. 119–23; Michael Wiedorn, 'Go Slow Now: Saying the Unsayable in Glissant's Reading of Faulkner', in *American Creoles: The Francophone Caribbean and the American Souths*, ed. by Martin Munro and Celia Britton (Liverpool: Liverpool University Press, 2012), pp. 183–96.

16    It is worth noting however, that Glissant elsewhere claims the right to write without any concern for his reader, with the sole aim of analyzing the Martiniquan situation: 'il arrive que l'œuvre ne soit pas écrite *pour quelqu'un*, mais pour démonter les mécanismes complexes de la frustration et des variétés infinies de l'oppression. Exiger qu'en ce cas elle soit immédiatement préhensible revient à commettre le même écart que tant de visiteurs qui, après deux jours passées à la Martinique, prétendent expliquer aux Martiniquais les problèmes de leurs pays' (*DA*, p. 200).

and claims that Faulkner's writing is influenced by the Creole folktales that he apparently listened to as a child. In contrast to the majority of earlier English and American critics, Glissant places Faulkner emphatically within the Creole world of the plantations.[17] *Faulkner, Mississippi* is also the only one of Glissant's essays of the 1990s to discuss at length the question of hidden meaning; and it does so because Faulkner is an exemplarily obscure figure: 'La "psychologie" de Faulkner n'opère que dans l'obscur [...] C'est une variance prodigieuse sur la ligne de crête de l'innommable' (*FM*, pp. 137–38); 'Faulkner remonte au plus obscur, au "plus essentiel", là vraiment où pas un ne va' (*FM*, p. 216). He uses the same techniques of the detour — the 'parole différée', as Glissant calls it in his case — as the other authors cited in 'Roman des Amériques'. Moreover, his writing as a whole can be summed up in the paradoxical formula that is repeated almost obsessively in *Faulkner, Mississippi*: 'dire sans dire tout en disant'. This paradox is what determines the style and structure of Faulkner's novels: it is responsible for his rambling narratives, and his characters, who are not classically defined but 'en proie à la béance, à un suspens de l'être, à un non-devenir' (*FM*, p. 38). The 'parole différée', moreover, is motivated by its link with a secret: 'Indiquer et dérober un secret ou une connaissance, c'est-à-dire en différer le relèvement, ce sera une grande part du projet de Faulkner et ce sera le motif, pour l'essentiel, des modes techniques autour desquels s'organisera son écriture' (*FM*, p. 14).[18]

There is however an essential difference between Faulkner on the one hand and, on the other, writers such as Carpentier, Walcott, Frankétienne, and Glissant himself. Whereas these make a conscious choice to construct their novels in such a way as to disorientate the reader, Faulkner's writing, according to Glissant, obeys a wholly unconscious logic. The reason for this is the particular form of historical 'vertige' that he experiences, and the specific position of Faulkner as an individual within that history. Although slavery is of course the basic reality upon which the whole of American-Caribbean history is built, the latter's incompleteness is attributed in 'Roman des Amériques' to a much vaguer set of circumstances: chronology has been 'oblitérée pour toutes sortes de raisons, en particulier coloniales' (*DA*, p. 254). But for Faulkner, in Glissant's analysis, it is clear that history very specifically means slavery. And Faulkner's social position as a descendant of one of the most prominent slave-owning families of Mississippi makes it impossible for him to speak openly about it, out of loyalty to his social class; but at the same time, a repressed feeling of guilt for the ancestral crime propels him to evoke it constantly in indirect, veiled ways: 'Faulkner ne le dit jamais (le criant si souvent, obscurément), parce qu'il souffre dans sa chair (dans son Sud) de le penser vraiment' (*FM*, p. 18).[19]

This means, therefore, that Faulkner's writing exhibits the same compulsive, constrained quality as the earlier notion of counter-poetics: Faulkner cannot completely control his discourse. It also shares with counter-poetics the idea of

17    For example, in 'Roman des Amériques': 'L'enracinement de Faulkner dans le *deep South* l'arrache à ce rêve d'européanité' (*DA*, p. 258).
18    See Chapter 11 for further discussion of this.
19    See Michael Wiedorn: 'For Glissant, slavery becomes the unsayable, the unspeakable, in Faulkner's novels' ('Go Slow Now', p. 188).

lack, in this case the lack of historical legitimacy following the defeat of the South in the Civil War, of which Glissant writes, 'L'œuvre de Faulkner est tout entière greffée sur ce manque, qu'il ne faudra pourtant jamais déclarer. Voilà par où se joue et s'accumule le différé: dire le manque sans le proclamer' (*FM*, p. 35). Unlike counter-poetics, however, these features do not stem from tensions between *langue* and *langage*: the contradiction and the lack of Faulkner's 'dire sans dire tout en disant' are entirely the result of the history in which he finds himself unavoidably implicated. The role of the unconscious is also more precise than it was in the case of counter-poetics, since here it explicitly involves a repressed semantic content: a meaning that one hides from oneself.

Glissant emphasizes several times that the textual effects of the 'dire sans dire' are what gives Faulkner's work — for which he has the greatest admiration — its literary value. He will later write, in *Mémoires d'esclavage*, that Faulkner has 'inventé de fond en comble une nouvelle littérature et une nouvelle technique de l'écriture et un style nouveau, qui sont bien de *dire sans dire tout en disant*' (*ME*, p. 61). In *Faulkner, Mississippi* he claims that Faulkner has thus influenced a large number of other writers (*FM*, pp. 344–45); and in an interview given in 2005 he goes as far as to state, somewhat contradictorily, that the specific techniques common to the 'roman des Amériques', which he had previously explained by the socio-historical realities of the region, are due simply to Faulkner's influence:

> Un Alejo Carpentier (Cuba), qui écrit en espagnol, un Wilson Harris (Guyana), qui, lui, écrit en anglais, un Aimé Césaire (Martinique) ou moi-même, qui écrivons en français, avons un langage commun qui est fait de confiance dans les mots, dans le pouvoir du verbe, dans les techniques d'écriture que *nous avons empruntées essentiellement à Faulkner*: accumulation, listage, redondances, entassements, révélations différées.[20]

In so far as this influence has actually played a role, it would seem that something which in Faulkner's writing results from unconscious pressures has been taken up and exploited on a completely conscious level by other writers of the Caribbean-American region.

The definition of slavery as that which 'se dit sans se dire' reappears in *Mémoires des esclavages*, and the book makes several references to Faulkner. But it generalizes the definition beyond him, and beyond literature, and even beyond the American-Caribbean region, including also slavery in the islands of the Indian Ocean. As its title implies, there are several different memories of slavery: Glissant constructs a typology which distinguishes between the memories of the individual, of the tribe, and of the world community; and these can all be either conscious or unconscious. And just as he had previously associated Faulkner with the 'roman des Amériques' alongside writers who were descended from slaves, here he is concerned with the memories of the French as much as those of their former colonial subjects. But while he analyzes the differences between them, he insists that for everyone the memory of slavery is traumatic, for reasons of guilt and/or shame, and is therefore

20   Tirthankar Chanda, 'La "créolisation" culturelle du monde, entretien avec Édouard Glissant', *Label France*, 38 (2000), 38–39 (p. 39, my emphasis).

to some extent repressed. Whoever is implicated in slavery, even from a distance of several generations, is incapable of remembering it in a 'natural' or 'neutral' way: our memory will necessarily be in the mode of the 'dire-sans-dire': '*Nous avons à nous dire tout esclavage, parce que nous essayons d'être lucides et d'être participants, sans nous le dire pourtant, parce que dans tous les cas nous en avons honte [...] et le disant quand même, parce que nous tenons au sens du temps et à la signification des histoires des peuples*' (*ME*, pp. 63–64).

There is very little on language in *Mémoires des esclavages*: it is memory and history that, even more than in connection with the 'roman des Amériques', are most central.[21] One could therefore argue that here we are dealing not with a hidden meaning but with a hidden history: 'c'est ce qu'on appellerait une histoire *cachée*, ou une histoire *qui se dit sans se dire tout en disant*' (*ME*, p. 56). But the elements that are hidden or repressed are not limited to simple facts: they always have a meaning, otherwise they would not be repressed. Moreover Glissant asks whether they have not perhaps left their mark on language: 'Dans les divers pays de la néo-América, la mémoire inconsciente du temps de l'esclavage a-t-elle passé dans les langages, dans quelles proportions et selon quels procédés secrets ou généralisés de transfert?' (*ME*, p. 148). In the Lacanian perspective of Dominique Chancé, the censorship of transportation and slavery requires that 'la quête politique passe par la quête de signifiants inconscients, et c'est en plongeant au cœur du langage [...] que les personnages et les auteurs mènent leur quête de sujet'.[22] She is talking here about Glissant's novels, but this observation applies with equal validity to *Mémoires des esclavages*.

If memory is to a large extent buried in the unconscious, it follows that the *madman* — the psychotic, who by definition does not repress anything — should have privileged access to it; and indeed Glissant calls madmen the 'maîtres du souvenir éperdu', and says of their delirium 'nous savons qu'il s'agit là de la recherche d'une vérité qu'ils détiennent, ils ont connu les esclavages et ils les expriment pour nous' (*ME*, p. 68). Here he is referring to his analysis of 'délire verbal' in *Le Discours antillais*, where it is treated as a variant of counter-poetics.[23]

In this way Glissant, as he so often does, recycles in *Mémoires des esclavages* several themes of his earlier essays that have already been discussed here. The stylistic techniques of the Creole folktale, for example, are now seen not as a way of obscuring meaning, but as combatting repression and rediscovering memory: 'la répétition et l'accumulation sont pour nous une forme inlassable de la connaissance' (*ME*, p. 83). Above all, the notion of the fundamental unity of the American-Caribbean region acquires a new importance in the context of the 'histoires transversales', which play a major role in the effort to overcome the problems of collective memory (and which also 'se disent sans se dire tout en se disant') (*ME*, p. 60). Glissant seeks to join

21   'Le lieu commun de tant de troubles et de contradictions non encore résolues restera dans tous les cas la mémoire, ses exigences diverses, ses distorsions ou ses manques et parfois ses maladies' (*ME*, p. 27).

22   Dominique Chancé, *L'Auteur en souffrance* (Paris: Presses universitaires françaises, 2000), p. 151.

23   *DA*, p. 242: 'Le délire verbal [...] est un des plus fréquents avatars de la contre-poétique mise en acte par le créole'.

up the histories — which until now, he argues, have been disconnected, unknown to each other — of the different countries that suffered from slavery and still suffer today from its after-effects on collective memory. We must reveal their common evolution and re-establish the continuity of their 'histoires transversales'; the normal tendency to treat them in isolation has meant that 'elles sont demeurées opaques et indistinctes', because their assumed separation is in fact quite illusory, 'alors que par exemple les mêmes bateaux négriers desservaient tour à tour les ports de la Caraïbe, des Carolines et des Virginies, et parfois même poursuivaient au Brésil' (*ME*, p. 147). The collective realization of the unity of the American-Caribbean region thus becomes extremely significant in the context of memory. Equally, the restoring of relations between the countries concerned demonstrates the liberating force of Glissant's Relation on a more general level: Relation can overcome ideological obliteration.

Whereas in Faulkner's case it is only the personal unconscious that is relevant, in *Mémoires des esclavages* it is also, and particularly, the collective unconscious. Glissant has already used this concept in *Le Discours antillais,* where he stresses that it is determined by social history.[24] This amounts to claiming that the collective unconscious is a wholly ideological phenomenon, in other words an integral part of the system of ideological oppression as a whole. It is therefore easy to see that it could collaborate with other ideological pressures in censoring the historical reality of slavery. However, the collective unconscious is in principle more difficult to distinguish from mere ignorance than is the individual unconscious; and education obviously plays an important role in the attempt to fill in the gaps in the memories of slavery. The project of restoring the 'histoires transversales' would seem to necessarily involve the acquisition of new knowledge. Nevertheless, Glissant insists on the limits of this approach, arguing that memory is 'difficilement améliorable par le moyen d'un enseignement: on apprend à se souvenir, mais on n'apprend pas à *se souvenir autrement* [...] du moins pas par les seules méthodes pédagogiques' (*MF*, p. 162).[25] We must, of course, remedy the deficiencies in our knowledge through 'objective' historical education, but we must also, at the same time, undertake a work of self-analysis on both the individual and the collective levels. The phenomenon of slavery will never be fully understood 'par les seules méthodes de la pensée objective', and these must be supplemented by a sustained effort to overcome our subjective rejection of the past — an effort in which 'le *risque* de la compréhension (ne serait-ce que par les excès d'une subjectivité trop partisane) engage, et force à affronter l'obscur et le différé' (*ME*, p. 42). Here, for the first time in all the texts that I have discussed, Glissant accords a central place in his analysis to the process — necessary and, above all, possible — of discovering and illuminating the meanings that we hide from ourselves.

The notion of hidden meaning thus takes on several different forms in the course

---

24   See *DA*, pp. 279, 285, already quoted above.
25   He also suggests that the inadequacies of the official school syllabus may be motivated by the unconscious: if history and geography are badly taught in France, it is perhaps 'parce que ces matières engagent trop à fond les inconscients collectifs' (*ME*, p. 126).

of Glissant's work. Some of these are the result of strictly linguistic phenomena — the conflictual coexistence of the French and Creole languages, the absence of an indigenous language — or else of a combination of historical, cultural, and linguistic factors, as in the case of counter-poetics. Others, however, stem rather from the specific realities of the American–Caribbean region, where the main issue is slavery. Moreover, within these forms and in their relations with one another, a complex dynamic is played out between the conscious level and that of unconscious compulsion: so, for example, when slavery is no longer a present reality, deliberate dissimulation is replaced by repression. Hiding from the other, hiding from oneself. But these different types of hidden meaning ultimately have one extremely important thing in common: they are all the result of the particular, and particularly obscure, conditions of plantation slavery and its social and cultural consequences.

# CHAPTER 8

❖

# Social Hierarchies in the
# Short Stories of Joseph Zobel

The position of Joseph Zobel in Martiniquan literature is an unusual combination of admiration and critical neglect. He produced a substantial literary corpus: four novels, five collections of short stories, and four volumes of poetry. By far the best known of these is the novel *La Rue Cases-Nègres*,[1] which is universally regarded as a classic of French Caribbean literature and taught in schools throughout Martinique; first published in 1950, it has been reprinted many times and translated into English, German, Italian, and Dutch.[2] In 1983 it was made into a film, directed by Euzhan Palcy, which received seventeen international awards. In its evocation of the everyday lives of the 'petit peuple' of Martinique, *La Rue Cases-Nègres* is seen as the founding text of the Martiniquan novel (far more so than René Maran's much earlier *Batouala*, published in 1921).[3]

But there is very little critical discussion of Zobel's work. Régis Antoine's *La Littérature franco-antillaise*, for instance, one of the standard reference works in the field, contains only three brief mentions of him;[4] and even Patrick Chamoiseau and Raphaël Confiant, who are perhaps his most direct descendants in terms of his influence on their own fiction, devote only eight pages to him in their *Lettres créoles* (pp. 142–49). There are a few examples of more specialized work on him, most of which are devoted to *La Rue Cases-Nègres*.[5] Zobel has some connections with the much-discussed Negritude movement (Césaire was the first to encourage him to write, and Zobel records his enthusiasm for the movement in 'Nardal', in *Et si la mer n'était pas bleue*); but his writing is entirely different from the Negritude authors: his social realism contrasts with their surrealism, their promotion of 'le merveilleux' and of primitivism, their view of Africa as the spiritual home of all

1    Joseph Zobel, *La Rue Cases-Nègres* (Paris: J. Froissart, 1950).
2    For the publication history of *La Rue Cases-Nègres*, see <http://www.worldcat.org/title/black-shack-alley-la-rue-cases-negres> [accessed November 2016].
3    René Maran, *Batouala, véritable roman nègre* (Paris: Albin Michel, 1921).
4    Régis Antoine, *La Littérature franco-antillaise: Haïti, Guadeloupe et Martinique* (Paris: Karthala, 1992), pp.185, 352, 357.
5    See for example Hal Wylie, 'Joseph Zobel's Use of Negritude and Social Realism', *World Literature Today*, 56.1 (Winter 1982), 61–64; Eileen Julien, 'La Métamorphose du réel dans *La Rue Cases-Nègres*', *The French Review*, 60.6 (May 1987), 781–87; Sylvie Kandé, 'Renunciation and Victory in *Black Shack Alley*', *Research in African Literatures*, 25.2 (Summer 1994), 33–50.

black people, and their interest in ethnography. One can of course only speculate on the reasons for academic critics' neglect of Zobel's writing. It may just be seen as too simple to provide a fruitful object of literary analysis; it is true that it lacks the intellectual sophistication and stylistic complexity of some other Antillean writers. But, in its low-key and unpretentious way, it certainly does not lack subtlety, or indeed complexity, as I hope to show in the following discussion.

Zobel is a skilled practitioner of the short story form, and I shall refer here to three of his collections: *Laghia de la mort* (1946); *Le Soleil partagé* (1964); and *Et si la mer n'était pas bleue* (1982).[6] Over this thirty-six year period, the dominant focus is always on village life in Martinique, and draws heavily on the author's own experiences (the village in question is often named as Petit-Bourg, where Zobel himself was born). But we also notice two important changes as his work develops over time. The first is a question of tonality: strong emotions and drama gradually give way to a more subdued pathos, irony, and humour.

The second change, which forms my subject matter in this essay, is an increasingly complex representation of the social hierarchies that structure village life.[7] Zobel shows how these hierarchies are organized along a number of different parameters. The most obvious of these are wealth and skin colour (not simply black versus white but all the carefully categorized shades in between — women are often even named accordingly: 'Mamzelle Chabine, Mamzelle Capresse, Mamzelle Coolie', *SP*, p. 95). Then there is the type of employment of the individual concerned (which confers differing degrees of respectability as well as wealth), from the plantation workers at the bottom, through domestic servants to shopkeepers and tradesmen, and then the local bourgeoisie. Education is another important parameter, as is speaking French rather than Creole, and the indices of respectability constituted by church attendance and marriage. Experience of the wider world beyond the village also confers prestige. These parameters are not all accorded the same importance by everyone: some people attach more importance to wealth than to skin colour, or vice versa. More importantly, their plurality creates the possibility of contradictions between them: some individuals 'score' highly in terms of educational success but not in family wealth, for instance; and it is above all this plurality that determines the complexity of these communities.

In *Laghia de la mort*, however, the interplay of such hierarchical structures is not very prominent. 'Il était un petit navire' shows a prostitute selecting her clients according to their rank in the army; and in 'Le Premier Convoi' Ferdinise is attracted to Isidore because he is a fisherman and so better off than the plantation workers — he tells her: 'Tu sais, je faisais la pêche avant la mobilisation. Je gagnais de l'argent ... Dans mon village, on m'aime tellement!' (*LM*, p. 41). (Fishermen traditionally have

6    Joseph Zobel, *Laghia de la mort* [1946], 2nd edn (Paris & Dakar: Présence africaine, 1978), hereafter referred to as *LM*; *Le Soleil partagé* (Paris & Dakar: Présence africaine, 1964), hereafter referred to as *SP*; and *Et si la mer n'était pas bleue* (Paris: Éditions caribéennes, 1982), hereafter referred to as *ES*.

7    Louise Hardwick comments that *La Rue Cases-Nègres* also 'offers a subtle economic critique of social class in the Antilles' in her *Childhood, Autobiography and the Francophone Caribbean* (Liverpool: Liverpool University Press, 2013), p. 127.

SOCIAL HIERARCHIES IN JOSEPH ZOBEL    91

more prestige than plantation workers because they are self-employed.) But most of the stories in this collection are concerned solely with the poor black inhabitants. The first one, 'Laghia de la mort', narrates a 'laghia', or ceremonial fight-dance: Régis Antoine describes it as a 'petit chef-d'œuvre' in which 'une intrigue désolante se dévoilait peu à peu, un drame œdipéen se jouant à l'occasion d'une danse de lutte entre un père et un fils non reconnu'.[8] The second, 'Défense de danser', set in the village's Christmas party at which a woman's ex-lover tries to force her to return to him, is equally dramatic and also depicts solely working-class life; in 'Coup de nuit', Léonal wins a card game with strangers and suspects that they will come after him and attack him: his fear, as he tries drunkenly to find his way along unfamiliar mountain paths in the darkness, is powerfully evoked. The remaining two stories, 'Le Syllabaire' and 'Mapiam', are both narrated by boys who suffer at school because of their black skin and poverty; later, in *Le Soleil partagé* and, especially, *Et si la mer n'était pas bleue*, Zobel will return to the topic of school but treat it in a far more nuanced way.

*Laghia de la mort* was written when Zobel was still young; the stories were first published separately in the local newspaper *Le Sportif* before appearing in book form in 1946, just before Zobel left Martinique for France where, apart from working as a civil servant in Dakar from 1957 to 1974, he lived until his death in 2006. The two later collections, *Le Soleil partagé* and *Et si la mer n'était pas bleue*, were thus written from a greater distance, both in time and in space; and it is perhaps this that explains their relatively more detached perspective. Also, not all these stories take place in Martinique; several are set in France and one in Senegal. But the Martiniquan ones also differ from those in *Laghia de la mort* in that they show a greater variety of social types and give a more detailed representation of the hierarchies: i.e. not simply black plantation workers versus the *béké* or mulatto bourgeoisie. They are also more analytical, but not in the sense that Zobel explains the meanings behind events, or comments in abstract terms on the society he is evoking. It is just that the events and characters themselves reveal the workings of a community that, although very small, is unexpectedly complex and in which status is very important, and is expressed in often subtle ways.

'Et si la mer n'était pas bleue', for instance (the first story in the collection of the same name), starts by introducing the relationship between the boy narrator's mother and her distant relative Tante Oberline, who is a dressmaker, and so relatively well-off ('Naturellement, sa maison était plus grande et plus belle que la nôtre', *ES*, p. 13). Tante Oberline comes to the mother's house to ask that the boy accompany her on a journey to Anse Mitan, by the sea. The mother is clearly not in a position to refuse Tante Oberline; they do not have a close relationship, but 'c'était ma mère qu'elle faisait appeler de temps en temps pour lui rendre quelques services' (p. 12). These 'services' usually take the form of tidying up Oberline's workroom, then asking 'Y-a-t-il quelque chose d'autre à faire pour vous?' (p. 13) and being sent out to do some shopping. The journey to Anse Mitan is undertaken so that Tante Oberline can visit Mamzelle Vital, whom the boy imagines as a school teacher or

---

8    Antoine, *La Littérature franco-antillaise*, p. 357.

a postmistress: 'Certainement une personne qui portait chapeau et non madras; qui ne marchait pas nu-pieds et parlait français' (p. 16). In fact, she turns out to be a client of Tante Oberline; and what is significant here is that the latter performs for her the same kind of 'petits services' that she herself expects from the boy's mother, saying to her, 'Laissez donc ça; je le ferai puisque je suis là' (p. 21). In other words, the relationship of subservience between the mother and Oberline is exactly the same as that between Oberline and Mamzelle Vital, but now with Oberline in the subordinate position: a hierarchy of three positions rather than two.

A similar three-level structure is observable in 'Joséphine', in *Le Soleil partagé*, where the narrator is again an unnamed boy. Joséphine's black mother wages a campaign to get her daughter married off to a young middle-class mulatto, Samuel; this involves, among other things, preparing a big party, and the boy's mother is asked to do the cooking. While this is an index of her inferiority to Joséphine's family, the fact that she can cook at this standard is also a mark of status insofar as it signals that rather than just a plantation worker she has been a domestic servant to a white family: 'Ma mère avait, en effet, une réputation de fine cuisinière. Elle avait servi chez les Blancs lorsqu'elle était jeune — situation très appréciable pour une négresse des plantations' (*SP*, p. 113). Being asked to cook the dinner, therefore, allows her to demonstrate her superior status in relation to the other village women: 'Avec son tablier blanc, elle se donnait un air plus digne, émergeant de sa condition de négresse des plantations pour vivre, l'espace de quelques heures, sa vocation de cuisinière [...] elle était pour ainsi dire en train de prouver sa supériorité sur toutes les femmes du bourg' (p. 117).

'Le Phonographe', also in *Le Soleil partagé*, similarly demonstrates the complication of an initial dual opposition by a third, intermediate, character. The first gramophone in the village is owned by the very middle-class Madame Deleuze, 'la femme du notaire', and is greatly admired by the whole village. But she acquires a rival in the shape of the working-class Odilbert Faustin, who on his return from the navy brings back another gramophone, with more records and better music (in the eyes of the village) than those of Madame Deleuze. The two owners of these prestigious objects have been able to acquire them for very different reasons: for Madame Deleuze, it epitomizes her social status and her cultural interests; whereas Odilbert is not only working-class, but has been the black sheep of the family until he joined the navy. This, however, allows him to travel — which endows both him and his family with a different sort of prestige: 'Les Faustin parlaient de croiseurs, de porte-avions, d'avisos, de ports dont les noms enchantaient l'imagination [...] la famille Faustin était vue par chacun en filigrane sur un fond de pays inconnus, lointains, merveilleux; ce qui, dans le bourg, en faisait des êtres à part' (*SP*, p. 146).

However, the triumph of the Faustin family in relation to the gramophone does not last long. To capitalize on it they organize, with great effort, a party to which all the village are invited, to dance to the gramophone, but the noise of the dancing is so loud that the music cannot be heard, and the father is reduced to going out to find the usual village accordionist to play for them instead; they have thus lost face far more than Madame Deleuze has, and the story ends on a note of comic anticlimax — thus contrasting markedly with the tone of *Laghia de la mort*.

Other stories deal with more serious issues and provide a broader perspective on the factors that determine the hierarchies. They show a society hovering between the traditional African-derived belief in sorcery and magic, and the influence of France, especially of the Catholic Church.[9] Thus in 'Joséphine', for instance, when the boy and his mother move house their new neighbours are friendly, but know not to help them with their furniture because 'nous ne les connaissions pas encore et qu'ils étaient par conséquent suspects de nous jeter un sort en y touchant' (*SP*, p. 89). Also, Joséphine's mother, although she goes to church, is suspected of being a 'sorcière': 'Malgré les preuves qu'elle pouvait fournir de dévotion, elle passait pour être un peu sorcière. D'ailleurs, elle ne s'en défendait point, ne fût-ce peut-être que pour bénéficier de la crainte et du respect attachés à une telle réputation' (p. 114). In other words, she is happy to combine the respectability associated with her church attendance with the very different kind of respect accorded to her as a witch. Elsewhere in the story, however, we see both her and her daughter trying to identify with French culture: in order to appeal to the bourgeois mulatto Samuel whom her mother is trying to persuade to marry her, Joséphine has a new dress made according to the latest French fashion, powders her face, and wears lipstick, and instead of her usual braids straightens her hair 'à coups de brosse et à grand renfort de vaseline' (p. 116). Equally, attendance at church is not always primarily proof of Catholic devotion: for Joséphine it is above all an occasion to impress the neighbours by dressing up, and to be seen by more upper-class people:

> Aller à la messe, c'était pour elle partir à la conquête de la petite église bourrée de tout ce que le village comptait de notables, d'élégantes, de beaux jeunes gens; et chaque robe neuve qu'elle arborait devait produire l'effet d'une arme nouvelle. (*SP*, p. 103)

But, as the ironic tone of these descriptions implies, Joséphine in fact makes herself look ridiculous; and the village is divided into those who admire her and those, like the narrator, who laugh at her (p. 105). Everyone, however, even the more genuinely devout, makes an effort to appear clean and well-dressed at church. A more sympathetic example of this occurs in 'Le Syllabaire' in *Laghia de la mort*, where poor people who have walked from the plantations into town are shown washing and changing their clothes before attending mass (*LM*, p. 74), and the narrator's mother tidies herself up and is touchingly proud of the result: 'Elle se sentit vraiment irréprochable: pauvre négresse, mais propre comme depuis son jeune âge sa mère [... ] lui a appris qu'une femme, fût-elle noire, pauvre et malheureuse, doit être' (p. 76).

Perhaps the most important aspect of the influence of the Church is its promotion of marriage; and marriage is, particularly, but not solely, for women, a major parameter of social status. Most of the plantation workers are not married; when the narrator realizes that Joséphine is — like 'une fille de bonne famille' (*SP*, p. 110)

---

9    The opening sentence of 'Le Cadeau', for instance, asserts the general belief in sorcery: 'Tant de choses se passaient que les grande personnes, les vieilles femmes, les vieillards, les portaient au compte de la sorcellerie, et nullement pour faire peur aux enfants que nous étions! Il y avait certainement des sorciers, des vrais' (*SP*, p. 126).

— aiming to marry Samuel, he comments: 'Autrement dit, au lieu d'aller un beau jour habiter ensemble dans une case, comme presque tous ceux qui travaillaient aux plantations ou à l'Usine, ils seraient les héros d'une cérémonie qui réunirait des hommes vêtus de noir, des femmes en robe de soie' (*SP*, p. 110).

The most developed example of the conjunction of Catholicism and marriage is to be found in 'Le Retour de Mamzelle Annette', in *Et si la mer n'était pas bleue*, which is set against the background of the visit, several years earlier, of 'la Mission', i.e. two French missionaries who came to the village to baptize the inhabitants, give religious instruction, and, above all, to persuade them to get married. Here, the parameters of the Church, Frenchness, and marriage come together very explicitly:

> Eux, les deux missionnaires, étaient spécialement venus de France (c'était un peu comme s'ils avaient été envoyés par Dieu lui-même) pour donner la première communion et marier tous ceux qui étaient dans le péché, et pour baptiser les pauvres enfants qui étaient nés du péché. (*ES*, p. 55)

But — and here again we can see the ambivalence of the hierarchies — they were not universally welcomed, being seen by some as a humiliating reminder of colonialism: 'tel et tel se demandaient si, en réalité, la Mission n'était pas une entreprise de charité qui, tout compte fait, ne pouvait qu'humilier les pauvres nègres' (*ES*, p. 56). However, they succeeded in getting almost everyone to marry. Moreover, this is seen as a victory for women: in other words, marriage also has an effect on the balance of power between genders: 'C'était alors une grande victoire des femmes sur les hommes lesquels, n'eût été la Mission, n'auraient jamais pris la décision de faire "bénir leur commerce"' (p. 57).

The text continues, however: 'Mais Mamzelle Annette était la seule qui n'eût pas remporté la victoire' (*ES*, p. 58). That is, there is just one man who refuses to marry the woman he has lived with for years: this is Ernest, the barber, who is a mulatto. Here we see how the prestige of marriage is also tied up with, and can be negated by, skin colour. Annette's friends tell her, 'C'est parce que tu es une négresse noire et qu'il est un mulâtre qu'il ne veut pas t'épouser' (p. 58).[10] The narrator's black parents quarrel about Ernest's decision, with the father criticizing him for refusing to marry a black woman, and then saying that he cannot understand why a black woman would want to marry a mulatto anyway, to which the mother responds, 'Si tu étais une femme tu serais bien fière de faire pour un mulâtre, un enfant qui n'ait pas les cheveux crépus. Tu sais qu'il n'y a rien qu'une négresse aime tant qu'un homme et un enfant à cheveux soyeux!' (p. 39), and concluding, illogically, 'Et bien, pendant que tu y es, dis simplement que tu regrettes de m'avoir épousée' (p. 39).

For Ernest, the respectability accorded by marriage, which would conform to his already respectable status as a barber, would be outweighed by the shame of marrying a black woman: skin colour so to speak trumps the Church. The converse

---

10  In a further twist, Annette decides she cannot bear the shame of being the only unmarried woman in the village, and leaves Ernest to go to the town and get a job as a servant to white people; she thus raises her status and takes her revenge on him: 'ainsi, elle avait quand même remporté la victoire, et Monsieur Ernest était resté sans femme' (*ES*, p. 59).

is also true, especially for women, that is, the shame of living in sin is negated if the male partner is white or mulatto.[11] Thus Mamzelle Charlotte, the dressmaker in 'Joséphine', gives herself airs (refusing, for example, to let her daughter speak 'patois', *SP*, p.101) because of her white lover: 'Elle était [...] trop "aristocrate"; elle faisait accroire, du seul fait qu'elle était entretenue par un petit Blanc qui gérait une plantation des environs' (p. 101). Joséphine herself is presumably the product of such a union: she is lighter-skinned than her mother, and we do not know who her father was. She and her mother fail in their attempt to get her married to a mulatto. But the end of the story shows them celebrating another kind of victory: Joséphine has a baby and her mother is sure that Samuel is the father. The text ends with her saying: 'Voyez un peu derrière sa tête. Héhéhé! C'est Samuel tout craché! ... Et la bouche! Dites-moi un peu si ce n'est pas la bouche de Samuel! Hihihi' (p. 122). In other words, Joséphine may have failed by the marriage criterion but she has won by that of having the child of a mulatto. Thus the various different parameters of Catholicism, marriage, skin colour, and the status of women in relation to men intertwine to produce a variety of outcomes.

A rather different type of inequality is that between children and adults; and the effect of having so many of the stories told through the eyes of children, i.e. by disempowered narrators, is to accentuate the reader's perception of social hierarchies in general. Childhood is far from an idyllic state in the village. Children are expected to be obedient to their elders — not only their parents, but all the adults in the village — and to run errands and do other odd jobs for them: 'Être serviable faisait partie des premiers devoirs des enfants envers les grandes personnes' (*ES*, p. 42). In 'Le Cadeau', for instance, the central theme is the relationship between the boy narrator and Monsieur Atis, the village watchmaker, whom the boy admires for his social position — 'Il n'était donc pas riche, mais il jouissait d'autant de prestige que ceux qui avaient des maisons à l'étage au haut du bourg' (*SP*, p. 128) — and for whom he is happy to deliver watches to customers and collect the money for them. Similarly, the narrator of 'Joséphine' is the only boy living on his street and so is forced to become 'le garçon de courses des habitants de Calebassier' (*SP*, p. 90); at first he is pleased to do this, but then begins to feel that he is being exploited, but he has no choice but to continue running these errands: 'Et pas question de refuser: on porterait plainte à ma mère, qui me battrait [...] et par surcroît j'aurais encouru l'opprobre de l'enfant qui refuse de rendre service aux grandes personnes' (p. 91). In other words, if the child refuses, its mother will punish it; and being or having a helpful, well brought-up child is another marker of prestige.

As a result, all the childless adults in the village can call on any child to do something for them. As the girl narrator of 'Le Retour de Mamzelle Annette' explains:

[Les grandes personnes] qui avaient des enfants assez grands pour faire les courses

---

11    Thus in 'Le Phonographe' the father of a girl invited to the Faustin family's party refuses to let her attend on the rather tenuous grounds that 'vous comprenez, je ne peux pas envoyer ma fille chez vous pour y rencontrer Manotte Gésira, dont la sœur est en ménage avec un homme marié qui n'est même pas un béké' (SP, p. 150).

> ne recouraient guère aux enfants des autres; en revanche, nous incombaient les
> courses et les corvées de toutes celles qui, n'ayant pas d'enfants, nous requéraient
> à chaque occasion. (*ES*, p. 42).[12]

As a result, the children all long to be grown up; but, ironically, it is often precisely through doing these kinds of odd jobs that they acquire something approaching adult status. This is particularly true of the narrator in 'Le Retour de Mamzelle Annette' who, after Annette leaves Ernest following his refusal to marry her, in effect becomes his housekeeper, tidying and cleaning his house and barber's saloon. Her parents are pleased that she is regarded by the village as 'une petite fille remarquablement propre et diligente, et qui [...] avait transformé la maison de Monsieur Ernest à ce point qu'on ne dirait jamais que c'est le travail d'un enfant' (*ES*, p. 39). But the girl herself also enjoys it, on the one hand because it proves that she possesses the housewifely skills of an adult woman (p. 43), and on the other — far more childishly — because she can imagine that it is *her* house: 'Alors, je fis comme si c'était quelque maison abandonnée que je venais de découvrir par la grâce du merveilleux, et que j'entreprenais de nettoyer avec toute l'application et la coquetterie que je pouvais déployer pour épater mes camarades' (p. 44). On another and less conscious level, however, it also becomes 'her' house in the sense that she seems to become sexually interested in Ernest, almost as though she is imagining herself as a replacement for Annette in this sense as well. She is fascinated by glimpses of his bedroom, which she dares not enter — 'La bonne éducation interdisant formellement aux enfants de pénétrer dans les pièces où les grandes personnes se mettent nues pour se laver, s'habiller et faire tout ce que les enfants ne doivent pas voir' (p. 48) — but stays outside its door after she has finished her work in order to listen to Ernest snoring during his afternoon siesta, then waking up and putting his trousers on (p. 49). It is also in his house that she sees herself in a mirror for the first time, and while he sleeps she looks at herself 'longuement' and concludes that 'J'étais drôle, jolie, admirable' (p. 47), as though hoping that Ernest might think so too. But then Annette returns from the town and moves back in with Ernest: the girl sees them together, again in a mirror, and witnesses the attraction between them: 'Lui la fixait d'un regard de plus en plus tendu, qui semblait l'attirer et la transpercer lentement' (p. 53). The girl feels rejected, and never goes back to the house. Through being an exploited child, she has become both a quasi-adult housekeeper and a quasi-adult sexual rival for Ernest.

Relations between children are just as much dominated by issues of prestige as are those between adults, as in the girl's desire to 'épater mes camarades'. The little boy in 'Et si la mer n'était pas bleue' uses Tante Oberline's empty cotton reels as wheels on the toy carts that he makes, and comments that 'Rien ne me posait mieux aux yeux de mes camarades; rien ne suscitait plus grande envie; rien ne me valait plus de fierté' (*ES*, p. 15). Conversely, when he is by the seaside for the first time, he is humiliated by the fishermen's children who laugh at him when he is knocked

---

12    This sentence is a good example of Zobel's consistent refusal to adapt his literary style to the demands of verisimilitude: the distinctively adult syntax and vocabulary of his child narrators might seem to detract from the realism that otherwise characterizes his writing.

down by a wave: 'Je me relevai dans mes vêtements mouillés, sous les rires et les moqueries des gamins' (p. 23).

But the main arena for competition between boys is school; and three of the stories are set in schools.[13] Education is the main route out of poverty and, specifically, out of working on the plantation or in the factory. This is made very clear by the mother in 'Le Syllabaire', in *Laghia de la mort*, who is determined that whatever the financial sacrifices her son will go to school in order to escape this fate: 'Le livre, ou mon enfant n'ira pas à l'école. Fera partie des "petites bandes" qui travaillent dans les plantations des békés. Comme moi depuis l'âge de sept ans. Non.' (*LM*, pp. 85–86).

Education is mainly open to boys: there are not many schools for girls. The narrator of 'Joséphine' feels superior to Joséphine because he can read and write and she cannot (*SP*, p. 99). School is also where children learn to speak French; Joséphine's attempts to gain prestige by singing songs in French is ridiculed by the boy, but she refuses to sing in Creole (p. 100). (She also sings, constantly, an English song, 'Isti longoué pitipéra oué', which, to him, 'pourrait être aussi bien du zoulou' (p. 100), but is decipherable to English-speaking readers as a mangled version of 'It's a Long Way to Tipperary'.) These rather pathetic attempts to compensate for her lack of education emphasize the importance of success at school.[14]

Zobel's treatment of the theme of education in relation to poverty changes significantly between *Laghia de la mort* and the two later collections. In the former, both 'Le Syllabaire' and 'Mapiam' depict a poor black boy at school, and in both he is humiliated.[15] In 'Le Syllabaire', his mother cannot afford to buy Aristide the necessary textbook; he is the only boy in the class who does not possess it, the teacher is exasperated with him, and the other boys, who refuse to let him look at their copies, shout and laugh at him in a 'chahut dont Aristide était resté mortifié' (*LM*, p. 80). 'Mapiam', meaning 'sores', is the derisive nickname given to the narrator Casimir by his fellow pupils: he wraps his feet in bandages, claiming that he has sores, but a school medical examination reveals that there is nothing wrong with his feet: the bandages were his attempt to disguise the fact that he could not afford to wear shoes. Casimir is a good scholar, and is always top of his class; the headmaster tells his mother that he will get his 'certificat d'études' and perhaps go even further (*LM*, p. 105), but this does not count for anything with his class-mates and even the other teachers because he is 'noir et laid' (p. 101); rather than showing him respect his fellow pupils make fun of him for being so clever (p. 102) and criticize his poor clothes (p. 103). Nor are the teachers any more sympathetic: when his pretence of having sores is revealed and he bursts into tears and confesses that he has done it because he cannot afford shoes, the head master just apologizes to the doctor for this 'regrettable et burlesque incident' (p. 110). Even more revealingly,

13   Education is also of course a major theme in *La Rue Cases-Nègres*.
14   The resulting prestige is apparent in a remark by a character in 'Le Phonographe': 'Parce qu'il a été un peu à l'école, proférait Cius, il se prend pour un Docteur' (*SP*, p. 144).
15   Hardwick discusses these two stories briefly in *Childhood, Autobiography and the Francophone Caribbean* from the point of view of this theme of the effects of poverty on children's experience at school (p. 124).

the fact that Casimir is top of his class is taken to mean that the class as a whole is no good: 'Cette classe n'a pas de chance: avoir pour premier cette espèce de nègre marron?' (p. 108). In other words, being black and poor cannot be offset by educational success.

But the situation presented by 'Le Cahier d'Édouard Tanasio', in *Et si la mer n'était pas bleue*, is very different. The narrator goes to school with two brothers, Eugène and Édouard Tanasio, whose father is a 'chef d'atelier' at the factory and so is fairly wealthy: the narrator comments: 'Ses parents étaient de ceux que des gens comme les miens saluaient respectueusement' (*ES*, p. 29). But the other boys do not look up to Édouard in any way. Not only is the narrator better than him 'en orthographe, en grammaire, en français et même en calcul' (p. 32), he even thinks that he is physically more attractive than him, despite the latter's lighter skin — 'Rien ne me paraissait préférable à mes jambes, plutôt grêles mais rapides à la course, à ma peau, pas boutonneuse comme la sienne *bien que plus noire*' (p. 30, my emphasis) — and he concludes that 'Édouard était de ceux qui comptaient le moins dans la classe' (p. 31).

The status of the older brother is more complex. He is virtually a grown man, 'le plus grand, le plus costaud et le plus fort de toute la classe' (*ES*, p. 27), with a moustache, and as such is respected and feared by the other boys. But they also realize that he is actually too old to be in school at all; he is still there only because he is incapable of passing the exams: in other words, he is stupid. And his manly appearance simply makes him look ridiculous when he is sitting in the classroom:

> A la vérité, je n'en revenais pas de voir Eugène sur un banc d'école, alors que tous les gars du village qui avaient son âge et sa corpulence, travaillaient aux champs ou à l'usine. Car Eugène Tanasio était, somme toute, un homme. (*ES*, p. 28)

His having to wear shorts rather than long trousers also adds to the ridicule (p. 29). But the fact that he is still attending school is not only a proof of his stupidity; it is equally proof of his parents' wealth, because they can afford to keep him at school. So his stupidity is compensated for, but not cancelled out, by his manliness and his family's wealth. Another ambiguous sign of his prestige is that, even though he 'avait fait sa première communion et assistait à la messe', he regularly has sex with grown women; this inspires in his class-mates 'un peu d'envie et de jalousie que nous dissimulions sous un faux dédain, affectant d'être scandalisés' (p. 29). Eugène, in other words, scores highly in terms of his physical manhood, his sexual activity, and his family's wealth, but negatively in terms of Catholic respectability and educational prowess. The tone of this story is very different from the heart-wrenching pathos of the two stories in *Laghia de la mort*; and it is clear that here, poor black boys can indeed gain prestige from their intelligence and their success at school, not only in terms of their future employment but also in their day-to-day relations with their fellow pupils.

What general conclusions can be drawn from Zobel's portrayal of life in the Martiniquan village? In the first place, our overall impression is perhaps rather negative; while Zobel does not overtly criticize his characters, and his humour is kindly and gentle, he nevertheless evokes a community in which status, competition, snobbishness, and envy are prevalent. The overall atmosphere is very different from that of *La Rue Cases-Nègres*, for instance, in which Man Tine's devotion to her grandson and his love for her are central themes. More surprisingly, it is also very different from the *French* village in which the first story in *Le Soleil partagé* is set: here, the main character is a Martiniquan man who has come to live in the village, who overcomes his neighbours' initial suspicion of him, and is surrounded by friendship and sympathy when he receives the news of his mother's death. There is little evidence of any such solidarity in the Martiniquan village that features in the stories that I have been discussing. Also, few individual characters stand out as morally admirable: Monsieur Atis, perhaps, in 'Le Cadeau', for his kindness to the narrator; and the heroically struggling mother of Aristide in 'Le Syllabaire'. The child narrators engage our sympathy because they are innocent and powerless. But for the most part in *Le Soleil partagé* and *Et si la mer n'était pas bleue* Zobel focuses on the factors that divide the village — but also hold it together in a kind of network of shared assumptions, values, and judgements. The village community, in other words, is structured by a number of hierarchies, as I have shown. But these are not stable or clear-cut, for various reasons: partly because the differences between people are often quite petty (Freud's notion of 'the narcissism of small differences' is very relevant here); partly because life for many of the villagers is precarious and their fortunes vary over time; but principally because the co-existence of a number of hierarchical parameters produces conflicts between them (the power of sorcery versus that of the Church, wealth versus educational success, marital fidelity versus the desirability of having a white lover, and so on). The interest of these stories therefore lies above all in the subtlety and complexity that Zobel reveals in the social hierarchies of the village.

CHAPTER 9

❖

# Secret Worlds: Incommunicability and Initiation in Three Novels by Ernest Pépin

Ernest Pépin is well-known in Guadeloupe as a novelist, poet, and critic, but as yet little has been written about his work.[1] This study of *Tambour-Babel*, *Le Tango de la haine*, and *L'Envers du décor* attempts, therefore, to open up a relatively new body of texts to analysis, and is thus based largely upon my own readings, and upon an interview that Pépin gave me.[2] His fiction is usually associated with the 'créolité' movement founded by Patrick Chamoiseau, Raphaël Confiant, and Jean Bernabé; indeed, Pépin describes himself as 'affiliated' to it in his article 'The Place of Space in the Novels of the *Créolité* Movement'.[3] In the same article he also stresses the continuity between the 'créolité' novels and those of Édouard Glissant; and it is easy to see how his own work, in its concern with Antillean history and popular culture, reflects the influence both of the 'créolité' writers and of Glissant. At the same time, however, Pépin is very aware of the 'serpentine path traced by French Caribbean literature between the ideological, aesthetic, and political claims staked out by the various literary movements or strata, from exoticism to *créolité* via *négritude* and *antillanité*'; and the literary affiliations of his own work are equally 'serpentine'.[4] Rather than simply reproducing the themes of his fellow-writers, the three novels which I shall be discussing also move into new and significantly different thematic

1 See, however, E. Anthony Hurley, 'Loving Words: New Lyricism in French Caribbean Poetry', *World Literature Today*, 71:1 (1997), 55–60; Catherine Khordoc, 'Babel: figure de créolisation dans *Tambour-Babel* d'Ernest Pépin', in *Les Langues du roman: du plurilinguisme comme stratégie textuelle*, ed. by Lise Gauvin (Montreal: Presses de l'Université de Montréal, 1999), pp. 129–45; Kathleen Gyssels, 'Du Tambour-Babel au Babil du songer' (1999), <http://www.lehman.cuny.edu/ile.en.ile/paroles/pepin_gyssels.html> [accessed September 2006]; Mary Gallagher, 'The Passion of Place and Passage: From Emile Ollivier's *Passages* to Ernest Pépin's *Tambour-Babel*', in *Ici-Là: Place and Displacement in Caribbean Writing in French*, ed. by Mary Gallagher (Amsterdam & New York: Rodopi, 2003), pp. 157–78. *Le Tango de la haine* was reviewed by Patrick Grainville in *Le Figaro* (22 June 1999), and *L'Envers du décor* by Lyonel Trouillot in *Matin* (Haiti) (13 July 2006).
2 Celia Britton, 'Entretien avec Ernest Pépin', *Francophone Postcolonial Studies*, 6:1 (2008), 24–39. The interview was carried out on 29 November 2006 at Le Gosier, Guadeloupe.
3 Ernest Pépin, 'The Place of Space in the Novels of the *Créolité* Movement', in *Ici-Là*, ed. by Gallagher, pp. 1–23 (p. 21).
4 Ibid. p. 2.

territory. In the course of this chapter, therefore, I shall suggest that Pépin echoes but also enlarges and even challenges the notions of the specificity of Antillean society and culture that inform the earlier work of Glissant on the one hand and that of the 'créolité' writers on the other.

All three of these novels are characterized by the mobility of their narrative point of view: the narration is assumed by a variety of characters as well as an anonymous, but not impersonal, narrative voice. Thus *Tambour-Babel*, which recounts the story of an old master-drummer and his son's struggle to become a worthy successor to him, intersperses third-person narration with four chapters narrated by the son, Napo (including one in which he is still in his mother's womb), one by his mother Hermancia, one by Basile, his father's rival, and one by the dancer Sosso. *Le Tango de la haine* describes the failed marriage of Abel and Nika, and Nika's persecution of her ex-husband: here the narrative voice slides fluidly back and forth between the two protagonists, often within a single chapter. *L'Envers du décor* revolves around the relationship between Anadine, an old Creole woman, and Jean-Paul, a young 'métro' who came to Guadeloupe to open a restaurant with his wife Sylvie: the business fails, his wife leaves him, and he is rescued from a state of destitution by Anadine who teaches him how to survive in the 'real' Guadeloupe. The narration is mainly from the point of view of Anadine (both first-person and free indirect discourse), but Jean-Paul also narrates several chapters and one chapter each is assigned to a Haitian immigrant, Sylvie's mother, and Anadine's dog Laya. In addition, in all three novels, the anonymous narrator comments on the action, addresses both the reader and the characters directly (sometimes both at the same time: 'Il vous faut savoir, chère Anadine et cher lecteur', *ED*, p. 63), and sometimes takes on the characteristics of the traditional *conteur*, evoking an oral story-telling situation rather than the writing of a novel, or sometimes both at once.[5] This narrator is not omniscient: he merely adds another voice to those of the characters, a voice that is both inside and outside the novel.[6] He also serves to convert the narration into a dialogue between several voices; it is his prompts, for instance, that stimulate the production of Anadine's narrative (as in 'Dis-nous, Anadine!', *ED*, p. 14).

This plurality of narrating subjects clearly resonates with the discursive structure of Glissant's *Mahagony* and *Tout-monde*,[7] or the central emphasis on diversity in the work of the 'créolité' group.[8] In fact, however, its significance in Pépin's writing is

---

5    *TB*, p. 136: '*Lecteurs (lectrices)*, la vie est un mal-tête qui surprendra toujours notre besoin de claireté. Elle fesse à terre nos certitudes pour nous donner une petite goutte de vérité, mais toute vérité n'est pas bonne à dire et en même temps mon estomac n'est pas un frigidaire qui peut garder en conserve un manger déjà tout près d'être rassis alors même que *l'auditeur* réclame explications pour comprendre les détours du racontement' (my emphasis).

6    As Pépin explains, 'C'est la voix de l'auteur, mais d'un auteur qui se veut masqué [...] c'est une voix un peu en dehors du texte, mais qui est finalement dans le texte également [...] qui sort le lecteur du fil de l'histoire pour qu'il prenne du recul; c'est ma manière de l'obliger à se distancer un peu' (Britton, 'Entretien avec Ernest Pépin', p. 29).

7    Édouard Glissant, *Mahagony* (Paris: Éditions du Seuil, 1987); *Tout-monde* (Paris: Gallimard, 1993).

8    See for example Bernabé, Chamoiseau and Confiant, *Éloge de la créolité*, where they write: 'Du fait de sa mosaïque constitutive, la Créolité est une spécificité ouverte. [...] L'exprimer c'est

somewhat different. For him, it reflects rather a vision of reality based on the key notion of *incommunicability*: no one point of view can encompass the whole situation because no one subject can understand the experience of others. In *Le Tango de la haine*, for instance, the independent narrator first justifies his existence by the claim that neither Abel nor Nika are capable of providing a true account of their relationship:

> Moi, je ne suis pas là pour dire la vérité puisque je suis un conteur-menteur. Je ne suis pas là non plus pour dire des mensonges puisque je suis un accoucheur de la vérité. Mais à dire vrai j'ai bien connu ces deux numéros-là. Comment? Ça n'a pas d'importance. Le fait est que je les ai connus et tout ce qu'ils peuvent raconter sera toujours à des années-lumière de la tête d'épingle de la réalité. (*TH*, p. 64)

But he then admits that his own understanding of it is far from complete: 'Moi-même, je ne l'ai jamais compris exactement' (p. 66), and engages in an argument with another anonymous voice about what the root of the couple's emotional problems really is (pp. 76–79). The narrative organization of the novels is thus one manifestation of a view of reality as consisting of separate 'worlds' that exist alongside each other without any communication between them. The titles underline this theme: the 'Babel' that evokes the mutual incommunicability of different languages, the 'haine' that separates husband and wife, and the opposition between the apparent and the real that is suggested in the phrase 'l'envers du décor'.

This emphasis on a world that is invisible to outsiders recalls Glissant's early formulations of opacity, defined as a strategy for the colonized cultures of the Caribbean to protect themselves against the invasive pressures of the colonizer's need to know, understand, and therefore control them. In *Tambour-Babel*, the world of the drummers is presented in similar terms: they are a secret aristocracy, unrecognized by the Guadeloupean middle class and by French society. Because of their poverty, 'tous ces grands des grands, hormis pour les initiés, vivaient des vies sans gloire [...]. Ils constituaient toute une aristocratie invisible' (*TB*, pp. 97–98). The secret world is that of a 'subaltern' group, unable to make itself heard within society as a whole.[9] Their only means of communication, and the only means of memorializing them, are the vernacular, almost clandestine 'annales de radio bois-patate, de radio télégueule et de bien d'autres radios que l'Histoire n'a jamais recensées' (*TB*, p. 123). This novel also suggests that the split between the apparent and the real — which becomes a central theme in *L'Envers du décor* — exists in a particularly acute form in Caribbean society, where it correlates with the opposition between French and African cultures. When Napo goes on tour with his group, he explains to an African spectator who cannot understand how they can have

exprimer non une synthèse, pas simplement un métissage, ou n'importe quelle autre unicité. C'est exprimer une totalité kaléidoscopique, c'est à dire *la conscience non totalitaire d'une diversité préservée*' (pp. 27–28).
9    See Gayatri Spivak, 'Can the Subaltern Speak?', in *Marxism and the Interpretation of Culture*, ed. by C. Nelson and L. Grossberg (London: Macmillan, 1988), pp. 271–313.

European names and play like Africans: 'Mon nom et mon tambour ne s'accordent pas pour toi [...] Nous sommes les hommes à deux visages. Celui que nous montrons et celui qui nous regarde à l'intérieur de nos pays d'avant' (*TB*, p. 233).

In *L'Envers du décor*, similarly, the secret world in question is Guadeloupean society as a whole. Jean-Paul and Sylvie represent typical 'métros' coming to start a new life in what they see as the tropical paradise of the Antilles. Guadeloupe appears to them completely knowable, constructed by its tourist industry as an alluring, unproblematic surface spread out in front of them and *for* them: blatantly offered to them as an object of consumption. In fact, however, it remains impenetrable to European outsiders because they cannot understand what they are seeing, hearing, or even eating (Anadine remarks, 'Justement, touristes ne veut pas dire connaisseurs', *ED*, p. 12). Although Jean-Paul scornfully distances himself from the tourists who 'tournent dans leur bocal de mirages préfabriqués' (p. 29), he and his wife are in fact guilty of exactly the same misrecognition of the 'world' of Guadeloupe — the world, that is, that exists beneath the touristic 'décor' that they take for reality itself. Jean-Paul and Sylvie's ignorance of the culture is compounded by the fantasies that motivated their coming to Guadeloupe; the images they see on their arrival already seem familiar to them, because 'Elles faisaient en quelque sorte partie de nous, venues d'un imaginaire que nous avions concocté sur les îles' (p. 23). The theme of misrecognition, central to the novel, is inextricably bound up with fantasy and desire: when they think they are seeing, they are merely dreaming with their eyes open, as the anonymous narrator warns us: '*Lecteur! Ce n'est pas tout dire dormir, c'est garder yeux ouverts qui fabrique le rêve!*' (p. 34). Anadine lists all the things they cannot see (pp. 44–48), and concludes 'Blanc, tu ne voyais que les beautés sans te douter que s'il y a l'endroit, il y a l'envers' (p. 49).

What the tourists see as an island is in fact a country: 'Il dit "île", moi je dis "pays"'(*ED*, p. 35); and Anadine's distinction is elaborated in *Tambour-Babel* into an opposition between nature and society:

> 'Une île!' crie le découvreur. Il ne sait pas encore qu'il a rencontré un pays. Les touristes vont dans les îles. Ils ne foulent que du sable. Ceux qui vont dans un pays échangent une poignée de mains avec des humains. (*TB*, p.189)

And hence also an opposition between geography and history. It is specifically knowledge of history which is seen as the corrective to fantasy and ignorance; here, too, Pépin echoes a prominent Glissantian emphasis on the importance of recovering history, although in Glissant's conception it is the Antilleans themselves who suffer from this lack, rather than outsiders.[10] In Pépin's novel it is Jean-Paul who has to realize that both the good and the bad aspects of Guadeloupean society are determined by its history, moving from his earlier dismissive 'Comment peut-on être triste dans un paradis? Nous ne comprenons pas [...]. D'ailleurs, pourquoi remuer cette histoire d'esclavage? Ne comprenons pas!' (*ED*, p. 32) to learning from Anadine that:

---

10  Glissant, *DA*, p. 88: 'Le temps martiniquais n'est pas non plus intériorisé par la collectivité. L'inconscient et lancinant besoin de se connaître se perd dans l'absence du sens ou de la dimension historiques. Non seulement l'histoire fut collectivement subie, mais encore elle fut "raturée"'.

> Nous n'étions ni le paradis, ni l'enfer. Nous étions une histoire! Une petite histoire aveuglée par des couleurs de peau, des maîtres, des esclaves, des injustices, des mensonges, des profitations, et qui cherchait son chemin parmi les étoiles du monde. (*TB*, p. 131).

History is thus finally equated with 'l'envers du décor', the island's history is what cannot be simply *seen* by the outsider. It is secret and invisible: 'Une histoire invisible parce que nous la cachions dans notre cœur' (p. 131).

Thus in both *Tambour-Babel* and *L'Envers du décor*, the 'real' culture of the Guadeloupean people is presented as opaque in Glissant's sense of the term, that is, hidden from European colonizers, tourists, and by implication the Europeanized middle class of the island, for all of whom it is in principle inaccessible. *Le Tango de la haine*, however, is not concerned with barriers between cultures, but with those between men and women in the same culture, and is thus significantly different from Glissant's opacity. It relentlessly juxtaposes the two separate, and extremely antagonistic, worlds of men and of women. On one level, the degree of inaccessibility from one to the other is not symmetrical: that is, women appear to understand men far better than men understand women, because their relative social status means that the woman needs to understand the man in order to survive, while the converse is not true. Knowledge in this case is not the means to power, but the reverse of power. Thus Nika can see inside Abel: 'A maintes reprises, elle avait découvert, à travers les soupiraux, les persiennes, les interstices, les fentes, les béances de ses émotions la complexité de son en-dedans. Et parfois elle pensait, avec tristesse, qu'elle le connaissait trop bien pour l'aimer' (*TH*, p. 40), whereas he has only a superficial view of her; the text continues: 'Abel, lui, ne la connaissait pas. Il percevait des moires de surface, des miroitements changeants' (p. 40). In addition to their superior social position, men's sexual desire for women also blinds them to their inner reality, limiting them to the woman's physical 'surface'; Abel eventually realizes that his 'grande erreur' has been that 'Il avait toujours considéré *l'extérieur* des femmes. La rondeur de leurs fesses, le pointu de leurs seins [...]. Tout ça n'était rien à côté des milliers de mondes invisibles qu'elles portaient en-dedans' (p. 109). Intersubjective relations are here conceived in spatial terms: the emphatic oppositions between depth and surface, inside and outside, reinforce the image of a secret world that can only be penetrated through its 'interstices', 'fentes' and 'béances'.

But they also have a temporal dimension which escapes both men and women, in so far as Pépin insistently connects contemporary sexual relationships with the history of slavery.[11] Just as in *L'Envers du décor*, in other words, history holds the key to understanding, in *Le Tango de la haine* the conflictual relations of the couple can only be resolved by coming to terms with the continuing after-effects

---

11    Pépin says: 'l'esclavage — y compris ce qui s'est passé apres l'abolition — a été un tel traumatisme qu'il a rendu difficiles, presque impossibles, les relations harmonieuses entre hommes et femmes dans cette culture créole [...] l'homme antillais, c'est un vaincu historique. C'est quelqu'un qu'on a pris quelque part et qu'on a amené ici dans des conditions atroces. Comment voulez-vous qu'une femme ait confiance en lui, se sente épaulée, accompagnée, par un homme qui a subi tout cela?' (Britton, 'Entretien avec Ernest Pépin', p. 34).

of the history of slavery. Caribbean women despise men because the male slave was unable to assert his masculinity and assume responsibility for his partner and children; and Caribbean men have continued to act out this symbolic impotence while compensating for it by the importance they attach to their physical virility and promiscuity.[12] Abel and Nika are equally unable to understand this: Abel complains that Nika misinterprets his constant infidelities as a sign that he does not love her (*TH*, pp. 60–61); and she, symmetrically, complains that he misinterprets her harshness as rejection of him whereas it is in fact an attempt to change him into someone whom she can really love (p. 154).

*Le Tango de la haine* thus departs from Glissant's conception of opacity as a form of protection for subaltern cultures. Rather than conceiving of 'real' Antillean society as sharing one homogeneous set of attitudes — as Glissant by implication does — the novel focuses on a major fault-line within the culture. Moreover, this split is itself presented as a consequence of the history of Guadeloupe, with the result that the Glissantian insistence on the importance of history is also both echoed, and harnessed to a different view of relationships within one culture. The novel shows how the same history can be 'lived' differently by groups which do not differ in their race, class, locality, or in fact anything except their gender; women, the anonymous narrator argues, occupied a different status within slavery and so were not psychologically affected by it in the same way. When his interlocutor objects, 'Mais elles sont des Antillaises, elles ont vécu la même histoire, elles portent en elles aussi des maîtres et des esclaves ...', he replies, 'C'est là le drame. Elles n'ont pas le même vécu de l'histoire. Elles ont toujours été du côté de la vie et la vie ne cherche ni maîtres, ni esclaves' (*TH*, p. 78).

In fact Pépin's emphasis on the multiplicity of these 'worlds' results in an extremely fragmented representation of society. Even within one community, reality is not knowable; it is not accessible to any common understanding or interpretation, but is an agglomeration of multiple, separate, secret worlds.[13] Anadine's comment on Jean-Paul and Sylvie's naivety produces an image which sums up the whole structure:

> Il y a des gens ainsi. Ils sont persuadés que le monde se résume à ce qu'ils voient. En ce qui me concerne, j'imagine des poupées russes. Chaque poupée, chaque monde, et c'est l'ensemble de ces mondes visibles, invisibles, incompréhensibles, absurdes, intentionnés, indifférents, attentifs, supérieurs et inférieurs qui constituent le monde! (*ED*, p. 37)

When Anadine defines 'l'envers du décor' as 'Une histoire invisible parce que nous

---

12    Pépin's presentation of this idea is very close to the thesis of Fritz Gracchus in his *Les Lieux de la mère dans les sociétés afro-américaines* (Paris: Éditions caribéennes, 1986), and he agrees that Gracchus has influenced his thinking (see Britton, 'Entretien avec Ernest Pépin', p. 34). Jacques André gives a slightly different analysis of the same complex, with reference to Gracchus, in his *L'Inceste focal dans la famille noire antillaise: crimes, conflits, structure* (Paris: Presses universitaires de France, 1987). These two texts will be discussed in greater detail in Chapter 12.

13    Within French Antillean literature, Maryse Condé's *Traversée de la mangrove* perhaps comes closest to this view of social reality: structured as a series of interior monologues by the inhabitants of the same village, it emphasizes the misunderstandings and lack of communication between them.

la cachions dans notre cœur', she adds, 'Voilà pourquoi je n'aime pas les livres. Ils n'auront jamais la vérité du cœur' (*ED*, p. 131). In other words, Jean-Paul cannot learn the secrets of Guadeloupean history by reading about them in a book; and this is in fact true of all the secret worlds — they are not accessible to rational knowledge. Rather, they require and generate a different kind of intuitive knowledge that takes various forms.[14] In *Tambour-Babel* the characters' senses are supernaturally acute, so much so that they shade into more mysterious forms of perception that can best be described as intuition — as Eloi grows older he reaches 'cette saison où l'on ne voit plus avec les yeux mais à l'aide de tous les sens connus ou inconnus' (*TB*, p. 40). Thus Hermancia 'avait développé un sens tout spécial pour savoir si le lewoz avait donné tout son lot de contentement' (p. 26). They can 'read' each others thoughts: unlike Abel and Nika, Eloi 'entendait tout ce que [Hermancia] voulait cacher et cacheter dans le profond de son cœur' (p. 21). Sometimes these intuitions are explicitly associated with a magic ability to perceive the invisible; when Hermancia was a girl, her mother sensed that she was reaching puberty 'avec la seule bougie de son cœur de mère et la voyance magique d'un sorcier-gadè-zafè' (p. 23). Although a similar intuitive capacity characterizes Anadine ('Anadine a dix mille sens!', *ED*, p. 15), in *L'Envers du décor* the dominant source of non-rational knowledge is not sensuous, but the experience of suffering; the tribulations of Anadine's life have left her with 'une science, une autre science, des accidents de la vie'(p. 16), whereas Jean-Paul and Sylvie 'ne pouvaient pas connaître cette science du malheur que ruminait la vieille' (p. 44). It is only later, when Jean-Paul learns how to survive as a homeless 'clochard' (he repeats 'J'ai appris' nine times, listing his new experiences, p. 166), that he finally gains access to 'l'envers du décor' (p. 167).

Just as rational knowledge cannot penetrate the secret worlds, so ordinary language is also sidelined in favour of a range of non-verbal languages that communicate that which is secret. One can see this, too, as a variation on a Glissantian theme, insofar as Glissant's characterization of Creole as a 'camouflaged language' stresses its clandestine quality and its distance from ordinary languages.[15] But Pépin's secret languages are not Creole, or indeed any kind of speech. Although Anadine and Jean-Paul have long dialogues with each other, it is their silent communication that most powerfully taps into 'l'énergie secrète des choses qui viennent d'en-bas. Conversation d'ombres, où seuls comptent le bruit des paupières et la maturation intérieure' (*ED*, p.161). Even Laya, the dog, 'speaks' to Jean-Paul, and Anadine comments: 'Tous les langages n'ont pas besoin de mots. Il nous trahissent souvent alors que le silence est pur' (p. 121). Hermancia, too, says 'Je n'ai jamais eu besoin de mots pour parler ni pour comprendre. Il me suffit de hausser mes antennes' (*TB*, p.

14    Pépin claims that he has 'une prédilection pour ces mondes souterrains, pour ce qui est inconscient, pour ce qui est non-rationnel', and believes that 's'il y a un savoir occidental très normé, très cartésien (bon, il y en a un autre aussi — il n'y a pas que cela — mais disons que c'est celui-là que l'on met en avant) ce n'est pas ce savoir-là qui régit notre représentation du monde et notre façon de voir' (Britton, 'Entretien avec Ernest Pépin', p. 26).

15    See for instance Glissant's chapter entitled 'Poétique naturelle, poétique forcée' in *Le Discours antillais* (*DA*, pp. 236–45). See also Chapter 7 here for further discussion of Creole as a 'camouflaged language'.

39); and the way in which she walks after making love to Eloi is a secret 'writing': 'Mais qui sait déchiffrer l'écriture invisible des femmes?' (p. 29). Napo eventually does learn how to decipher it:

> J'ai compris les femmes (à commencer par Hermancia!), traversées par tant de violences qu'elles ont appris la force du silence. Elles parlent avec leurs corps qui enfle et désenfle [...] qui étouffe le cri du plaisir pour mieux porter la charge des jours. (*TB*, p. 175)

Another form of body-language is dance, also illustrated in *Tambour-Babel*. But the strangest example of it occurs in *L'Envers du décor*. When Jean-Paul dances to the Haitians' music, his movements enable him to enter their world, losing his individual subjectivity in an almost *vodou*-like possession: 'Ses compères haïtiens avaient l'habitude des métamorphoses. Simplement, ils ne savaient pas que les Blancs aussi pouvaient entrer dans le corps d'un oiseau' (*ED*, p. 55). In this state, Haiti speaks to him ('Elle lui parla de sa splendeur passée', p. 55). Here, in other words, the dance communicates secret knowledge to the dancer: the 'speaking' subject is in fact *receiving* the message embodied in the non-verbal language of his own bodily movements.

Dance is of course also an art, and other artistic practices in Pépin's novels are also characterized as languages communicating intuitive knowledge of secret worlds. Towards the end of *Le Tango de la haine* Abel takes up painting and discovers that it provides him with a new 'language': 'Le monde me parlait dans une langue que je n'avais jamais pris la peine de déchiffrer auparavant' (*TH*, p. 188). He paints a portrait of Nika, and the portrait itself reveals to him 'comme en surimpression [...] l'aura d'une souffrance incomprise et son besoin camouflé d'être aimée' (p. 189). But not only is his understanding of Nika thus transformed: more generally, the painting 'm'apporta la révélation de mes erreurs. Toutes mes théories sur l'amour ont été fausses. [...] Il me fallait tout reprendre au point de départ' (p. 194). The most fully elaborated example of an art form as a secret language is, however, drumming in *Tambour-Babel*, whose 'Prelude' announces that '*Ce que langue ne peut dire, le tambour le déparle*'. Drumming is presented as a kind of super-language: it has its own syntax, but its constituent elements are not arbitrary signs, but imitations of nature ('Il détachait des sons expressifs comme des onomatopées. Il les reliait entre eux en de longues séquences', *TB*, p. 118); therefore, it subsumes all ordinary languages — the drummers collectively 'créaient une langue pour remplacer toutes les langues' (p. 111) — and is itself, as the title suggests, a multiplicity or 'Babel' of languages. It enables the drummer and his audience to communicate with secret worlds: Eloi, for instance, 'répétait une frappe de façon obsessionnelle, cherchant à atteindre l'âme secrète de tout ce qui portait la vie dans son entourage' (p. 13). The drums open up a world that is denied to white people who can only read books: 'Les blancs lisent de grands livres pour chercher la clé du monde, nous, nous frappons à la porte de nos tambours et tout devient d'une claireté' (p. 45).

Jean-Paul in *L'Envers du décor* is, however, an example of a white man who does learn how to decipher the secret language of Guadeloupe and is initiated into its world. That is, in Pépin's novels it is possible for outsiders to penetrate the opacity of the separate worlds; in fact, this theme of initiation is prominent throughout. Even Napo has to undergo a classic trajectory of initiation: he goes off alone into the forest and meets a mysterious old man who teaches him the secrets of the natural world and makes him smoke a pipe of magic herbs, after which he can hear the inaudible sounds of an ant walking on a leaf, the sap rising in the trees, etc. (*TB*, p. 143). In *Le Tango de la haine*, some women can initiate men into the social reality from which their infantilism otherwise excludes them, and that is the main difference between Nika and Abel's new lover Marie-Soleil:

> Il comprit alors ce qui avait manqué à Nika (*mais ce n'était pas sa faute à elle!*). Elle n'avait pas eu la force de l'enfanter et de l'expulser dans ces mondes-là, où vivre n'était plus une jouissance mais un voyage [...]. Une initiation à la condition humaine. (*TH*, p. 110).

As in this example, initiation is often a kind of rebirth; for Napo in *Tambour-Babel* and Jean-Paul in *L'Envers du décor*, gaining access to the secret worlds equally involves a transformation of the self. Napo only 'becomes' his father's true son when he has been initiated into the knowledge that enables him to be a master-drummer, and Anadine's teaching of Jean-Paul culminates in him symbolically becoming her son: 'Je venais de naître!' (*ED*, p.171). The specific kind of intuitive knowledge that initiation brings, in other words, is not merely the acquisition of additional insights, but the construction of a new identity: as Jean-Paul gradually learns about Guadeloupe, 'il perdait sa vieille peau de Blanc-France pour rentrer dans celle d'un Guadeloupéen' (p. 126).

The centrality of the theme of initiation distances Pépin's novels further from the concept of opacity, which not only does not envisage the possibility of outsiders entering the secret world of slave society and its later forms, but would by implication see this as a negative outcome. Opacity is for Glissant entirely beneficial: it is a means of protecting vulnerable social groups from the oppression inherent in surveillance and invasive attempts to 'understand' them.[16] Pépin's promotion of initiation, on the other hand, defines a form of understanding that because it is intuitive, based on experience and identification, is not aggressive: it does not alter the culture that is the object of understanding, but brings about a profound alteration in the subject who learns to understand.

In many ways, Pépin's novels would appear to be closer to the thematic concerns of the 'créolité' movement, with its emphasis on the recovery and preservation of traditional folklore. This is particularly true of *Tambour-Babel*, where the community of drummers is presented as an idyllic world rooted in the traditional rural culture of Guadeloupe with strong links to the African past, and the narrator bemoans the fact that 'une sorte de lèpre rongeait la vie créole' (*TB*, p. 152). *L'Envers du décor*, too, whose heroine is a wise old Creole woman acting as spokesperson for her culture (not unlike Marie-Sophie in Chamoiseau's *Texaco*) unambiguously presents

---

16    Glissant, 'Il y a dans ce verbe comprendre le mouvement des mains qui prennent l'entour et le ramènent à soi. Geste d'enfermement sinon d'appropriation. Préférons-lui le geste du donner-avec, qui ouvre enfin sur la totalité' ('Pour l'opacité', in *PR*, p. 206).

that traditional authentic culture as its main positive value.[17] In both these novels, however, as well as in the more contemporary *Le Tango de la haine*, the echoes of 'créolité' coexist with a very different attitude towards the wider, and more modern, world. In the first place, the characters' recourse to traditional folklore and magic is often described with gentle irony, as in, for example, both Hermancia's and Nika's visits to the 'quimboiseur' (*TB*, p. 124, and *TH*, pp. 167–70). The attempts of the 'créolistes' to propagate Creole are also ridiculed by Anadine: 'J'ai entendu à la radio: "Nous kay asseoir, autour de la table, pou nou diskité de la masse salariale évè le patronat." Ça c'est créole alors?' (*ED*, p. 11); and their campaign to promote a self-consciously Creole identity is parodied by her dog: 'Bien sûr, nous, chiens créoles, nous n'avons pas droit à tout cela, mais ça viendra. Nous nous battrons pour faire reconnaître notre identité, notre culture et notre histoire. Nous ferons avancer notre cause' (*ED*, p. 117).

More importantly, the secret worlds in the novels are not limited to Guadeloupean subalternity, and nor do they belong only to the past. *Le Tango de la haine*, despite its emphasis on the psychological determining influence of history, is set in a distinctively modern Guadeloupe: here the principal secret world is the changing historical situation of women, that men cannot understand. Indeed, the notion of a secret language is itself parodied: the women invent 'une langue à elles, que l'homme ne comprenait plus' (*TH*, p. 201), but rather than a mysterious non-verbal communion with nature, it consists of the very contemporary, urban, middle-class, and public discourse of feminism: 'des mots bizarres et barbares comme fidélité, égalité, divorce, justice, pensions alimentaires, dommages et intérêts, droit de vivre, droit de jouir et droit d'être le chef de famille' (p. 201).

The relationship between Jean-Paul and Anadine in *L'Envers du décor* does position him principally as the recipient of her knowledge of traditional Guadeloupean life, which constitutes the secret world of this novel. But it is not a purely one-way relationship; not only does he teach her about French society ('sous nos langues, l'histoire, les coutumes, les savoirs voltigeaient en de grandes étincelles d'un genre nouveau pour moi', *ED*, p. 127), but he also enlarges her understanding of the Caribbean, and even of herself. Anadine's opinion of the Haitians reflects the traditional Guadeloupean prejudice towards them (pp. 56–57, 103), and it is Jean-Paul who realizes what motivates this prejudice:

> Ce qu'Anadine refusait dans l'Haïtien c'était elle-même! Ce n'était pas parce qu'elle le supposait différent qu'elle le rejetait. C'était parce qu'elle savait qu'ils étaient mêmes et pareils. Et elle avait mis tant de cœur, tant de rage à sortir de la nasse, et voilà que l'autre venait lui tendre un miroir où elle se voyait telle qu'elle avait toujours été: une pauvre négresse secourue par les Blancs. (*ED*, p. 58)

In *Tambour-Babel* there are no white characters, and the community of drummers is indeed an archetypally traditional one. Nevertheless it is here that we find the most striking example of Pépin's refusal to remain within the secret world of Antillean folklore and 'créolité'. The drums are intimately linked with the natural world of Guadeloupe (as, for example, in the long lyrical description on pp. 111–12) and with

17   Patrick Chamoiseau, *Texaco* (Paris: Gallimard, 1992).

the African past, but they also relate to American music:

> Ils savaient que la terre d'avant [i.e. Africa] ne pouvait que consentir à cette messe. Ils savaient aussi que tout près les Américains noirs juchés haut sur la crête des blues, embusqués dans les temples du gospel, plongés dans les rapides du jazz, prenaient le même chemin. (*TB*, p. 112)

In the same way, although Napo has to be immersed by the old man of the forest in the sounds of nature, he also — explicitly in order to become a proper traditional Guadeloupean drummer — has to initiate himself into all the other 'musiques venues des quatre coins du monde' (*TB*, p. 126): 'Celui qui n'aime qu'une musique n'aime pas la musique' (p. 188). Indeed, the old man himself turns out to be less an autochthonous sage such as Chamoiseau's 'Mentô' figures in *Texaco*, and more a proponent of Glissant's 'Tout-monde': he has travelled all over the world, is familiar with the good and bad effects of globalization (p. 137) and tells Napo, 'Laisse descendre ton cœur dans le cœur du tout-monde et tu connaîtras la pêche merveilleuse d'aimer et de vivre' (p. 134). Even his religion has the global, ever-evolving character of the 'Tout-monde' as he constantly builds new temples for new gods (p. 141). Similarly, the solution to Napo's dilemma is not just the 'secret' of the Guadeloupean drums, but a whole range of secrets: 'Napo [...] écoutait toutes les musiques, à la recherche d'un secret, mais derrière le secret il trouvait d'autres secrets en enfilade' (p. 145). And what is most striking is that these other kinds of music include classical European music: moreover, it is this secret language that he tries hardest to penetrate:

> Cela sonnait pour lui comme un emmêlement de flutes et de hautbois, comme une langue violoneuse qui ne lui parlait pas. Il y avait là mystère d'un casse-tête sans fin dont il n'a pas la clé. Longtemps, il écouta dans une touffaille obscure, cherchant le sel, quémandant l'ordre caché qui ne se révélait. (*TB*, pp.147–48)

Finally, he can listen to Ravel's *Bolero* with 'le sentiment que ce morceau avait été composé pour lui', and this new enthusiasm, far from rooting him in his own culture, takes him beyond it: no other Guadeloupeans share it, in fact they make fun of him (p. 149). But it is a necessary component of his ultimate success as a drummer.

Here in other words the 'secret world' in question is not the more obviously mysterious world of magic, folklore, and popular Caribbean tradition, but that of European high culture, which is described as just as impenetrable, concealing as many precious secrets, as the world of the 'quimboiseurs' and the drummers, and as equally accessible to the intuitive, non-rational, life-transforming knowledge that is more usually associated with 'primitive' cultures.

In conclusion, it is this even-handedness, the refusal to privilege traditional Caribbean culture, that most sharply distinguishes Pépin's novels from those of writers such as Chamoiseau and Confiant. Similarly, his reworking of Glissant's 'opacity' moves it away from its implication in a homogeneous, closed Creole community, towards a conception of community as both internally fragmented and, through the prominence of the 'initiation' theme, potentially open to outsiders who are prepared to learn its various secret languages. His originality is to have combined the involvement with folklore, magic, and the past that characterizes the 'créolité' novels, and Glissant's conception of the opacity and camouflage of specifically Caribbean culture, with a more balanced and dynamic relationship between knowledge and ignorance, inclusion and exclusion, that opens out onto the Glissantian relationality of the 'Tout-monde'. In Pépin's novels, the secret worlds are always *relative* to each other.

CHAPTER 10

❖

# Place, Textuality, and the Real in Édouard Glissant's *Mahagony*

All of Édouard Glissant's novels are characterized by extreme richness and inventiveness at the level of their textuality. They build up complex, constantly expanding networks of interconnected elements, which may be stories, images, or phrases. Glissant's term for these networks is the 'trame' or 'weave';[1] and the connotations of weaving are entirely appropriate to the fashion in which the text is constructed from many distinct but inextricably intertwined strands.

Evocations of place have a crucial role in this, and nowhere more so than in his novel *Mahagony* (1987). A plurality of separate places is drawn together in the 'weave', as echoes and resonances are set up between them. Places become textualized — evolving configurations of words which participate in the construction of the text. Conversely, the text is also imaged as a kind of landscape of natural, proliferating vegetation: for instance, Longoué's story is 'seulement une branche d'une végétation interminable [...] dans l'entour incertain de Trou-à-Roches' (*Mahagony*, p. 95). This process of textualization involves both similarity and difference. Different words are used to refer to the same place: 'Cases-L'Étang' also has another name, 'Trou-à-Roches' (p. 104).[2] Conversely, different places are described in the same words, a process that will be analyzed in the final part of this chapter. Either way, there is no stable one-to-one correlation between word and referent but, rather, a shifting network of intratextual relations and variations.

However, places are also important in Glissant's novels — and perhaps particularly *Mahagony* — for an entirely different reason: because of what has happened in them. This involves the diegetic level of the novel, that is, its creation of a realist fictional world in which events matter. Places, in other words, also engage with the real. For

1    Rendered as 'weave' in Betsy Wing's translation of *Poétique de la Relation* (Édouard Glissant, *Poetics of Relation*, trans. by Betsy Wing (Ann Arbor: University of Michigan Press, 1997). Glissant links the 'trame' or 'weave' with his other key concepts of opacity and Relation, for instance: 'Des opacités peuvent coexister, confluer, tramant des tissus dont la véritable compréhension porterait sur la texture de cette trame et non pas sur la nature des composantes' (*PR*, p. 204).
2    Different words are also used to refer to the same trees: 'Les trois ébéniers sont en même temps acajous, et parfois — par une aberration légitime — acacias, sans qu'on y trouve à comprendre' (p. 230). There is in fact a very close connection between places and trees in *Mahagony*, all the important places are marked by trees.

instance, the ebony trees are significant *because* Anne Béluse killed Liberté Longoué under them, and because Maho was shot under them; Malendure is significant because both Maho and Mani think about leaving the island from there but then decide against it, and so on.

As these examples suggest, the significance of place is also intimately connected with the passing of time. Juris Silenieks theorizes this connection in terms of the Bakhtinian notion of the 'chronotope'.[3] He quotes Bakhtin's definition of this concept — 'the intrinsic connectedness of temporal and spatial relationships that are artistically expressed in literature' — and comments, 'it is essential to emphasize the inseparability of time/space as a formally constitutive category of literature. Glissant's landscape is diachronic, a sort of cadastre where the experiences of a people are recorded'.[4] Thus it is because the mahogany tree is so old, and has witnessed so many key events, that it constitutes the most significant place around which *Mahagony* is structured.

This causal relation operates generally throughout Glissant's fiction. The more things that have happened in a place, the more important the place is. It is relevant here that the island of Martinique has, on the one hand, a long and dramatic history and is, on the other, extremely small. The combination of these two factors means that a large number of things have happened in a limited number of places; in many of these places, therefore, many things have happened. This phenomenon is exploited in the novels to produce a strong emotional reaction in the reader, in that the accumulation over time of things happening in the same place produces a particular kind of uncanny effect. An early example of this occurs in *Le Quatrième Siècle*, when, at the end of the second chapter, we discover that Papa Longoué's shack is exactly where the first Longoué spent his first night on the island, after escaping from La Roche (QS, pp. 59–60). In *Mahagony*, too, the same effect is created in connection with the mahogany tree: the power of the final description of this tree, now surrounded by the banality of a tourist hotel complex, derives from our knowledge that it was precisely here that Gani, Maho, and Mani all hid from their pursuers, over a period of nearly a hundred and fifty years (*Mahagony*, p. 248).

The resonance of a place, in other words, stems from the sedimentation in it of layers of different incidents and different periods of past time.[5] And for this to be perceptible, we have to know that it was indeed 'the same place', and for us to know this, the text has to operate on a realistic level as well as on that of the freely generative textuality which, as I have shown, is equally characteristic of the representation of places. Relations of fictional reference are also crucial, in order to allow the reader to identify particular places.

3    Juris Silenieks, 'Pays rêvé, pays réel: The Martinican Chronotope in Edouard Glissant's Œuvre', *World Literature Today* 63.4 (1989), pp. 632–37.

4    Mikhail Bakhtin, *The Dialogic Imagination: Four Essays*, ed. by Michael Holquist, trans. by Caryl Emerson and Michael Holquist (Austin: University of Texas Press, 1981), p. 84; quoted in Juris Silenieks, 'Pays rêvé, pays réel', p. 632.

5    As Nathaniel Wing comments, 'Le lieu n'est jamais une surface plane où se joue les actions, mais une profondeur dans la mémoire et dans les passions des protagonistes' ('Écriture et relations dans les romans d'Édouard Glissant', in *Horizons d'Édouard Glissant: actes du colloque international, octobre 1990 (Porto)*, ed. by Yves-Alain Favre (Pau: J & B Éditions, 1992), pp. 295–302 (p. 299).

There is in *Mahagony*, therefore, a dynamic relation between reference and textuality. This in turn creates a parallel dynamic between *sameness* and *difference*. In much of Glissant's theoretical writing, and in the novels and poems, it is difference that is valorized, and sameness carries a very negative connotation.[6] But focusing on his representation of place enables us to see that, alongside the oppressive philosophical and ideological universalism, there is a different kind of sameness that has a powerful positive value in his fiction. The sameness of place however, does not exclude change, hence difference. The meaning of a place changes as different things happen in it. But the new meanings do not obliterate the old ones; rather, a kind of palimpsest is formed through a process of superimposition and accumulation. The condition for this whole process, moreover, is the identity of the place over time; it is only because it is different that one can see that the place has changed, but it is only because it is recognizably the same place that one can talk about change at all. The notion of change requires both identity and difference. The mahogany tree itself is the best image for this combination of change and permanence, which figures prominently in all the descriptions of it: 'les arbres qui vivent longtemps changent toujours, en demeurant' (p. 16); 'Et le mahogani seul a perduré dans son personnage changeant' (p. 230).

There are two passages from *Mahagony* which show with particular clarity how this interplay of textuality and the real, and of difference and sameness, works out in detail. They also — and this is surely no accident — illustrate in a rather oblique fashion the importance of the relationship in Glissant's work between places and people. Glissant, in all his writing, has a strong, almost Proustian sense of the equal importance of places and people, and the similarity between them. In *Mahagony*, of course, the connection between place and person is made very specifically via the theme of the tree that is planted over the placenta of every newborn baby. The text exploits the anagrammatic echoes in *place/plant/placenta*, as when Eudoxie says, 'Tout homme femme a son plant mêlé avec son placenta' (p. 52). More generally, Mathieu speaks of 'lieux qui sont autant de personnages débutants' (p. 24), and even admits that 'je suis plus enclin à saisir des reliefs de végétation changeante qu'à mettre en scène [...] des êtres humains que j'aurais imaginés. Les types de personnages nous importent moins que le vent glissant sous les acacias' (p. 28).

---

6    For instance, in the section entitled 'Le Même et le Divers' in *Le Discours antillais*, where Glissant argues that the universalist European ideology of 'le Même' underpinned colonial expansion and exploitation: 'pour nourrir sa prétention à l'universel, le Même a requis (a eu besoin de) la chair du monde. L'autre est sa tentation. Non pas encore l'Autre comme projet d'accord, mais l'autre comme matière à sublimer. Les peuples du monde furent ainsi en proie à la rapacité occidentale, avant de se trouver l'objet des projections affectives ou sublimantes de l'Occident. Le Divers [...] signifie l'effort de l'esprit vers une relation transversale, sans transcendance universaliste' (*DA*, p. 190). In his later work, 'le Même' is sometimes reformulated as 'la pensée du système', and combatted by concepts such as 'le chaos-monde' et 'la pensée archipélique', of which Glissant writes that: '[elle] s'accorde à ce qui du monde s'est diffusé en archipels précisément, ces sortes de diversités dans l'étendue, qui pourtant rallient des rives et marient des horizons. Nous nous apercevons de ce qu'il y avait de continental, d'épais et qui pesait sur nous, dans les somptueuses pensées de système qui jusqu'à ce jour ont régi l'histoire des humanités, et qui ne sont plus adéquates à nos éclatements, à nos histoires ni à nos non moins somptueuses errances' (*TTM*, p.31).

Nevertheless, as far as the structure of the novel is concerned, individual people play a dominant role as narrators of the different sections. All except three of the chapters have as their title either the name of the narrator or a description of him or her. Of the other three, one, 'Un coq à Esculape', soon makes it clear that its narrator is Mathieu. But the remaining two are not narrated in the first person at all. They are anonymous accounts, set in unnamed places, of the actions of an unnamed man, in the first case, and in the second, of a woman who is only named right at the end, as Marie Celat. (The context allows us to guess that the man is Maho, but this is not confirmed until much later in the novel (p. 186), by Marie Celat, who also names the place — a steep wooded descent to the sea — as Malendure.)

The chapters are called 'La Descente' — the first chapter in Part II of the novel — and 'Remontée', which occurs towards the end of Part III. What links them together is, in the first instance, simply their shared differences from all the other chapters: the third-person narration, the different kind of title, and the fact that although the places in which they are set are described in great detail, they are not identified. Beyond this, however, the textualization of these two enigmatic sites seems to create a kind of subjectless dialogue between them: 'Remontée' 'answers' 'La Descente'. This is reinforced by the way in which each chapter alludes to the other's title: 'La remontée est à fur et mesure plus facile' ('Descente', p. 101) and 'elle était descendue' ('Remontée', p. 236). The symmetrical relationship extends, in fact, to their psychological significance: 'going down' (perhaps 'going under') seems to be recounting a failure of nerve, insofar as Maho lacks the courage to leave the island, whereas 'coming back up' narrates Marie Celat's recovery from madness, 'C'est ainsi que [...] pour la première fois elle revint à elle-même [...] Réelle enfin' (p. 236).

But a more detailed analysis reveals that there are far more connections between the two chapters on a purely textual level, thus illustrating the major role played by places in the textual productivity of Glissant's writing. The chapters are linked by a whole web of intricate echoes which serve to weave the two places together. Thus, very near the beginning of 'La Descente' we read: 'les arbres sont de toutes sortes mêlées, qui font de l'ombre dans l'ombre, en couches ascendantes jusqu'au rai provoquant du jour' (p. 99); and this image of layers of leaves and shade is precisely echoed very near the beginning of 'Remontée': 'À l'entrée du gouffre une seconde couche de vert opposait son épaisseur. Non plus pâle mais moirée de toutes les atteintes de l'ombre' (p. 234). In the next but one sentence of 'La Descente', 'le vertige si soudain' (p. 99) corresponds to 'Le vertige [...] la fit vaciller' ('Remontée', p. 234); similarly, 'il [...] s'agrippe à n'importe quoi, pour remonter la pente' ('Descente', p. 101) and 's'agrippant pour ne pas tomber' ('Remontée' p. 235).

Other links are more complex. For instance, in 'La Descente', 'Leurs feuilles sont argentées d'un dépôt grenu et fragile, qui n'est pas le sel ni l'embrun de mer' (p. 100) is indirectly linked to 'une mince tige d'argent bruni' ('Remontée', p. 234): leaf has become stem, and the sea-spray has generated an echo in 'bruni'. In a larger-scale example, the word 'poids' enters into two different contexts in each section; in 'Remontée' they occur close together:

> Pour la première fois elle revint à elle-même. Transparente, pesant d'un *poids* inattendu sur les ombrages qui descendaient. Réelle enfin sur l'éparpillement. La toute minuscule chose qu'elle avait dessouchée restait dans sa main. Preuve qu'elle était descendue au fond du vertige et avait ramené un *poids* rassurant, trop connu déjà. (*Mahagony*, p. 236, my emphasis)

Thus the first occurrence refers to the literal weight of her body, the second ambiguously to the literal weight of the plant but also, metaphorically, to the reassuring solidity of her newly recovered sense of herself. If we juxtapose this passage with two separate extracts from 'La Descente' — 'L'homme balance dans le vide, il hésite entre la mer et le mont. Le *poids* tenace des ombres le pousse vers le bas' (p. 100), and 'Des nids de feuilles parasites l'aident pourtant à gravir, si gros qu'il peut *peser* sur eux de tout son corps' (p. 101) — we see a reversal on one level: here the *second* reference to weight is the literal weight of his body, while the first is a metaphorical weight pulling him down to the sea. But there is also a parallel: in both cases, the first 'weight' is associated with movement downwards ('ombrages qui descendaient', 'le pousse vers le bas'), and with a disturbing sense of transparency and void; while the second occurrence in both cases stresses solidity and upward movement ('ramené', 'gravir').

Other examples of this 'weaving' together of the two texts, hence of the two places, extend further, expanding into the rest of the novel. For instance, one of the rare occurrences of direct speech in each chapter refers to the snake, known as 'l'ennemi': 'Ne mettez jamais votre main dans un trou. L'ennemi dort peut-être dedans' ('Remontée', p. 235) corresponds to '"il ne manquerait plus que l'ennemi", songe-t-il' ('La Descente', p. 102). But, equally, the adolescent Mani, in one of several chapters narrated by Mathieu, exactly repeats Maho's words in 'La Descente': 'Il ne manquerait plus que l'ennemi' (p. 224). Another example concerns phrases previously used by Marie Celat in the chapter that bears her name: 'nous sommes tout autant éparpillés' (p. 117); 'Ce temps-là était bien heureux, une légèreté d'herbage' (p. 117), both of which recur in 'Remontée', 'Réelle enfin sur l'éparpillement [...] il y avait dans l'air une légèreté d'herbage, qui contrastait pour elle avec le sentiment de sa densité toute nouvelle' (pp. 236–37). Also in the 'Marie Celat' chapter, the 'vonvons' and 'moustiques' of 'La Descente' (p. 102) are picked up in a way that not only establishes Malendure as the site of 'La Descente' and Maho as its protagonist, but also links 'La Descente' with 'Remontée': talking about Maho, Marie Celat says, 'Même quand il *descendait* Malendure, l'eau de la mer ne rafraîchissait plus ses pieds. Il mettait trop de temps à *remonter* dans les vonvons les moustiques' (p. 186, my emphasis).

All of the above examples demonstrate the productivity of the text, and hence the importance of place as textuality. There is another example that initially falls into this category, but — and this is why it is particularly significant — then *also* brings into play the diegetic dimension of fictional reference that I have argued is equally essential in that it enables us to recognize an identity of place.

Its starting point is a number of repetitions of the words *roches, terre, rouge, racines, violets*. The first page of 'La Descente' contains the sentence: 'Les roches retiennent de grands arpents de terre rouge entre des racines violettes' (p. 99). Some elements of this are picked up in 'Remontée', scattered across separate sentences on p. 235: 'tige ou branche ou racine'; 'rouge sang'; 'poils [...] violets'. Then on the next page, 'racines' is woven together with the missing 'roche' and 'terre': 'Le tronc continuait en une résille multipliée de fines racines, courant l'une sur l'autre, brillantes dans leur couleur marron, qui enveloppaient absolument une roche ensouchée dans la terre' (p. 236). Further down the page, a version of 'violet' reappears together with 'roche' and the 'tige' from p. 235: 'Elle jeta au loin la roche et la tige violacée'. The original sentence from 'La Descente' thus unfolds and develops into a more complex structure in 'Remontée'.

However, some of its elements have already figured much earlier on. Right at the beginning of the novel, Mathieu's first section of narrative includes a description of the site of the mahogany and the ebony trees at Cases L'Étang, which starts: 'Les ébéniers avaient éclaboussé leurs branchages et leurs *racines* partout alentour en forêt inachevée mais inviolée, marquée de fulgurances *rousses et violettes*' (p. 17). This section thus contains textual elements which recur in both 'La Descente' and 'Remontée'.[7] But we know that Mathieu is describing Cases L'Étang, and that 'La Descente' is set at Malendure, which is not the same as the site of the mahogany tree ('Cases L'Étang, à l'écart de Malendure', p. 221). We do not know where 'Remontée' is set, *unless* we pick up the further connections that Mathieu, in this same description, goes on to make. These are textual links to 'Remontée' but *not* to 'La Descente' — and they are referentially far more precise than the allusions to roots and the red and mauve colours that occur in both: that is, they have to be describing the same place. His description of Cases L'Étang continues:

> Fulgurances rousses et violettes qui s'avivaient dans les éclairs de pluie; la savane qui s'étendait plus loin et qui ondulait entre les maigres touffes de vétiver changeant de couleur avec les sautes du vent [...]. Derrière l'embroussaillage des ébéniers une odeur de four de charbon grossissait inépuisable. (*Mahagony*, pp. 17–18)

And in 'Remontée' we read: 'Une odeur de four de charbon envahissait jusqu'au cœur [...] les vétivers sur la savane barraient de leurs touffes les longues traînées argentées soulevées par le vent dans la déclive du champ' (p. 237). 'Remontée' (Marie Celat's recovery from madness), in other words, takes place at the key site of the whole novel: Cases L'Étang, by the mahogany tree, despite the striking fact that the tree, normally so prominent in the text as a whole, is never mentioned in 'Remontée'.

Mathieu's final chapter returns to Cases L'Étang and repeats the words he has already used ('savane', 'vent', 'touffes'), but this time he adds to them more elements from the version in 'Remontée': 'Peut-être apercevez-vous une grande étendue de savane, roulée par le vent. Les traînées d'herbe argentée se couchent en houles

---

7    There is, in fact, a further occurrence of some of its elements, where a list of different places is held together textually by the recurrence of a cluster of words: 'Sans doute la bleuité des fonds avait-elle enfin cédé au rouge têtu des terres défrichées. Une poussière portée par le vent caressait les feuilles sans se poser nulle part. On la sentait virer en plein devant le visage et obliquer vers la fumée violette des chaudières de la Fabrique. Les roches des rivières se veinaient d'entailles enfouies' (*Mahagony*, p. 93).

rythmées, butent contre des touffes, reprennent aussitôt leur course' (p. 247). This referential identification produces a particular effect which, although it is based on a similar process of picking up textual echoes, is very different from that of the 'weaving' of variable connections on the purely textual level, because it results in a 'real' discovery about the location of 'Remontée'. The discovery, moreover, is not at all obvious; so the textual repetitions have here a hermeneutic function, becoming in effect clues which enable the reader to solve the 'mystery' of the location of 'Remontée'. The effect is a slight shock of recognition, and it is dependent on sameness: the revelation that the setting of 'Remontée' and Cases L'Étang are the same place. The recognition effect on the level of the real is arguably all the more powerful because it is achieved through purely textual means — the repetition of certain words — rather than plainly stated.

Conversely, the similarities which the text creates between Cases L'Étang and Malendure overlay but do not erase their differences on the level of the real. The 'écart' that separates them ('Cases L'Étang, à l'écart de Malendure') is the space across which 'La Descente' and 'Remontée' weave their textual connections; whereas in 'Remontée' textual connections to Cases L'Étang in Mathieu's narration are based on referential identity.

One finds in *Mahagony* a range of different, sometimes quite complex, interactions between the two levels of textuality and diegetic reference. My final example starts with a simple textual echo between the two chapters. At the end of 'La Descente' we read: 'de gros vonvons *qui s'écartent* parfois, vers la profondeur absurde des cavernes en *abîme* creusées entrée les branches' (p. 102); and this is picked up at the beginning of 'Remontée': 'la main les [les feuilles] *écarta*, cherchant au fond de *cet abîme*' (p. 234). The same image recurs several times, with slight variations, in the rest of the novel. In the chapter narrated by Lanoué, 'abîme' becomes, more prosaically, 'trou': 'Depuis le jour où le planteur de nos corps a écarté les feuilles de caco portées par la pluie des sables, crié fouillant le trou, ramenant le vent autour de la souche tant minuscule' (p. 71). Lanoué is referring here to the planting of the mahogany tree over Gani's placenta. Eight pages later, Gani finds himself a hiding place, again by the mahogany tree, and repeats the gesture of pushing aside leaves that cover a space hidden behind them: 'À droite de l'éboulement un trou de terre était masqué par des orties géantes que l'enfant écarta sans danger' (p. 79). Then, much later, Mani, also at Cases L'Étang, finds what is now called 'the' hole: 'Mani penche vers le trou, caresse les herbes à l'entrée de la case' (p. 221).

Various elements of all three of these sentences are echoed in 'Remontée', adding to the link established by the original sentence quoted above ('la main les écarta, cherchant au fond de cet abîme'). The 'trou' is introduced, again with a definite article as though it has already been mentioned — 'elle sentit sa tête chavirer vers le trou si banal, invisible presque' (p. 234) — and Marie Celat puts her hand in it, echoing the verb 'pencher' used of Mani thirteen pages earlier: 'La main [...] pencha plus au fond dans la ténèbre' (p. 235). She then pulls up a plant growing in the hole, in a gesture which is the exact opposite of the planting of the mahogany tree on p. 71, and once again the text underlines the link between the two actions by echoing the words used: 'la souche tant minuscule' (p. 71) reappears as 'La toute minuscule chose qu'elle avait dessouchée restait dans sa main' (p. 236). In this way, a symbolic connection is established between the mahogany tree that is planted over Gani's placenta (p. 71) and the miniature 'tree' that Marie Celat, in an obscure act of exorcism of the past, perhaps, pulls up over a century later.[8] They cannot, of course, literally be the same tree. But given the other indications that 'Remontée' is set at Cases L'Étang, we are, I think, meant to assume that the 'trou' is literally the same hole. The evolution of this image through the novel, therefore, mixes purely textual resonances between Cases L'Étang and Malendure, a psychological equivalence in Marie Celat's mind between the original mahogany tree planted over a new-born baby's placenta and another 'baby' tree a century later, and a referential identity of place in the situating of the 'trou'.[9]

This essay has been concerned with detailed textual correspondences between two very short and enigmatic sections of *Mahagony*. But this small-scale study raises some much larger issues surrounding the status of the real in Glissant's fiction. My analysis here would suggest that the real — here exemplified by the identity of the place in which 'Remontée' is set — is problematic but not unattainable: the reader can ultimately discover that this chapter is describing Cases L'Étang. Conversely, the similarly diegetic information that the setting of 'Remontée' and that of 'La Descente' are *not* the same is conveyed considerably more quickly and easily. At the same time, the two chapters describe these different places in strikingly similar terms; as I have shown, many words and phrases are repeated from one chapter to the next. This kind of textual echoing contrasts with the more straightforward way (more typical of conventional realist discourse, perhaps) in which we are simply told that Cases L'Étang is 'à l'écart de Malendure'.

But the fact that 'Remontée' *is* set at Cases L'Étang is communicated solely through the play of lexical repetitions between two separate sections of the text: the same kind of 'poetic' discourse, in other words, as that which links 'La Descente' with 'Remontée', hence Malendure with the referentially non-identical place Cases L'Étang. (In fact, the two passages in question are far more widely separately within the novel as a whole (pp. 17–18 and pp. 236–37) so that making the connections between them requires even greater attention on the part of the reader.) From a stylistic point of view, one cannot distinguish in Glissant's fiction between a realist

8    Bernadette Cailler stresses the equivalence of the two trees, commenting: '[Marie Celat] will go so far as to mischievously uproot the mahogany stem, the sacrosanct symbol of all the heroic commitments of earlier days', in 'Édouard Glissant: A Creative Critic', *World Literature Today* 63.4 (1989), pp. 589–92 (p. 591).
9    It also allows us to make one final, much larger-scale, link between the two chapters I have been comparing and the structure of the novel as a whole. The 'trou' mentioned in 'Remontée' recalls the other name of the site of the mahogany tree: not Cases L'Étang but Le Trou-à-Roches. And the other chapter, 'La Descente', is set at Malendure. Thus a curiously asymmetrical relation is revealed between these two chapters and the first two parts of the novel, whose titles are, precisely, 'Le Trou-à-Roches' and 'Malendure'. 'La Descente' is in 'Malendure', but 'Remontée' is in the third part of the novel, 'Le Tout-Monde', rather than in 'Le Trou-à-Roches'. The textuality of places is thus not only a question of small resonances and recurrences, but also engages with the overall organization of the novel into three parts, subdivided into chapters.

diegetic discourse and a non-realist, purely textual generativity which creates patterns of verbal echoes that have no referential correlate. It is only the particular choice of lexical items — the referential specificity of 'vétivers', 'four de charbon', 'le trou', etc. — that makes the difference. One might see this as an indication that his writing has moved on beyond the opposition between realist and non-realist fictional discourse that underpinned much of the debate surrounding the French novel in the 1970s and 1980s (and that has in a sense structured this essay). In this highly unobtrusive fashion, Glissant is working towards a new relationship between textuality and realism.[10]

---

10    *Tout-Monde*, in 1993, develops this further in questioning the boundary between the diegetically and the autobiographically 'real', also to a significant extent in connection with the representation of place. See 'Fictions of Identity and the Identities of Fiction in *Tout-Monde*', Chapter 9 of Britton, *Language and Literary Form in French Caribbean Writing*, pp. 127–37.

# CHAPTER 11

❖

# The Theme of the Ancestral Crime in the Novels of William Faulkner, Édouard Glissant, and Maryse Condé

William Faulkner, Édouard Glissant, and Maryse Condé all come from that part of the world that we can define as the American Tropics, and therefore share a common history of plantation slavery. Within that history, however, they occupy very different positions — Faulkner as the descendant of slave-owners, Glissant and Condé as the descendants of slaves. In addition, the American South and the Caribbean have very different attitudes towards the question of racial mixing, pejoratively known as miscegenation in the United States and positively as *métissage* or creolization in the Caribbean. The South's fear of miscegenation leads to an obsession with what Glissant calls 'filiation', that is, maintaining clear continuous lines of descent, especially male descent, which he sees as the opposite of creolization; these two antagonistic principles are a prominent theme in many of his essays.[1]

Glissant has also written on Faulkner throughout his career, culminating in 1996 with *Faulkner, Mississippi*, and the opposition and interplay of filiation and creolization are central to his account of Faulkner. He sees Faulkner's novels as showing the inevitable perversion of filiation, and the impossibility of founding a 'pure' lineage. Thus Faulkner's *Absalom, Absalom* is a particularly important text for Glissant, because of its hero Thomas Sutpen's desperate desire to found a lineage, and the tragic consequences of this (*FM*, p. 151). In other words, he reads Faulkner's work as dominated by the issue of the origin of Southern society; Faulkner's sense of the damnation of the South, he argues, stems from the impossibility of founding a legitimate filiation, and this in turn is impossible because the whole society has been brought into existence by a crime, an 'original sin'.

What this crime is, however, is never entirely clear. Looking at Faulkner's work as a whole, Glissant shows how it sometimes appears to be simply miscegenation: 'Dans la métaphysique délirante du Sud, il est une logique indéniable: que c'est impossible de fonder lignée à partir du mélange' (*FM*, pp. 122–23). Elsewhere, however, the 'curse' might be something the settlers brought with them to America

---

1    See for example 'Culture et identité' in Glissant's *Introduction à une poétique du divers*.

(p. 163); or it might stem from the way in which they acquired land (pp. 163–64); but this — stealing land from the native Americans — is in turn juxtaposed with another original sin: the institution of slavery. Thus, after evoking the first question of how Faulkner is to represent the crime of stealing land, Glissant adds, 'S'ajoute une autre béance [...] comment comprendre ou au moins envisager cette "damnation" du Sud? Est-elle liée à l'obscur enchevêtrement de *l'esclavage*, de ses racines, de sa tourmentée histoire?', and concludes that Faulkner never gives an answer to these 'questions primordiales' (p. 37).

So there are three possible candidates for the status of original sin: miscegenation, the theft of the land, and slavery. Throughout *Faulkner, Mississippi*, they reappear in varying combinations: miscegenation is the result of slavery — 'la damnation, le métissage, né du viol de l'esclavage' (*FM*, p. 124) — but is that the only reason why slavery is a crime? In fact, slavery is more often seen as a parallel crime to the appropriation of land, a 'perversion', which undermines the attempt to found a legitimate community, but one which is 'liée (sourdement, obscurément), à une injustice, une oppression, en l'occurrence, l'esclavage' (p. 169). The two crimes are brought together in *Go Down, Moses*, where the Indian chief sells to the white settlers both the land which is not his to sell, and slaves, as Glissant points out (*FM*, p. 165).[2] But in general terms there is no necessary link between them.

Moreover, none of these entangled possible causes is ever stated explicitly. They combine to create a pervasive sense of damnation and rottennness, as in Hamlet's Denmark (*FM*, p. 181); *but* 'Faulkner ne le dit jamais (le criant si souvent, obscurément), parce qu'il souffre dans sa chair (dans son Sud) de le penser vraiment' (p. 181). Here, Glissant raises the question of how Faulkner's own position affects his representation of Southern society, and argues that because of his implication in and intense emotional attachment to the South his novels cannot confront the question openly.[3] As a citizen, Faulkner shared the conventionally loyalist and racist views of the Southern plantocracy in general. In his writing, however, the conflict between his moral principles — in particular, his hatred of injustice — and his social position produces a fundamental ambiguity of which he does not seem to be fully conscious (*FM*, pp. 308–09). Thus, Faulkner is not in control of his writing (p. 137), which as a result both reveals and conceals the original crime(s), constantly gesturing towards a truth whose revelation is constantly deferred: 'ce que l'écrivain William Faulkner s'est attaché, avec une si sauvage ténacité, à occulter tout en le révélant: le différé de la damnation du Sud' (p. 28).

This 'différé' is, according to Glissant, a major structural principle of Faulkner's work. It underlies various prominent features of his writing, such as the curious indeterminacy of his characters (*FM*, pp. 37–38) and the inconclusive nature of his narratives (p. 53). But its central dynamic is the concealment-revelation of the secret crime: 'Indiquer et dérober un secret ou une connaissance, c'est-à-dire en *différer* le relèvement [...] ce sera le motif, pour l'essentiel, des modes techniques autour

---

2    William Faulkner, *Go Down, Moses* (New York: Random House, 1942).
3    Faulkner's attitude to the legacy of slavery in the American South, and its effect on his novels, has already been discussed in Chapter 7.

desquels s'organisera son écriture' (p. 14). Thus the crime is figured in the novels by a secret truth buried in the past and only revealed towards the end of the novel, after a long and convoluted process of partial disclosures, hints, and clues; but, even then, the revelation of this particular secret — for example Sutpen's first marriage to the not-wholly-white Eulalia Bon in *Absalom, Absalom* — is only implicitly and ambiguously connected to the basic crime which causes the damnation of the South. This kind of compulsive ambiguity and deferment is reminiscent of the theory of the Marxist critic Pierre Macherey, with his emphasis on the determining force of the 'silences' in the work; in the chapter of his *Pour une théorie de la production littéraire* entitled 'Dire et ne pas dire', he argues that what is overtly present in the literary work emerges from a 'fond de silence' which is 'ce qui donne un sens au sens'.[4] The work says what it does because of what it cannot say, and this structure is produced by a contradiction between the author's ideology, determined by his or her class position, and the ability of literary form to distance and put into question that ideology.[5]

As Macherey would, Glissant explains Faulkner's work as determined by his social position as a member of the Southern white landowning classes in the lengthy aftermath of their defeat in the Civil War. Had Faulkner not been so loyal to traditional white Southern society and so troubled by its decline, he would not have needed to repress or 'différer' the truths of its original sins. Therefore, despite the fact that Faulkner and Glissant are both formed by the history of plantation slavery in the American Tropics, one would not expect to find any similarities between their novels, because their social positions within this geographical-historical complex are so different: as a black descendant of slaves, Glissant has no reason to feel implicated in the crimes of the white plantation owners.

In fact, however, critics such as J. Michael Dash and Chris Bongie, while also stressing the differences between the two writers, have argued that Glissant's early fiction is heavily influenced by Faulkner.[6] The clearest example of this is the novel which Bongie describes as 'Glissant's resolutely Faulknerian *Le Quatrième Siècle*' (*IE*, p. 167). In their discussion of *Le Quatrième Siècle*, both Bongie and Dash point to the overwhelming influence of the past on the present — a past, however, that cannot be represented straightforwardly or with any certainty.[7] Dash adds to this the concern with filiation and legitimacy, and conversely with interracial contact (p. 75); Bongie notes 'the importance of family genealogies' to both *Le Quatrième Siècle* and *Absalom, Absalom* (*IE*, pp. 167–68), and mentions Glissant's analysis of the secret and its revelation in Faulkner's novels (p. 167).

There is, however, another Faulknerian echo in *Le Quatrième Siècle*, which relates more directly to Glissant's analysis in *Faulkner, Mississippi*: the motif of the ancestral crime or 'original sin'. One of the more surprising features of *Le Quatrième Siècle* is

---

4    Macherey, *Pour une théorie de la production littérarie*, p. 106. Macherey's theory has been adapted to a specifically postcolonial context by Gayatri Spivak in her 'Can the Subaltern Speak?' (see p. 286).
5    See Chapter 4 for further discussion of Macherey's theorization of the text.
6    See J. Michael Dash, *Édouard Glissant* (Cambridge: Cambridge University Press, 1995), pp. 74–79; Bongie, *IE*, pp. 167–69, 189–93).
7    Dash, *Édouard Glissant*, pp. 74–75; Bongie, *IE*, p. 189.

that in it Glissant chooses to appropriate and rework Faulkner's obsession with the crime that lies buried at the source of a community's evolution over time; the crime, in other words, that is 'original' in the sense that it has to do with the foundation of a lineage — in fact, in *Le Quatrième Siècle*, of two lineages. The novel tells the stories of two families who are descended from two African captives brought to Martinique on the same slave ship; the fact that we never learn their original African names is in itself a sign that transportation breaks the chain of filiation and so necessitates the founding of new lineages, named as the Longoués and the Béluses. The first Longoué and the first Béluse are enemies because of something that happened in Africa before they were captured, but for most of the narrative we do not know what that was. Only the narrator, Papa Longoué, knows; and he does not disclose it to his listener, Mathieu Béluse, until three-quarters of the way through the novel (QS, pp. 245–46), when we and Mathieu learn that the two African ancestors were once close friends, but that after 'Longoué' was chosen to be the new chief of the tribe 'Béluse', out of envious rage, sold his friend to the slave raiders, but then was also taken himself, and they ended up on the same ship. The whole Béluse family, in other words, is descended from the man who betrayed his friend by selling him into slavery. This, then, is the ancestral crime that haunts *Le Quatrième Siècle*. The similarities with Faulkner are clear: the narrative of founding a new lineage, not here as a result of colonization but of the trauma of transportation (hence the novel's repeated emphasis on the theme of 'enracinement'); and, particularly, the fact that the Béluse lineage is based on an original crime that is secret, unknown to the descendants and revealed only belatedly and briefly.

It does not follow, however, that Glissant's novel is also driven by the principle of the 'différé', the compulsive, constrained need to 'say without saying' that drives Faulkner's tortuous scenarios of gradual revelation; Glissant himself is not caught up in the moral and social contradictions that in his reading of Faulkner's work underlie the dynamic of the 'différé'. One indication of this is the contrast between Faulkner's lack of clarity concerning the nature of the original crime — hesitating, as I have shown, between slavery, miscegenation, and the theft of land — and the way in which in Glissant's novel it is quite unambiguously defined as African complicity in slavery, with a lucidity which suggests a much freer, less constrained authorial position.

At several points in *Faulkner, Mississippi*, however, Glissant emphasizes his view that the 'différé' is the most positive feature of Faulkner's writing, because the fracture that it introduces into the novels opens them up to the possibility of future change, including an intuition of creolization (FM, pp. 225–26, 304–05). This may explain why, in addition to his reworking of the story of the original crime, Glissant also adopts the 'différé' as a structural principle. The revelation of Béluse's treachery in *Le Quatrième Siècle* is deferred until almost the end of the novel, just as the revelation of Charles Bon's mixed blood is in *Absalom, Absalom*. In Glissant's novel, however, the deferral strikes the reader less as an obscure impulse to delay or play down the truth than as a calculated *mise en scène* of repression: no longer the author's repression, in other words, but that of the characters. As in Glissant's reading of Faulkner, the repression is to do with slavery; unlike in Faulkner's case, however, it is not the result of guilt: there is no reason why the descendants of slaves (apart from individuals such as Béluse who raise the sensitive issue of African complicity in it) should feel guilty about slavery.[8] But Glissant has elsewhere written a great deal about their repression of the *shame* of slavery and the importance of overcoming it, most recently in *Mémoires des esclavages*. In this text he makes a direct connection between Faulkner's 'différé', now described as 'une nouvelle technique de l'écriture et un style nouveau, qui sont bien de *dire sans dire tout en disant*' (*ME*, p. 61), and slavery, not just in Faulkner's work but in a far more general manner: no-one who has been in any way implicated, however distantly, in any system of slavery, he argues, is capable of having a normal, 'neutre et serein' (p. 63), memory of it. Rather, he continues in a long italicized sentence:

> Nous avons à nous dire tout esclavage, parce que nous essayons d'être lucides et d'être participants, sans nous le dire pourtant, parce que dans tous les cas nous en avons honte [...], et le disant quand même, parce que nous tenons au sens du temps et à la signification des histoires des peuples. (*ME*, pp. 63–64)

In this sense the deliberate appropriation of Faulkner's 'différé' allows Glissant to stage the *different* drama of the slaves' descendants' repression of the trauma of slavery. But he also makes another use of it, one that is far more ironic. In *Le Quatrième Siècle* the deferred revelation of the original Béluse's crime is strangely anti-climactic: one the one hand the reader finally finds out the reason for the enmity between Longoué and Béluse, but the impact of the revelation is immediately followed by the realization that it is simply not relevant to the present-day characters' lives: referring to the slave ship that brought the two ancestors to Martinique, Papa Longoué finishes his story by saying 'Mais lequel ici se souvient du bateau?' (*QS*, p. 247). This ironic, empty anti-climax is the sign of a conception of history which is very different from that of Faulkner. On the one hand, Glissant accuses Faulkner of depriving black people of their history, criticizing 'cette manière de "chosification" qui "sort" une communauté de son histoire' (*FM*, p. 84); and his own novels very consciously reinstate black people as agents of history.[9] But while *Le Quatrième Siècle* does indeed emphasize the need to retrieve a lost history, it accords equal importance to the need to leave it behind: as Mycéa says: 'le fait est qu'il faut apprendre ce que nous avons oublié, mais que, l'apprenant, il faut l'oublier encore'

8    It is worth noting, however, that in a brief chapter in *La Case du commandeur* Glissant returns to this theme, tracing another genealogy, that of the Celat family, back to the same crime: their ancestor Odono is one of two friends who give themselves the same name, but then fall in love with the same woman; out of jealousy, one of them sells the other into slavery (*La Case du commandeur*, pp. 138–42). As in the earlier novel, both end up in Martinique. But here no-one knows which one was the victim and which the betrayer; the guilt of complicity in slavery is in this case not limited to one particular individual, but hangs ambiguously over the community as a whole.

9    As Bongie notes, *Le Quatrième Siècle* 'critically supplements [*Absalom, Absalom*], in its revisionist emphasis on the centrality of a black experience that remains for the most part on the silent or inarticulate margins of the Southern writer's œuvre' (*IE*, p. 189) and 'offers us the hope of a solution that, as Glissant points out, is apparently absent from Faulkner's novels (*L'Intention poétique*, p. 178) [...] in which the past becomes the redemptive ground out of which a different set of relations — and a revolutionized future — might be thought to emerge' (*IE*, p. 191).

(*QS*, p. 285). Thus, whereas the South for Faulkner is trapped in a static historical impasse, Glissant's characters have the 'resilience and creativity', in Dash's words, to instigate change.[10]

Moreover, the way in which *Le Quatrième Siècle* demonstrates that time moves on is centrally to do with the original crime of the first Béluse. There is no indication that Mathieu feels responsible for, or shocked by, the betrayal perpetrated by his ancestor. The enmity between the families dies out and Papa Longoué 'adopts' Mathieu, because his own son has been killed fighting in the First World War. Thus, while his situation as the last of his line could be seen as an eminently Faulknerian example of failed filiation, here the failure is repaired by the adoption of the descendant of the original traitor Béluse; and this in turn means that where Glissant differs most strikingly from Faulkner is in the complete absence of the idea of damnation. Indeed, the Béluse family, far from being cursed, develops and thrives, adapting to new historical circumstances; it is the Longoués, descended from the original innocent victim, who die out as a distinct lineage.

But this — the end of the Longoué filiation — *does not matter* because, as we read on the last page of *Le Quatrième Siècle*, they are somehow diffused into the lives of everyone else: 'Taris, les Longoué reposaient en tous'. It is also extremely significant that the two examples which the text goes on to give of this process of diffusion concern, first, the descendants of the original enemy, Béluse, and secondly those of the mixed-race Targin family: 'Dans un Béluse, dont le vertige et l'impatience portaient la connaissance jusqu'au bord du chemin où elle était bientôt partagée entre tous. Dans un Targin, corps impavide, créé pour l'acte' (*QS*, p. 287). Filiation, in other words, has given way to the creolization that is so antipathetic to Faulkner (see *FM*, p. 117). Creolization has 'mixed up' the original African lines of filiation and given them new sources of strength, as Mycéa reflects: 'Puisque la mer avait *brassé* les homme venus de si loin et que la terre d'arrivage les avait fortifiés d'une autre sève' (*QS*, p. 285, my emphasis). Faulkner's sense of damnation, in other words, is dependent upon the supremacy of filiation, which in Glissant's fiction, as in his essays, gives way to the reality of creolization in which the notion of an ancestral curse affecting subsequent generations of one particular family can no longer be sustained.

Maryse Condé's allusions to Faulknerian themes in her novels are equally ironic, but differ from Glissant's in that she is not at all interested in the idea of founding a lineage: the hidden crimes, in her case, are not original, but they are ancestral. Also, unlike Glissant, Condé has not written extensively on Faulkner, but in interviews has spoken of his influence on her novels. Critics such as Michael Lucey, and indeed Condé herself, have linked her *Traversée de la mangrove* to Faulkner's *As I Lay Dying* because of their structural similarity: multiple interior monologues organized around a death.[11] But elsewhere Condé emphasizes that her interest in

10    'There is generally a resilience and creativity in Glissant's characters that make them very different from Faulkner's doomed protagonists' (Dash, *Édouard Glissant*, p. 74). Dash also contrasts Glissant's 'open-ended universe' with Faulkner's atmosphere of doom (p. 77).

11    Michael Lucey, 'Voices, Accounting for the Past: Maryse Condé's *Traversée de la mangrove*', in *L'Héritage de Caliban*, ed. by Maryse Condé (Pointe-à-Pitre: Jasor, 1992), pp. 123–32; Françoise

Faulkner centres on the notion of a transgression and guilt that affect people who have not committed the transgression themselves, but in some sense inherited it.[12] This is a theme that is far more prominent in *Absalom, Absalom* than in *As I Lay Dying*; and there are in fact close links between *Traversée de la mangrove* and *Absalom, Absalom*. *Traversée de la mangrove* alludes to Faulkner's novel in the name of Mira's son: Quentin, like Quentin Compson, one of the narrators of *Absalom, Absalom*, but also a child who will never be able to get to know his father Sancher, just as Charles Bon (for different reasons) never gets to know Thomas Sutpen. More generally, a comparison of *Absalom, Absalom* with Condé's *Traversée de la mangrove* allows us to see that the latter constitutes another reworking, parallel to Glissant's, of the theme of the ancestral crime.

For instance, Condé's presentation of miscegenation bears a distinctly ironic relation to Faulkner: it used to be a crime — the white ancestor of the Lameaulnes family had to flee Martinique for Guadeloupe because he married a black woman in 1904 (*Traversée de la mangrove*, p. 20) — but is no longer; the mulatto Lameaulnes family are now the richest and most socially powerful in the whole village, and we are told that 'dans la Guadeloupe d'aujourd'hui, ce qui comptait, ce n'était plus la couleur de la peau [...] Non, ce qui comptait, c'était l'argent' (p. 135). Conversely, the elderly Man Sonson is angry with her son for marrying a white woman, but he laughs at her and she reflects that 'Peut-être que ces mots-là, noirs, blancs, ne signifient plus grand-chose!' (p. 82).

In *Absalom, Absalom* filiation is undermined not only by miscegenation, but also by incest. Sutpen's repudiation of his first wife and son — Eulalia and Charles Bon — has tragic consequences not only for Charles but also for Judith and Henry, Sutpen's son and daughter by a second marriage, because the secret of Charles's parentage makes possible his engagement to his half-sister Judith, in other words raising the possibility of incest, and leading ultimately to Charles's murder by Henry. In fact, throughout most of the novel, incest is the central issue regarding guilt; only near the end do we learn, in a typical example of the 'différé', why Sutpen repudiated Eulalia: that is, he discovered that she, and therefore also Charles, was of mixed race. So, in gradually uncovering its layers of secrets, the novel intertwines miscegenation and incest as parallel sexual crimes, both threatening the ideal goal of legitimate filiation. While miscegenation in this instance is ultimately seen as 'worse', incest has an ominously pervasive quality that makes it equally sinister: in

Pfaff, *Conversations with Maryse Condé* (Lincoln & London: University of Nebraska Press, 1996), p. 74. William Faulkner, *As I Lay Dying* (New York: Jonathan Cape & Harrison Smith, 1930). In fact the similarities are fairly limited: the interior monologues in *Traversée de la mangrove* take place simultaneously during the 'veillée' of Sancher, while those of *As I Lay Dying* follow each other over a period of time and are more concerned with present events than memories of the past; also the character of Addie Bundren is not a source of mystery in the way that Sancher is.

12   'Transgression and guilt constitute one of the profound and essential themes of any literature. If you consider Faulkner, whom I have read quite a bit, you notice that he depicts many characters affected by a fault that is not within, but rather outside them, in the community to which they belong [...]. What interests me is the anguish of human beings who [...] wonder whether they are here for a reason that escapes their understanding, such as a transgression committed at some previous time' (Pfaff, *Conversations with Maryse Condé*, p. 51).

*Absalom, Absalom*, the Charles-Judith relationship is echoed by strong suggestions of incestuous feelings between Judith and Henry.[13]

*Traversée de la mangrove*, on the other hand, features a prominent incestuous relationship between Mira and her half-brother Aristide. Here incest is not a horrifying possibility, but an actual relationship which has been going on for some time; nor is it the unknowing consequence of a secret or a misunderstanding; and it is itself not a secret but is generally known throughout the village (*TM*, p. 180). One can see it as a metaphor for the closed community of Rivière au Sel — Mira prefers Sancher to Aristide because 'il venait d'Ailleurs' (p. 63) — just as for Faulkner it serves as a metaphor for the inbreeding of the white South. But Condé's closed community is a threat not to filiation but to individual self-determination: Aristide's reaction to the end of his 'guilty love' for Mira is to decide to leave, 'Ne prenait-il pas le départ de sa vraie vie?' (p. 80). Above all, the presentation of this incestuous relationship is extremely undramatic — it attracts disapproval ('son amour peu ordinaire', p. 73), but nothing like the kind of horror that attaches to it in *Absalom, Absalom*. Loulou, the authoritarian father of Aristide and Mira, does not try to stop it, for example (Aristide even thinks his father is jealous, p. 80), and Dinah, Mira's stepmother, merely prays that God will forgive her (p. 107). Incest is seen as embarrassing and rather unhealthy, but not as a terrible crime that must be prevented at all costs.

However, there are ancestral crimes in *Traversée de la mangrove*, and they have more indirect but nevertheless intriguing connections with other aspects of *Absalom, Absalom*. The tragedy in Faulkner's novel is in actual fact precipitated not by Eulalia's racial status per se but its consequence, that is, Sutpen's decision (although he does not see it as a choice) to repudiate both her and their child; and this finds an echo in *Traversée de la mangrove*'s theme of parents who reject or mistreat their children, or whose children suffer because of their misdeeds. Dodose believes that her son's cerebral haemorrhage, which leaves him permanently brain-damaged, is God's punishment for her adultery (*TM*, pp. 211–12); when Mira becomes pregnant by Sancher, Dinah interprets this as God's punishment for *her* adultery with Sancher: 'Les malheurs des enfants sont toujours causés par les fautes cachées des parents' (p. 104); and Rosa, Vilma's mother, echoes this comment when (just as Dodose does with Sonny, p. 214) she blames herself for not having loved Vilma enough: 'C'est moi qui suis coupable, responsable de tout ce malheur. Car, il ne faut pas chercher, le malheur des enfants est toujours causé par les parents' (p. 166). It is typical of Condé that the ancestral curse assumes the more twentieth-century, psychologistic form of the cycle of abuse: Rosa cannot love her children because she was not loved herself (p. 169); Loulou treats his sons harshly because he himself was rejected by his mother (pp. 122–23), and so on.

However, *Traversée de la mangrove*'s central example of the Faulknerian ancestral curse is rather different. It concerns Sancher: all the men in his family die

---

13    The temptation of incest also hovers over brother-sister relations in other novels by Faulkner, such as Quentin and Caddy in *The Sound and the Fury* (New York: Jonathan Cape and Harrison Smith, 1929).

prematurely, supposedly because of a crime that one of his ancestors committed. We learn that this crime was committed in Guadeloupe, and that Sancher has come there in order to die, with no children to succeed him, and thus to 'terminer une race maudite' (*TM*, p. 87): in other words, to break for ever the chain of filiation. Fragments of the ancestor's story gradually emerge, and Sancher's conviction that his death is imminent because of the curse put on the family is repeated several times. Also, Sancher is terrified of Xantippe, the mad outcast who lives in destitution outside the village and whom he sees as a figure of avenging death, saying to him: 'Est-ce que tu ne connais pas le pardon? La faute est très ancienne. Et puis, je n'en suis pas l'auteur direct' (p. 118). But the exact nature of the original crime remains a mystery to the reader and to the other characters for most of the novel; there is just one rumour, cited quite late on, that it concerns slavery: 'À l'en croire, Francis Sancher se prendrait pour le descendant d'un béké maudit par ses esclaves et revenant errer sur les lieux de ses crimes passés' (p. 244). But it is only in the last of the main chapters of the novel, at the end of Xantippe's interior monologue, that it acquires the status of a real event rather than a lurid rumour, and that it is revealed as the torture and massacre of the ancestor's slaves. Xantippe has found the evidence: 'Je sais où sont enterrés les corps des suppliciés. J'ai découvert leurs tombes sous la mousse et le lichen' (p. 245); and he knows (somehow) that Sancher is responsible for his ancestor's crime: 'À chaque fois que je le rencontre, le regard de mes yeux brûle les siens et il baisse la tête, car ce crime est le sien' (p. 245). Thus a direct link is created between the crime of slavery and its punishment, the curse of the dying out of the Sancher lineage.

This revelation is by far the most dramatic moment in Condé's consciously undramatic novel. There is nothing here of the ironic playing down of incest and miscegenation. Instead, the novel puts in place something very similar to Glissant's mimicking of the structure of the 'différé', in order to say something about the original crime of slavery and its present-day repercussions; the 'différé', in other words, once again functions not in relation to the author but on the level of the characters. Thus, throughout *Traversée de la mangrove*, on the one hand, slavery is rarely mentioned (although there is a brief reference to one of the Lameaulnes ancestors amusing himself by shooting his slaves in the head (*TM*, p. 124), prefiguring the crime of Sancher's ancestor); while on the other, Xantippe's sinister, silent appearances not only frighten Sancher but also make everyone else feel vaguely uneasy. Then in the last chapter, as we finally have access to his interior monologue, Xantippe assumes the more precise role of a reincarnation, a ghost of the slaves, come to Rivière au Sel to avenge their deaths. Thus, an earlier cryptic remark by Sancher about Xantippe — 'ce n'est pas moi qui ai fait couler son sang avant de le pendre à la tête du mapou lélé' (p. 118) — turns out, in the final revelation, to be a reference to the ancestral crime, in which Xantippe also identifies himself with the victims: 'C'est sur les racines en béquilles de ses mapous lélé que la flaque de mon sang a séché. Car un crime s'est commis ici, ici même, dans les temps très anciens' (p. 244). In other words, the revelation of the ancestral crime of the slave massacre has been foreshadowed all along, we realize in retrospect, by the presence of Xantippe, lurking unacknowledged in the background, as though perhaps not just the massacre but the fact of slavery itself forms a Machereyan 'unsaid' in the novel as a whole, until it finally bursts into the open with Xantippe's revelation.

Unlike in *Absalom, Absalom,* however, but as in *Le Quatrième Siècle,* the ancestral crime in *Traversée de la mangrove* is in some sense absolved by the end of the novel: Xantippe forgives Sancher on behalf of the slaves whose deaths he would have wanted to avenge, 'Il peut dormir tranquil cependant [...] je ne lui ferai rien. Le temps de la vengeance est passé' (p. 245). One could argue therefore that in Condé's novel the atmosphere of damnation which in the novels of Faulkner attaches permanently to the ancestral crimes is either absent from the start — incest is a banal misdeed rather than a source of horror and miscegenation is not a crime at all — or in the case of slavery, the curse is lifted.

This would mean seeing Xantippe's act of forgiveness as the equivalent of *Le Quatrième Siècle*'s coming to terms with the past but then moving on, diffusing the sins of filiation in the new historical reality of creolization. But there is, I think, in *Traversée de la mangrove* (despite Condé's consistent stress on modernity and her refusal of nostalgia) significantly less confidence in the notion of collective historical change. At the end of *Le Quatrième Siècle* there is a strong sense that things have moved on for the whole community; but in *Traversée de la mangrove,* because Xantippe's interior monologue is not shared with any of the other characters, both his revelation of the crime of slavery and his act of forgiveness remain purely private; it is impossible to conclude that the community's repression of the collective memory of slavery has been affected, and Xantippe's forgiveness does not, of course, prevent Sancher's death.

Glissant's novel therefore perhaps enacts a more upbeat reworking of its Faulknerian theme, while Condé's remains more pessimistic. Both, however, share a focus on slavery as the only original sin that counts, a far more explicit and lucid focus than Faulkner allows himself to have. Both combine the kind of ironic reworking of Faulknerian themes that we have come to expect from postcolonial writers with a perhaps more striking, because less usual, transformation of Faulkner's compulsive need to defer revelation, to 'say without saying', into a controlled representation of the repression of the trauma of slavery; and both, finally, replace the Faulknerian sense of permanent damnation and entrapment in the past with the idea that sins will eventually be absolved, or at least dissolved, and with characters who at least realize the desirability of being able to move on and leave the past behind.

CHAPTER 12

❖

# Sexuality and Racial Politics in Maryse Condé's *La Belle Créole*

In *La Belle Créole* Maryse Condé continues the systematic undermining of exoticist clichés about the Antilles that characterizes most of her other novels. Here, Guadeloupe is a place of crime, unemployment, power cuts, and dilapidation, and has been deserted by the tourist industry. The action of the novel takes place against a backdrop of strikes and violent unrest that has resulted in ever-present armed guards on the streets, as Condé sums it up in an interview she gave me: 'robberies, rapes, strikes, in particular a power strike and a strike of the refuse collectors. So everything happens in darkness. And it stinks everywhere'.[1] Even when the street lighting is on in the capital, the effect is equally unsettling: the city centre is 'illuminée comme un camp de concentration ou une township sud-africaine' (*BC*, p. 153). Dawn Fulton comments on the novel: 'Condé's narrative marks a deliberate divergence from the clichéd image of a peaceful Caribbean village suggested by its title', and, 'To refute the postcard vision of a tranquil, uncomplicated Caribbean island, Condé thus expresses her trademark insolence in a deliberate reflection on the poverty, corruption and despair of present-day Guadeloupe'.[2] The traditional exotic stereotypes have become nothing more than nostalgic fantasy: Ana, the American student of ethnology who comes to Guadeloupe to research traditional folklore, 'découvre très vite qu'elle traquait un pays du rêve et de l'imagination, un pays mythologisé' (*BC*, p. 86). As in Condé's other novels, again, this contrasting of exotic stereotype and reality is based on a temporal contrast between past and present. She herself stresses the importance of this theme in her writing: 'you have to try to write in the present. As long as you remain in a sort of nostalgia, in the past, you lapse into exoticism. When you try to stick closely to the present, to the reality of today, the exoticism disappears' ('Interview', p. 173).[3]

One major example of the degradation of contemporary social reality is the

1    Celia Britton, '"Writing in the Present": Interview with Maryse Condé', in *Language and Literary Form in French Caribbean Writing*, pp. 169–76 (p. 175). Hereafter referred to as 'Interview'.

2    Dawn Fulton, *Signs of Dissent: Maryse Condé and Postcolonial Criticism* (Charlottesville & London: University of Virginia Press, 2008), pp. 111, 122.

3    Cf. the title of Nicole J. Simek's 'The Past is *passé*: Time and Memory in Maryse Condé's *La Belle Créole*', in *Memory, Empire and Post Colonialism: Legacies of French Colonialism*, ed. by Alec G. Hargreaves (Lanham, MD: Lexington Books, 2005), pp. 51–62.

sphere of left-wing politics. The independence movements of the past now struggle to retain any relevance: Boris, the leader of a trade union which supports independence, discovers that 'la perspective de lendépans, loin d'exalter ses interlocuteurs, les faisait trembler' (*BC*, p. 172), because the poor of Guadeloupe are now so dependent on the subsidies they receive from France ('Plus de D.O.M.? Partant plus de SS. Ni de R.M.I. Ni de C.N.A.F. Ni de C.N.A.V., etc.', p. 172) that they believe independence would be a disaster. And although Boris castigates them for their 'éloge de la marâtre [i.e. metropolitan France]' (p. 172), he also realizes that he himself has lost faith in the struggle for independence:

> Pour la première fois, Boris se regarda au fond des yeux et dut convenir que sa foi d'antan n'était plus en vie [...] Sans doute, elle n'avait pas résisté à des années de piétinement, d'échecs, de volte-face et elle s'était éteinte à son insu. (*BC*, p. 167)

But, of course, racial politics is still relevant in trying to combat the continuing inequality of the black population of the island.

One of the original founders of the main independence party, the P.P.R.P., was Pierre Serbulon (*BC*, p. 45). The contrast between him and his son Matthias provides further evidence of the degradation of politics: whereas Pierre in his youth had been a militant activist, his son has become a suave Armani-wearing member of the bourgeoisie, a lawyer who is in no way politically active. But Matthias still exploits, entirely cynically, the old rhetoric of the left in the speech he makes at the trial of Dieudonné, the central character of *La Belle Créole*, who is accused of the murder of his mistress (in both senses) Loraine Féréol de Brémont, a *békée* who employed Dieudonné as a gardener and who became his lover. Matthias succeeds in getting Dieudonné acquitted by presenting his case as an example of the exploitation and oppression of the black population by the *béké* caste. To do so, he draws on the history of slavery in a way which, he thinks, echoes the discourse of Césaire and Fanon: 'Matthias était plutôt fier de son argumentation qu'il jugeait césairienne, voire fanonienne. La maîtresse békée cruelle. L'esclave sans défense. La maîtresse humilie, manie le fouet. Un jour, l'esclave se libère. En tuant. Baptême du sang' (p. 44). After the trial, however, he realizes that he had merely been reactivating a stereotyped and melodramatic version of a historical past that bore no relation to present-day reality — 'Ses acteurs s'étaient bornés à reprendre les vieux rôles du répertoire, à endosser les costumes archi-usés par la tradition' — and that in fact something entirely different, 'un drame moderne, entièrement moderne' (p. 44), was behind the murder. This recourse to dramatic invention and the use of out-dated stereotypes is, of course, particularly shocking in the legal context of the trial, where truth is supposedly paramount. Equally, he had been wrong to politicize the murder by inscribing it in the context of slavery and racial oppression, as Boris comments, 'Il avait su agrandir ce fait divers, cette histoire individuelle, à la dimension d'un drame collectif' (p. 164).[4]

---

4    Cf. Fulton, who writes that Condé '[demythologizes] not only exoticized visions of Guadeloupe but also the legal and racial politics at work in the defense strategy that sets the defendant free' (*Signs of Dissent*, p. 113). The murder is also subjected to other politicized misreadings in the novel, as when

Dieudonné's killing of Loraine was precipitated by the reappearance of her former lover, Luc. Ironically, Dieudonné is the only one of this love triangle for whom race is irrelevant. Loraine, in addition to her three European husbands, has apparently had a string of black lovers, and she sees this as a rebellion against her *béké* upbringing; she claims that now times have changed, the legacy of slavery has become irrelevant and it is perfectly possible for a white woman and a black man (i.e. Luc) to be in love: 'Ce sont des imbéciles qui s'imaginent que l'esclavage est toujours vivant, qui ne peuvent pas concevoir qu'un nègre de ce pays peut aimer d'amour une békée' (*BC*, p. 179). But her sexual relationships with both Dieudonné and Luc are really just as exploitative as Matthias Serbulon, in Dieudonné's case, in fact claims. This is certainly how Luc sees them; he regards his own financial exploitation of Loraine (she supports his work as an artist) as justified revenge for her sexual exploitation of him and her other black lovers. He says to Dieudonné: 'Les blancs nous ont toujours eu, depuis l'esclavage. Et ce n'est pas fini. Aujourd'hui, les hommes volent notre sueur, notre force, pour s'enrichir. Les femmes, notre virilité pour jouir' (p. 113). But Dieudonné 'ne partageait pas cette rancune' (p. 220), and is always made uneasy by discussions about race because he feels that his own relationships with white people (Loraine of course, but also the Cohen family for whom his mother worked when he was a child and who treated him as part of the family) are being criticized: 'toute conversation au sujet des "blancs" le remplissait de malaise, mettant en question son attachement d'enfant pour des "blancs", les Cohen et surtout son amour pour une "blanche", Loraine' (p. 131).

More generally, he is not interested in politics and is bored by the constant attempts of Boris and his friend Benjy to convince him that he is 'oppressed' (p. 75). Also, he feels completely disconnected from his own trial; he refuses to give Matthias Serbulon any information and so in effect gives him carte blanche to 'édifier ce mauvais scénario' (p. 137). Afterwards, he feels that his life has been taken over by the publicity surrounding the trial, so that his whole personality no longer has any 'truth': 'Il n'avait pas de vérité, il n'était rien, qu'un bwa-bwa de carnaval, habillé d'oripeaux, travesti des fantasmes de ses compatriotes' (p. 52).[5] And this appeal to truth seems to go beyond the opposition between (modern) reality and (nostalgic) stereotype that is so prominent in this and most of Condé's other novels. The central question of *La Belle Créole* is: what is the truth behind the murder? This involves above all the mystery of Dieudonné's feelings for Loraine, in other words 'truth' here is not just an issue in relation to modern society and racial politics, but engages with the more traditional theme of the unknowability of emotions. Hence Dieudonné's 'sempiternelle question' to Loraine: 'Et moi? Qu'est-ce que je suis pour toi?' (p. 184); and the narrative more generally stresses this unknowability:

the daughter of Milo, Dieudonné's biological father, attacks Dieudonné for preferring white women: 'Depuis qu'ils sont beaux comme ça, c'est après les blanches qu'ils courent! Les filles de couleur ne sont plus assez bonnes pour eux! Il leur faut des blondes!' (*BC*, p. 188).
5    Cf. Nathalie Gaillot: 'The story of Dieudonné, the protagonist, is compromised by a legal language (the language of his defense attorney) characterized as deceptive' ('Mothering Nation: Caribbean Women Writers Interrogating National Identity through Works of Fiction' (unpublished PhD dissertation, University of Minnesota, 2007, p. 157.)

'Le cœur! Le cœur! De quelle matière est-ce qu'il est fait? Comment peut-il s'étirer pour abriter des désirs, des émotions contradictoires?' (p. 209).

The importance of this question is heightened by the fact that, more concretely, the truth about the murder is not revealed until p. 226, less than thirty pages from the end of the novel (and when it finally comes, it is extremely brief, barely two pages).[6] This deferral is facilitated by the novel's narrative structure, which covers the twenty-four hours following the trial, but is constantly interrupted by long flashbacks to Dieudonné's earlier life as he remembers events from his past in a more or less random order. Condé skilfully teases the reader, leading us to expect several times that we are going to get the account of the murder, only to be disappointed.[7]

Loraine throws Dieudonné out when she finds him physically attacking Luc (p. 116). She assumes that this attack is an act of jealousy motivated by Luc's relationship with her; but in reality it is Dieudonné's reaction to Luc's sexual advances to *him*. These remind him of a period in his childhood when the neighbourhood homosexual, an old man nicknamed Mamzel Marie, would give him toys in return for sexual favours; Luc's attempted seduction 'rameuta ces souvenirs enfouis au plus profond de la honte et du secret' (p. 115), i.e. memories repressed not only because of his disobedience to his beloved mother, who had warned him not to go near Mamzel Marie, but above all because of 'le *plaisir* qu'il y avait pris' (p. 115, my emphasis). Subsequently, and despite his initial horrified repulsion, Dieudonné does have sex with Luc. But the reader discovers this only when, stung by her contempt for him, Dieudonné tells Loraine about it, only to realize that she has always known about Luc's bisexuality: 'Car elle le connaissait, son Luc! Elle savait qu'il allait à la voile, à la vapeur, séduisant tous ceux qui l'approchaient, hommes, femmes' (p. 226); moreover, Dieudonné also comes to the conclusion that this was probably the real reason why she had thrown him out (p. 226).

Enraged by his revelation, she takes the pistol she keeps by her bedside (which Dieudonné had believed she would never use) and shoots at him, out of jealousy over Luc; and it is at this point that Dieudonné kills her in an act of self-defence. The police find the two bullets and other signs of struggle, but Dieudonné refuses to tell them what has really happened, or to say anything at all to exculpate himself. He later tells himself that this is because he does not want to incriminate Loraine ('avouer cela aurait constitué l'ultime trahison', p. 227). But another and equally important reason would seem to be that he cannot publicly admit to his own homosexual feelings for, and acts with, Luc; indeed, the night that they spend together turns out to be a far more passionate experience than he had ever had with Loraine, 'La lune les regardait choquée peut-être de tant de passion' (p. 224).

---

6   This can be seen as another example of the Faulknerian 'différé', as taken up and modified by Glissant and Condé, discussed in Chapter 11, with the difference of course that in this instance the crime was not committed in the distant past. But the possible relevance to the crime of the 'ancestral' legacy of slavery — apparently disproved but, as I shall argue in the final part of this essay, ultimately reinstated — does provide an echo of the Faulknerian narrative structure.

7   As Simek comments, '[Dieudonné's] status as a murderer [...] remains unclear, and must be continually reassessed and reconfigured as the novel progresses' ('The Past is *passé*', p. 53).

In fact the text repeatedly tells us that, until he meets Loraine, Dieudonné has never been sexually attracted to women: 'Lui-même ne faisait pas l'amour et n'en souffraient pas trop. Tout l'effort de la séduction le dépassait' (p. 31); given his own physical attractiveness, girls are disappointed by his lack of interest in them (p. 31, p. 37); and his friend Rodrigues, in the course of the trial, gives evidence that Dieudonné 'n'avait pas goût aux femmes' (p. 44). When, as a child, he was unable to have sex with his cousin Hélène, the other cousins taunted him, 'Makoumè! Makoumè!' (p. 24), the standard insult thrown at men perceived to be homosexual. But no-one really thinks that Dieudonné is a homosexual, not least because he was only ten at the time. Nor does he, of course, despite the later evidence of his awakening desire for Luc, 'le désir inavoué, inavouable, de rester dans la chaleur et la lumière que dispensait Luc' (p. 220). The way in which this 'inavouable' desire is further described emphasizes its repressed nature, for example, 'une faim s'était éveillée en lui dont il ne savait pas nommer le nom, qu'il ne voulait pas regarder en face' (p. 218); and in his ambivalent recollection of their night together: 'Car ce qui s'était passé avec Luc [...] se situait dans *une autre région de lui-même, région périphérique,* peu essentielle à vrai dire. Un peu de désir. Un peu de plaisir. Même beaucoup' (p. 177, my emphasis).

In contrast, it is made quite clear that despite his intense love for her, his relationship with Loraine is not primarily sexual. Whereas Luc calls her a nymphomaniac, Dieudonné believes that she mainly just wants his company. Above all, he looks after her, tending to all her needs, undressing her, and putting her to bed every night when she is drunk (p. 243). What is most significant about this is that he sees it as a continuation of his relationship with his mother Marine, who was paralyzed in an accident when he was still young and whom he cared for devotedly until her death. He is quite well aware of the similarity: 'Et, la servant ainsi [i.e. Loraine], il croyait servir Marine ressuscitée' (p. 60); 'Les femmes, il les avaient toujours servies. Marine d'abord. Puis, Loraine' (p. 194). After Luc's appearance on the scene he wonders, 'S'était-il trompé en croyant qu'elle [Loraine] avait besoin de lui, autant qu'autrefois Marine avait besoin de lui?' (p. 78).

This parallel suggests an answer to the puzzling question of why he is so happy with Loraine despite the fact that she has always treated him badly. If she 'ne lui manifestait jamais qu'une rude condescendance' (p. 68), and 'ils n'avaient pas échangé de mots tendres. Elle ne lui avait jamais dit: "Je t'aime"' (p. 243), why does he consider his time with her before Luc's arrival to have been one of 'extraordinaire félicité' (p. 71)? But perhaps this contradiction can be explained if we realize that his love for Loraine is not so much for her own sake as fundamentally a projection of his love for his mother.[8] Loraine is much older than him, presumably about the same age as his mother. And he and Marine had had a very close relationship of mutual love and tenderness: Marine 'avait idolâtré son garçon' (p. 146) while 'Dieudonné avait adoré Marine' (p. 158). Equally the fact that he, now an adult, almost always

---

8    This of course provides yet more evidence that the racial dimension of his love for Loraine is completely irrelevant: he is not attracted to her because she is white, but because she allows him to relive his relationship with his mother.

refers to Marine as 'sa maman' rather than 'sa mère' suggests that this infantile affection persists. On the other hand, Dieudonné hates his father Milo; he discovers his identity only after the trial and his reaction is a furious desire to kill him, which he imagines in lengthy and lurid detail:

> Je le larderai de coups, han-han-han, comme la sale bête qu'il est. Vingt-deux coups de couteau. Un pour chaque année de ma vie. Plus quarante-six, pour les quarante-six années de la vie de ma maman. Parce que c'est lui qui l'a tuée... Je ferai couler son sang comme celui d'un cochon. Je m'en barbouillera les babines.
> (BC, p. 160)

In other words, he makes it quite clear that this hatred is intimately linked to his love for his mother.[9]

Moreover, if Dieudonné's deep love for his mother lies at the root of his apparently inexplicable love for Loraine, it can also be seen as motivating his homosexual attraction to Luc. In classic Freudian theory, an over-intense attachment to the mother can make it impossible for the son to form sexual attachments with other women, leading him to turn to men instead since they are not seen as rivals to the mother. Is this the dynamic that is at work in the novel? (If so, the publisher's description of it on the back cover as 'Sorte d'Amant de Lady Chatterley sous les tropiques' is singularly misplaced: Sons and Lovers might have been a more appropriate reference.)[10]

But this Freudian interpretation would imply that there is a repressed *sexual* element to Dieudonné's love for his mother. There is nothing in Condé's descriptions of their relationship that would indicate that this is the case.[11] However, I want to argue that the text does in fact suggest it, very indirectly but nonetheless compellingly, through a strand of imagery connected to the sea. The basic homonym *mer/mère* is reinforced by the mother's name, Marine; and although she herself is afraid of the sea it becomes, after her death, an object of deep attachment for Dieudonné. In fact Boris says despairingly that it seems to be the only thing he is interested in: 'Comme trait de son caractère, on ne pouvait guère retenir que son attachement à la mer' (p. 36); 'attachement' is a far less usual emotion in relation to the sea than to the mother, so that the pun *mer/mère* almost becomes explicit here. Every morning Dieudonné goes for a long swim in the sea. He himself feels that this 'attachement' to

---

9    Somewhat contradictorily, however, Dieudonné is also proud to discover that he is the son of a rich businessman: 'En même temps, une jubilation amère l'emplissait. Il n'était pas un rien du tout. Sans s'en douter, il était lié au monde des nantis' (BC, p. 183). And he links this to his lack of political consciousness, continuing: 'Est-ce pour cela qu'il n'avait jamas haï à la manière de Rodrigue ou de Boris?' (p. 183).

10    This picks up on Ana's naïve and stereotyped interpretation of Dieudonné's love for Loraine as 'cette version tropicale des amours de Lady Chatterley' (BC, p. 89).

11    Although it is perhaps relevant that Marine is beautiful and sexy: she is 'une jolie négresse, peau de sapotille comme on dit, trente-deux dents de perle' (BC, p. 25), and Milo remembers her as 'une sacrée négresse! Dans sa jeunesse, elle aurait mis le feu à un bénitier et leurs nuits flambaient' (p. 190). In this, moreover, she is unlike almost all the other women in the novel, cf. the waitress in the café, whose attempts to seduce Dieudonné are mocked by the text: 'à son grand désespoir, il ne répondit jamais à ses avances. Sourires assassins, koudzyé [i.e. coups des yeux], balancement de hanches, rien n'y fit' (p. 37).

the sea is a consequence of his prior loss both of his 'adoptive' parents, the Cohens (who had taken him with them on their trips on their boat *La Belle Créole*), and of his real mother, whom the wording of the text directly juxtaposes with the sea: 'il avait d'abord perdu les Cohen, ses parents adoptifs, puis sa maman, Marine. Seule la mer ne l'avait pas abandonné' (p. 37). Also, when he has finally decided to commit suicide by drowning, the sea is again linked to Marine, and contrasted with Loraine:

> [Loraine] était morte figée dans la violence, peut-être dans la haine. Il allait rejoindre celle qui ne l'avait rudoyé ni méprisé, celle qui ne s'était jamais trompée sur son compte. Elle le prendrait contre elle et il suffoquerait dans ses bras. Peut-être, dans l'inconnu qui l'attendait, trouverait-il Marine. (*BC*, p. 243)

The sea in other words becomes a substitute object for his love of his dead mother. But it is also, ambiguously, a lover. The quotation cited above (on p. 37) starts by positing the sea as a mother substitute, one who will always be there and never desert him. But this is immediately followed by a sentence which implies an *erotic* love: 'toujours prête à s'enrouler autour de son corps et à le saluer du baiser humide de sa bouche' (p. 37). And this erotic dimension becomes more explicit later in the text, where the sea is described, in Dieudonné's interior monologue, quite unambiguously as a sexual lover:

> La mer! Celui qui a connu son étreinte ne peut plus s'en passer. Ni homme ni femme ne lui suffisent plus. Il lui faut à tout prix retrouver le sel de sa bouche, l'odeur de frais de son corps et s'accrocher pour jouir à ses grands cheveux épars. [...] Elle était là qui lui offrait la caresse de son ventre, lui ouvrait les profondeurs moites de son pubis, couronné de varech. Il pouvait la posséder et se perdre en elle, s'il le voulait. (*BC*, p. 162).

In other words, the sea is both mother and lover for Dieudonné, and this supports the interpretation of his love for his mother as containing a strong sexual component.[12]

However, the sea also features in Dieudonné's memory of the night that he and Luc spent together, in Luc's room on the coast:

> Le chant de la mer les assourdissait, rageur comme si la maîtresse en titre se plaignait de sa trahison. Pourtant, il ne l'avait pas trahie, elle non plus. Il n'avait fait que voler une miette de bonheur à la vie. (*BC*, p. 224)

If the sea is Dieudonné's 'official mistress', this would seem to be identifying it with Loraine, who is indeed furious when he tells her that he has slept with Luc. But, as I have shown, the sea is usually linked not with her but with Marine; and the 'elle non plus' perhaps suggests that he has two 'maîtresses en titre', that is, having sex with Luc is betraying both Loraine and his mother. It would thus reinforce the connection I have made above between sexual desire for the mother and homosexuality.

12    Another aspect of this cluster of images concerns the boat 'La Belle Créole' which is clearly associated with the sea. But it is also, for Dieudonné, 'comme une femme aimée dont il aurait été séparé pendant longtemps' (*BC*, p. 207).

This connection is of course a very general one, found in all European societies as well as in America and the Caribbean. But there is also a specific psycho-social phenomenon which has been attributed to Caribbean and African-American communities and nowhere else: this is the concept of the matrifocal society, in which the mother plays the central and dominant role in the family, and the father is either absent or marginalized. From the early twentieth century onwards, many sociologists and anthropologists, largely Anglo-American, have worked on this.[13] But it has also been explored from a psychoanalytical perspective by Jacques André, a French psychoanalyst who lived in Guadeloupe for many years, in his *L'Inceste focal dans la famille noire antillaise*.[14] André writes: 'Si la matrifocalité est une réalité psychique, c'est en tant qu'elle est constituée d'une configuration de désirs dont le désir de la mère est le désir princeps'.[15] In other words, the lack of an effective father figure in the family precludes the formation of a 'normal' Oedipal stage in the son's development whereby he comes to recognize the father's dominant claim on the mother as sexual partner and relinquishes his own infantile sexual attachment to her. In the matrifocal family, in contrast, with no rival for the mother's love, it is far more difficult for the son to outgrow this attachment, and so he is perpetually on the verge of having to acknowledge his incestuous desire for her. The corollary of this, in turn, is that he is also subject to experiencing homosexual desire for other men, following the dynamic that I have outlined above. André refers to 'une homosexualité aussi latente que refoulée, dernier mot de la sexualité masculine — quand il ne s'agit là que d'une élaboration intermédiaire, masquant un niveau plus enfoui'.[16]

André also goes on to comment that 'la focalité de la mère exige la marginalisation de la figure paternelle. Aimer le père, c'est défier plus que la mère: la structure', which seems to imply that the father's marginal position in the family may be as much a result as a cause of the matrifocal structure: that is, the father finds himself actively excluded from the mother-son couple.[17] In *La Belle Créole*, Dieudonné's almost exaggerated hatred of his father is paralleled by his inability or refusal to assume a paternal role himself — as though his role as son is still so dominant that he cannot become a father as well. The one occasion on which he had sex with

---

13    See for example E. Franklin Frazier, *The Negro Family in the United States* (Chicago, IL: University of Chicago Press, 1929); Nancie L. Solien Gonzalez, *Black Carib Household Structure* (Seattle: University of Washington Press, 1969); Raymond T. Smith, *The Negro Family in British Guiana* (London: Routledge and Kegan Paul, 1956); and *The Matrifocal Family: Power, Pluralism and Politics* (New York: Routledge, 1996); F. Henriques, *Family and Colour in Jamaica: The Social Context of Reproduction* (London: Eyre and Spottiswoode, 1953).

14    Condé knew André and says that 'He and I had a lot of discussions together' ('Interview', p. 175); also, in her collection of interviews with Françoise Pfaff, she comments specifically on his book, saying: 'We have lived with the illusion that these things didn't happen in our societies. At the appearance of the very good book by Jacques André, *L'inceste focal en Guadeloupe et en Martinique* [*sic*] we said to ourselves, "This is not true. It's a white man talking". Now the truth is crystal clear' (Pfaff, *Conversations with Maryse Condé*, p. 135.)

15    André, *L'Inceste focal dans la famille noire antillaise*, p. 365.

16    Ibid., p. 139.

17    Ibid., p. 179.

Ana, which he has almost forgotten about, resulted in her pregnancy and the birth of her son Werner, and when he discovers this, Dieudonné is far from pleased: he refuses to take any responsibility for Werner and hopes that Ana will take him back with her to the United States, which she has no intention of doing. He can hardly believe that he is the father: 'Il était à lui, cet enfant? Sorti de son sperme? [...] il ne ressentait pas la moindre affection pour ce petit braillard. Pas le moindre sentiment de responsabilité. Aucun mouvement de son cœur ni de son corps' (*BC*, p. 182). The fact he cannot relate to the baby ('les bébés le mettaient mal à l'aise', p. 180) is, significantly perhaps in view of his attachment to his own mother, attributed by him to the reaction of babies in general to their expulsion from the mother's womb: 'Est-ce la nostalgie du ventre de leurs mères, paradis qu'ils ne regagneront jamais, qui les rend nerveux, agités, fantasques?' (pp. 180–81). His representation of the basic family group — father, mother, baby — in fact rejoins the novel's more general theme of the opposition of charming stereotype and unpleasant reality: 'Une maman tend le sein à son bébé. Le père regarde. N'est-ce pas l'image du bonheur? Image conventionnelle et menteuse. Dans la réalité, tout se passe autrement. Le père n'aime pas la mère, n'aime pas le bébé' (p. 182).

The reality, in other words, is the matrifocal family; and its prevalence in Caribbean societies is exemplified in the novel by several other cases of paternal failure in Guadeloupe. Luc, for instance, never knew his father (p. 225). Milo abandons Dieudonné along with Marine when he leaves them, and has never had anything to do with his son or provided any financial support. It is true that after the trial, under pressure from his devoutly Catholic wife who insists that he act responsibly, he goes to Arbella, Dieudonné's grandmother and says that he wants to make amends for his past neglect of Dieudonné, and that the latter should come to see him; but when Dieudonné fails to appear, 'Il éprouvait un réel soulagement' (p. 187). It is also noticeable that Milo's relations with the daughters born within his legitimate marriage are hardly involved or caring: 'Il ne comprenait jamais rien aux conversations de ses filles' (p. 188). Even the far more sympathetic Boris fails to be present at the birth of his child because he is both attending a political meeting and searching for Dieudonné; and when he learns that he has a son, his reaction is guilty but also distinctly underwhelmed. Benjy comes to collect him after he has been released from the police station following his arrest, and eventually, after several drinks in a neighbourhood bar, remembers to tell him that his wife has given birth to a son weighing just under three kilos, but all Boris says is, 'Deux kilos huit cents [...] Il n'est pas gros!' (p. 120), and then bursts into tears, 'comme un enfant'.

Male homosexuality has always existed in Caribbean societies, but only as an object of repulsion and a standard insult.[18] Homosexual men such as Mamzel Marie were rejected by their communities and ridiculed, even dehumanized: a 'mamzel Marie' is a dragonfly, and Dieudonné remembers him as 'un homme aux allures

18    André interprets this as a consequence of the greater danger of homosexuality in the matrifocal family: '*pourquoi prohiber ce qui ne serait pas désiré?* La force du tabou, sa virulence, la répugnance que provoque l'allusion à une activité homosexuelle sont à la mesure de la menace — du péril interne de son refoulement' (*L'Inceste focal dans la famille noire antillaise*, p. 158).

efféminées qui, au carnaval, se déguisait en libellule' (p. 114). But the relatively overt and relaxed homosexuality of Luc and his friends is a very different and far more recent phenomenon in the Caribbean.

In contrast, if one follows the logic of the proponents of the matrifocal family structure, the spectre of repressed mother-son incest is an entirely traditional feature of these societies. Moreover, this is usually explained by the fact that the basis of the matrifocal family, i.e. the marginalization of the father, is seen as a historical consequence of *slavery*.[19] Under the regime of plantation slavery, the female slaves looked after their children, at least while they were still very young (after which they might of course be sold off to other plantations); but the children's biological fathers were not usually allowed any contact with them. No family structure was possible for the slaves, and their subjugation to the white master precluded the men from asserting themselves as fathers, or indeed as husbands. As the Guadeloupean Fritz Gracchus puts it in his analysis of sexual desire and family relations in Caribbean and African-American societies, 'La psychanalyse nous enseigne qu'un Père n'existe que si sa parole est entendue et transmise par la Mère, sinon l'enfant en fait peu cas'.[20] Thus both because of his lack of contact with his children and his inability, as a slave, to assume the paternal role in a psychoanalytical sense, the absence of the father leads directly to the emergence of the matrifocal family, as a way of doing without him. But all of this in turn is a consequence of slavery. (The matrifocal family only occurs among people of African descent; the other ethnic communities in the Caribbean, such as those originating in India or the Middle East, never exhibit it. The reason for this is claimed to be that although they may be as poor and uneducated as the Afro-Caribbeans, they were never subject to plantation slavery.)

So far I have argued that the relationship between Dieudonné and Loraine, and its culmination in the murder, had nothing to do with racial politics because it was motivated not by the fact that she was white, but by his repressed incestuous desire for his mother. In other words, it had nothing to do with the kind of coercive, interracial sado-masochism that might have its roots in a collective memory of slavery. But on another level, and far more indirectly, if one analyzes Dieudonné's relationship to Marine in terms of the theory of the matrifocal family, then that incestuous desire can itself be seen as part of a traditional Caribbean social phenomenon which is ultimately caused — in a very different sense that is entirely unconnected with relationships between black and white people — by the historical and psychological legacy of slavery. Rather than the simple, implausible claim made

19   Fritz Gracchus's *Les Lieux de la mère dans les sociétés afro-américaines* is based on the idea that the male slave is, because of his status as slave, unable to perform the role of father to his biological children.

20   Gracchus, *Les Lieux de la mère dans les sociétés afro-américaines*, p. 127. He in fact makes a rather different argument: that the white master assumes the Lacanian role of Symbolic father for all the slaves, so that the female slaves desire to have his child rather than the child of a black fellow slave. I have commented on this at greater length in my *Race and the Unconscious: Freudianism in French Caribbean Thought* (Oxford: Legenda, 2002) pp. 85–94; and also discussed Gracchus with Condé in my interview with her ('Interview', pp. 174–75).

by Matthias Serbulon, that Dieudonné murdered Loraine because she in effect treated him as her slave, one can establish a far more tortuous chain of causality in which plantation slavery creates the matrifocal family, which leads to the son's incestuous desire for his mother, which in turn results in his homosexuality, which in Dieudonné's case arouses Loraine's furious jealousy with regard to Luc, so she tries to shoot him, and so he kills her in self-defence. The racial politics represented in the novel do not of course engage with the matrifocal family at all. Nevertheless, and despite the absence of any explicit comment in the novel on 'inceste focal', if one follows this trail of connections, one is led to the deeply ironic conclusion that the murder of Loraine was not such a 'modern drama' and was indeed, after all, ultimately caused by the legacy of slavery.

# BIBLIOGRAPHY

❖

ACHEBE, CHINUA, *Morning Yet on Creation Day* (London: Heineman, 1975)

ALBERS, IRENE, 'Mimesis and Alterity: Michel Leiris's Ethnography and Poetics of Spirit Possession', *French Studies*, 62 (2008), 271–89

ALTHUSSER, LOUIS, 'Lettre sur la connaissance de l'art', *La Nouvelle Critique*, 175 (April 1966), 36–41

—— 'Letter on art', in *Lenin and Philosophy and Other Essays*, trans. by Ben Brewster (New York: Monthly Review Press, 1971), pp. 203–19

—— *Pour Marx* (Paris: François Maspéro, 1965)

—— *For Marx*, trans. by Ben Brewster (Harmondsworth: Allen Lane, 1969)

ANDRÉ, JACQUES, *L'Inceste focal dans la famille noire antillaise: crimes, conflits, structure* (Paris: Presses universitaires de France, 1987)

ANTOINE, RÉGIS, *La Littérature franco-antillaise: Haïti, Guadeloupe et Martinique* (Paris: Karthala, 1992)

ARANJO, DANIEL, 'L'Opacité chez Édouard Glissant ou la poétique de la souche', in *Horizons d'Édouard Glissant*, ed. by Yves-Alain Favre (Pau: J & D Éditions, 1992), pp. 93–112

ARMEL, A., *Michel Leiris* (Paris: Fayard, 1997)

BAKHTIN, MIKHAIL, *The Dialogic Imagination: Four Essays*, ed. by Michael Holquist, trans. by Caryl Emerson and Michael Holquist (Austin: University of Texas Press, 1981)

—— *Problems of Dostoevsky's Poetics*, ed. and trans. by Caryl Emerson (Minneapolis: University of Minnesota Press, 1984)

BARTHES, ROLAND, *Mythologies* (Paris: Éditions du Seuil, 1957)

BERNABÉ, JEAN, PATRICK CHAMOISEAU, and RAPHAËL CONFIANT, *Éloge de la créolité* (Paris: Gallimard, 1989)

BLANCHOT, MAURICE, *La Communauté inavouable* (Paris: Éditions de Minuit, 1984)

BONGIE, CHRIS, *Islands and Exiles: The Creole Identities of Post/Colonial Literature* (Stanford, CA: Stanford University Press, 1998)

—— *Friends and Enemies: The Scribal Politics of Post/Colonial Literature* (Liverpool: Liverpool University Press, 2008)

BRATTAIN, M. 'Race, Racism, and Antiracism: UNESCO and the Politics of Presenting Science to the Postwar Public', *American Historical Review*, 112:5 (2007), 1386–1413

BRITTON, CELIA, *Edouard Glissant and Postcolonial Theory: Strategies of Language and Resistance* (Charlottesville & London: University Press of Virginia, 1999)

—— 'Entretien avec Ernest Pépin', *Francophone Postcolonial Studies*, 6.1 (2008), 24–39

—— *Language and Literary Form in French Caribbean Writing* (Liverpool: Liverpool University Press, 2014)

—— *Race and the Unconscious: Freudianism in French Caribbean Thought* (Oxford: Legenda, 2002)

—— *The Sense of Community in French Caribbean Fiction* (Liverpool: Liverpool University Press, 2008)

BURTON, R. D. E., 'The French West Indies *à l'heure de l'Europe*', in *French and West Indian: Martinique, Guadeloupe and French Guiana Today*, ed. by R. D. E. Burton and F. Reno (Basingstoke: Macmillan, 1995), pp. 1–19

CAILLER, BERNADETTE, 'Édouard Glissant: A Creative Critic', *World Literature Today*, 63.4 (1989), 589–92

CAILLOIS, ROGER, 'Illusion à rebours', *Nouvelle revue française*, 24 (December 1954), 1010–1024, & 25 (January 1955), 58–70

CÉSAIRE, AIMÉ, *Cahier d'un retour au pays natal* (Paris: Présence africaine, 1939)

—— *Soleil cou coupé* (Paris: Éditions K, 1948)

—— *Discours sur le colonialisme* [1950] (Paris & Dakar: Présence africaine, 1955)

—— *La Tragédie du roi Christophe* (Paris & Dakar: Présence africaine, 1963)

CÉSAIRE, AIMÉ, and ROGER TOUMSON, 'Aimé Césaire et Roger Toumson: entretien sur Michel Leiris', in *Michel Leiris: le siècle à l'envers*, ed. by Francis Marmande (Tours: Farrago; Paris: Léo Scheer, 2004), pp. 71–75

CHAMOISEAU, PATRICK, *Texaco* (Paris: Gallimard, 1992)

CHAMOISEAU, PATRICK, and RAPHAËL CONFIANT, *Lettres créoles: tracées antillaises et continentales de la littérature: Haïti, Guadeloupe, Martinique, Guyane, 1635–1975* (Paris: Hatier, 1991)

CHANCÉ, DOMINIQUE, *L'Auteur en souffrance* (Paris: Presses universitaires françaises, 2000)

CHANDA, TIRTHANKAR, 'La "créolisation" culturelle du monde, entretien avec Édouard Glissant', *Label France*, 38 (2000), 38–39

CLIFFORD, JAMES, *The Predicament of Culture: Twentieth-Century Ethnography, Literature, and Art* (Cambridge, MA: Harvard University Press, 1988)

CONDÉ, MARYSE, *La Belle Créole* (Paris: Mercure de France, 2001)

—— 'Order, Disorder, Freedom and the West Indian Writer', *Yale French Studies*, 83:2 (1993), 121–35

—— *Traversée de la mangrove* (Paris: Mercure de France, 1989)

CORIO, ALESSANDRO, 'The Living and the Poetic Intention: Glissant's Biopolitics of Literature', *Callaloo*, 36.4 (2013), 916–30

CROWLEY, PATRICK, 'Édouard Glissant: Resistance and Opacity', *Romance Studies*, 24:2 (2006), 105–15

DAHOMAY, JACKY, 'Cultural Identity versus Political Identity in the French West Indies', in *Modern Political Culture in the Caribbean*, ed. by H. Henke and F. Reno (Kingston, Jamaica: University of the West Indies Press: 2003), pp. 90–108

DASH, J. MICHAEL, *Édouard Glissant* (Cambridge: Cambridge University Press, 1995)

—— *The Other America* (Charlottesville & London: University Press of Virginia, 1998)

—— 'Caraïbe fantôme: The Play of Difference in the Francophone Caribbean', *Yale French Studies*, 103 (2003), 92–105

—— 'Le Je de l'autre: Surrealist Ethnographers and the Francophone Caribbean', *L'Esprit créateur*, 47 (2007), 84–95

DELEUZE, GILLES, and FÉLIX GUATTARI, *Mille plateaux* (Paris: Éditions de Minuit, 1980)

DUBOIS, W. E. B., *The Souls of Black Folk* [1903], 2nd edn, ed. by Brent Hayes Edwards, Oxford World Classics (Oxford: Oxford University Press, 2008)

FANON, FRANTZ, *Peau noire, masques blancs* (Paris: Éditions du Seuil, 1952)

—— *Les Damnés de la terre* [1961], 2nd edn (Paris: Gallimard, 1991)

FAULKNER, WILLIAM, *The Sound and the Fury* (New York: Jonathan Cape & Harrison Smith, 1929)

—— *As I Lay Dying* (New York: Jonathan Cape & Harrison Smith, 1930)

—— *Absalom, Absalom* (New York: Random House, 1936)

—— *Go Down, Moses* (New York: Random House, 1942)

FRAZIER, E. FRANKLIN, *The Negro Family in the United States* (Chicago, IL: University of Chicago Press, 1929)

FREUD, SIGMUND, 'The Uncanny', in *The Standard Edition of the Complete Works of Sigmund Freud*, ed. by J. Strachey and others, 24 vols (London: Hogarth Press, 1957–74), XVII, 217–52

FULTON, DAWN, *Signs of Dissent: Maryse Condé and Postcolonial Criticism* (Charlottesville & London: University of Virginia Press, 2008)

GAILLOT, NATHALIE, 'Mothering Nation: Caribbean Women Writers Interrogating National Identity through Works of Fiction' (unpublished PhD dissertation, University of Minnesota, 2007)

GALLAGHER, MARY, 'The Passion of Place and Passage: From Emile Ollivier's *Passages* to Ernest Pépin's *Tambour-Babel*', in *Ici-Là: Place and Displacement in Caribbean Writing in French*, ed. by Mary Gallagher (Amsterdam & New York: Rodopi, 2003), pp. 57–78

GLISSANT, ÉDOUARD, 'Assimilation ou antillanité?', *Afrique-Asie*, 245 (3 April 1981), 46–47

—— *La Case du commandeur* (Paris: Éditions du Seuil, 1981)

—— *La Cohée du Lamentin* (Paris: Gallimard, 2005)

—— *Le Discours antillais* (Paris: Éditions du Seuil, 1981)

—— *Faulkner, Mississippi* (Paris: Stock, 1996)

—— *L'Intention poétique* (Paris: Éditions du Seuil, 1969)

—— *Introduction à une poétique du divers* (Paris: Gallimard, 1996)

—— *La Lézarde* (Paris: Éditions du Seuil, 1958)

—— *Mahagony* (Paris: Éditions du Seuil, 1987)

—— *Malemort* (Paris: Éditions du Seuil, 1975)

—— *Mémoires des esclavages: la fondation d'un centre national pour la mémoire des esclavages et de leurs abolitions* (Paris: Gallimard, 2007)

—— 'Michel Leiris ethnographe', *Les Lettres nouvelles* 14:43 (1956), 609–21

—— *Une nouvelle région du monde* (Paris: Gallimard, 2006)

—— *Poétique de la relation* (Paris: Gallimard, 1990)

—— *Poetics of Relation*, trans. by Betsy Wing (Ann Arbor: University of Michigan Press, 1997)

—— *Le Quatrième Siècle* (Paris: Éditions du Seuil, 1964)

—— *Soleil de la conscience* (Paris: Éditions du Seuil, 1956)

—— *Tout-monde* (Paris: Gallimard, 1993)

—— *Traité du Tout-monde* (Paris: Gallimard, 1997)

GLISSANT, ÉDOUARD, and PATRICK CHAMOISEAU, *Quand les murs tombent: l'identité nationale hors-la-loi?* (Paris: Galaade/Institut du Tout-monde, 2007)

GRACCHUS, FRITZ, *Les Lieux de la mère dans les sociétés afro-américaines* (Paris: Éditions caribéennes, 1986)

GYSSELS, KATHLEEN, 'Du Tambour-Babel au Babil du songer' (1999), <http://www.lehman.cuny.edu/ile.en.ile/paroles/pepin_gyssels.html> [accessed September 2006]

HALLWARD, PETER, *Absolutely Postcolonial: Writing Between the Singular and the Specific* (Manchester: Manchester University Press, 2001)

HAND, SEÁN, 'Hors de soi: politique, possession et présence dans l'ethnographie surréaliste de Michel Leiris', in *L'Autre et le sacré: surréalisme, cinéma, ethnologie*, ed. by C. W. Thompson (Paris: L'Harmattan, 1995), pp. 185–95

—— *Michel Leiris: Writing the Self* (Cambridge: Cambridge University Press, 2002)

HARDWICK, LOUISE, *Childhood, Autobiography and the Francophone Caribbean* (Liverpool: Liverpool University Press, 2013)

HENRIQUES, F., *Family and Colour in Jamaica: The Social Context of Reproduction* (London: Eyre and Spottiswoode, 1953)

HINTJENS, H., 'Constitutional and Political Change in the French Caribbean', in *French and West Indian: Martinique, Guadeloupe and French Guiana Today*, ed. by R. D. E. Burton and F. Reno (Basingstoke: Macmillan, 1995), pp. 20–33

HURLEY, E. ANTHONY, 'Loving Words: New Lyricism in French Caribbean Poetry', *World Literature Today*, 71.1 (1997), 55–60

HUTCHENS, B. C., *Jean-Luc Nancy and the Future of Philosophy* (London: Acumen, 2002)

JULIEN, EILEEN, 'La Métamorphose du réel dans *La Rue Cases-Nègres*', *The French Review*, 60.6 (May 1987), 781–87

KANDÉ, SYLVIE, 'Renunciation and Victory in *Black Shack Alley*', *Research in African Literatures*, 25.2 (Summer 1994,) 33–50

KHORDOC, CATHERINE, 'Babel: figure de créolisation dans *Tambour-Babel* d'Ernest Pépin', in *Les Langues du roman: du plurilinguisme comme stratégie textuelle*, ed. by Lise Gauvin (Montreal: Presses de l'Université de Montréal, 1999), pp. 129–45

KULLBERG, CHRISTINA, *The Poetics of Ethnography in Martinican Narratives* (Charlottesville & London: University Press of Virginia, 2013)

LAPLANCHE, J., and J.-B. PONTALIS, *Vocabulaire de la psychanalyse* (Paris: Presses universitaires de France, 1968)

LEIRIS, MICHEL, *Afrique fantôme* [1934] (Paris: Gallimard, 1981)

—— 'Antilles et poésie des carrefours', in *Zébrage* (Paris: Gallimard, 1992), pp. 67–87

—— 'A travers *Tristes tropiques*' [1956], in *Cinq études d'ethnologie*, 2nd edn (Paris: Gallimard, 1988), pp. 113–27

—— *Cinq études d'ethnologie* [1969], 2nd edn (Paris: Gallimard, 1988)

—— *Contacts de civilisations en Martinique et en Guadeloupe* (Paris: Gallimard/UNESCO, 1955)

—— 'L'Ethnographe devant le colonialisme', [1950], in *Cinq études d'ethnologie*, 2nd edn (Paris: Gallimard, 1988), pp. 83–112

—— 'Préface', in Alfred Métraux, *Le Vaudou haïtien* (Paris: Gallimard, 1958), pp. 7–10

—— *Race et civilisation* [1951], in *Cinq études d'ethnologie*, 2nd edn (Paris: Gallimard, 1988), pp. 9–80

—— 'Regard vers Alfred Métraux' [1964], in *Cinq études d'ethnologie*, 2nd edn (Paris: Gallimard, 1988), pp. 129–37

—— *La Règle du jeu*, ed. by Denis Hollier and others (Paris: Gallimard, 2003)

—— *Le Siècle à l'envers*, ed. by Francis Marmande (Paris: Farrago, 2004)

LEUPIN, ALEXANDRE, *Édouard Glissant, philosophe: Héraclite et Hegel dans le Tout-Monde* (Paris: Hermann, 2016)

LÉVI-STRAUSS, CLAUDE, *Les Structures élémentaires de la parenté* (Paris: Presses universitaires de France, 1949)

—— *La Pensée sauvage* (Paris: Plon, 1962)

LUCEY, MICHAEL, 'Voices, Accounting for the Past: Maryse Condé's *Traversée de la mangrove*', in *L'Héritage de Caliban*, ed. by Maryse Condé (Pointe-à-Pitre: Jasor, 1992), pp. 123–32

MACHEREY, PIERRE, *Pour une théorie de la production littéraire* (Paris: François Maspéro, 1966)

MARAN, RENÉ, *Batouala, véritable roman nègre* (Paris: Albin Michel, 1921)

MARDOROSSIAN, CARINE M., 'From Fanon to Glissant: A Martinican Genealogy', *Small Axe*, 13:2 (2009), 12–24

—— '"Poetics of Landscape": Edouard Glissant's Creolized Ecologies', *Callaloo*, 36.4 (2013), 983–94

MÉNIL, RENÉ, *Antilles déjà jadis, précédé de Tracées* (Paris: Jean Michel Place, 1999)

—— 'Une quête de courants souterrains', CARÉ, 10 (April 1983), 27–31

—— *Tracées, identité, négritude, esthétique aux Antilles* (Paris: Pierre Laffont, 1981)

—— 'Vincent Placoly s'en va: adieu, frère volcan', *Tranchées, Revue politique et culturelle du Groupe Révolution socialiste*, (January 1993), 11–12

NANCY, JEAN-LUC, *La Communauté désœuvrée* [1986], 2nd edn (Paris: Christian Bourgois, 1990)

—— *The Inoperative Community*, trans. by Peter Connor and others (Minneapolis: University of Minnesota Press, 1991)

——— *Être singulier pluriel* (Paris: Galilée, 1996)

NESBITT, NICK, *Voicing Memory: History and Subjectivity in French Caribbean Literature* (Charlottesville: University Press of Virginia, 2003)

NGAL, GEORGES, *Lire le Discours sur le colonialisme* (Paris & Dakar: Présence africaine, 1994)

NOUDELMANN, FRANÇOIS, 'La Trame et le tourbillon', in *Autour d'Édouard Glissant,* ed. by S. Hassab-Charfi and S. Zlitni-Fitouri (Bordeaux: Presses universitaires de Bordeaux, 2008), pp. 119–23

PÉPIN, ERNEST, *L'Envers du décor* (Paris: Le Serpent à plumes, 2006)

——— 'The Place of Space in the Novels of the *Créolité* Movement', in *Ici-Là: Place and Displacement in Caribbean Writing in French,* ed. by Mary Gallagher (Amsterdam & New York: Rodopi, 2003), pp. 1–23

——— *Tambour-Babel* (Paris: Gallimard, 1996)

——— *Le Tango de la haine* (Paris: Gallimard, 1999)

PFAFF, FRANÇOISE, *Conversations with Maryse Condé* (Lincoln & London: University of Nebraska Press, 1996)

PRICE, SALLY, 'Michel Leiris, French Anthropology and a Side-Trip to the Antilles', *French Politics, Culture and Society,* 22.1 (2004), 23–35

RAO, RAJA, 'Language and Spirit', in *The Postcolonial Studies Reader,* ed. by Bill Ashcroft, Gareth Griffiths, and Helen Tiffin (London & New York: Routledge, 1995), pp. 296–97

SILENIEKS, JURIS, 'Pays rêvé, pays réel: The Martinican Chronotope in Edouard Glissant's Œuvre', *World Literature Today,* 63.4 (1989), 632–37

SIMEK, NICOLE J., 'The Past is *passé*: Time and Memory in Maryse Condé's *La Belle Créole*', in *Memory, Empire and Post Colonialism: Legacies of French Colonialism,* ed. by Alec G. Hargreaves (Lanham, MD: Lexington Books, 2005), pp. 51–62

SMITH, RAYMOND T., *The Negro Family in British Guiana* (London: Routledge & Kegan Paul, 1956)

——— *The Matrifocal Family: Power, Pluralism and Politics* (New York: Routledge, 1996)

SOLIEN GONZALEZ, NANCIE L., *Black Carib Household Structure* (Seattle: University of Washington Press, 1969)

SPIVAK, GAYATRI, 'Can the Subaltern Speak?', in *Marxism and the Interpretation of Culture,* ed. by C. Nelson and L. Grossberg (London: Macmillan, 1988), pp. 271–313

——— *The Postcolonial Critic: Interviews, Strategies, Dialogues,* ed. by Sarah Harasym (New York & London: Routledge, 1990)

TIFFIN, HELEN, 'Post-Colonial Literatures and Counter-Discourse', in *The Post-Colonial Studies Reader,* ed. by Bill Ashcroft, Gareth Griffiths, and Helen Tiffin (New York & London: Routledge, 1995), pp. 95–98

TOUMSON, ROGER, *La Transgression des couleurs: littérature et langage des Antilles,* 2 vols (Paris: Éditions caribéennes, 1989)

WALLERSTEIN, IMMANUEL, 'Post-America and the Collapse of the Communisms', *Rethinking Marxism,* 51 (1992), 90–102

WIEDORN, MICHAEL, 'Go Slow Now: Saying the Unsayable in Glissant's Reading of Faulkner', in *American Creoles: The Francophone Caribbean and the American South,* ed. by Martin Munro and Celia Britton (Liverpool: Liverpool University Press, 2012), pp. 183–96

WING, NATHANIEL, 'Écriture et relations dans les romans d'Édouard Glissant', in *Horizons d'Édouard Glissant: actes du colloque international, octobre 1990 (Porto),* ed. by Yves-Alain Favre (Pau: J & B Éditions, 1992), pp. 295–302

WYLIE, HAL, 'Joseph Zobel's Use of Negritude and Social Realism', *World Literature Today,* 56.1 (Winter 1982), 61–64

ZOBEL, JOSEPH, *Et si la mer n'était pas bleue* (Paris: Éditions caribéennes, 1982)
——*Laghia de la mort* [1946], 2nd edn (Paris & Dakar: Présence africaine, 1978)
——*La Rue Cases-Nègres* (Paris: J. Froissart, 1950)
——*Le Soleil partagé* (Paris & Dakar: Présence africaine, 1964)

# INDEX

❖

www.ingramcontent.com/pod-product-compliance
Lightning Source LLC
LaVergne TN
LVHW061327060426
835511LV00012B/1898